Productive Reflection at Work

Thinking about learning at work is rapidly evolving. *Productive Reflection at Work* identifies the importance of reflection at work, tracing it from an emphasis on training, through a focus on how organizations learn, to a concern with the necessary shared learning that needs to occur for organizations and work groups to operate effectively today.

This book articulates a new, collective, focus on what it terms productive reflection. That is reflection that serves the needs of the variety of stakeholders involved. It emphasises productivity, combined with satisfying the lived experience of work life. It points the way to a new focus on learning at work that moves away from an individual focus on reflection towards a collective one that critically mirrors the current context of production in workplaces.

The editors and contributors bring together insights from the worlds of education, management, psychology and organizational science, drawing extensively from examples set in Europe, the Middle East, North America and Australia. *Productive Reflection at Work* will benefit students, scholars and practitioners concerned with human resource development in organizations and continuing professional education.

David Boud is Professor of Adult Education in the Faculty of Education, University of Technology, Sydney. He is widely published in the areas of adult, higher and professional education.

Peter Cressey is a Reader in Sociology in the Department of Social and Policy Science at the University of Bath. He has researched and published widely in the field of industrial relations, work organization, workplace learning and European social dialogue.

Peter Docherty is Visiting Professor in Services Operations Management at the Royal Institute of Technology, Stockholm. His research is mainly in the fields of learning at the individual, group, organization and network levels, and the organization and management of sustainable organizations.

Productive Reflection at Work

Learning for changing organizations

Edited by David Boud, Peter Cressey and Peter Docherty

Routledge
Taylor & Francis Group

LONDON AND NEW YORK

First published 2006
by Routledge
2 Park Square, Milton Park, Abingdon, Oxon, OX14 4RN

Simultaneously published in the USA and Canada
by Routledge
270 Madison Ave, New York NY 10016

Routledge is an imprint of the Taylor & Francis Group

Transferred to Digital Printing 2007

© 2006 David Boud, Peter Cressey and Peter Docherty

Typeset in Baskerville by
HWA Text and Data Management, Tunbridge Wells

British Library Cataloguing in Publication Data
A catalogue record for this book is available from the British Library

Library of Congress Cataloging in Publication Data
A catalog record for this book has been requested

ISBN 0–415–35582–6 (hbk)
ISBN 0–415–35583–4 (pbk)

Contents

Figures

Tables

Notes on contributors

Ariane Berthoin Antal, Ph.D. is program director for Organizational Learning and Culture at the Social Science Research Center Berlin (WZB), Adjunct Professor at the Technical University of Berlin, Visiting Professor at Henley Management College, and Distinguished Research Professor at Audencia école de management, Nantes. Her areas of expertise are business and society, cross-cultural management, and organizational learning and change. ABAntal@wz-berlin.de

Monica Bjerlöv, Ph.D. is a senior researcher at the National Institute for Working Life in Stockholm. An educational psychologist, her main research interests are in the organizing of work, and sustainable change and development, with specific focus on the processes of sense making and dialogue. monica.bjerlov@niwl.se

David Boud is Professor of Adult Education in the Faculty of Education, University of Technology, Sydney. He is widely published in the areas of adult, higher and professional education. David.Boud@uts.edu.au

Monica Breidensjö, MA in behavioural science, is senior advisor to the Swedish Confederation of Professional Employees in trade union policy in health and safety issues. She has also a special competence in field development, learning and competence development at the workplace. She was formerly a member of the Board of the European Union's Foundation for the Improvement of Living and Working Conditions and of the European Commission's Committee of Health and Safety. monica@breidensjo.se

Svend Brinkmann is a Ph.D. scholar in the Department of Psychology at the University of Aarhus, Denmark. He is interested in the ethics and politics of psychology, particularly concerning educational issues. svendb@psy.au.dk

Peter Cressey is a Reader in Sociology in the Department of Social and Policy Science at the University of Bath. He has researched and published widely in the field of industrial relations, work organization, workplace learning and European social dialogue. p.cressey@bath.ac.uk

Peter Docherty (Ph.D., D.Sc.) is a senior research fellow at the Institute for Management of Innovation and Technology and formerly a senior researcher at the National Institute for Working Life, Stockholm. His research is mainly in the fields of learning at the individual, group, organization and network levels and the organization and management of sustainable organizations. peter.docherty@niwl.se

Kenneth H. Doerr is an Associate Professor of Operations Management in the Graduate School of Business and Public Policy at the Naval Postgraduate School in Monterey, California. His research focuses primarily on work design and the valuation of technology for operations. His research has appeared in *Management Science*, the *Journal of Applied Psychology*, and other journals. khdoerr@nps.edu

Bente Elkjaer (BA, MA, Ph.D.) is a Professor of Organizational and Workplace Learning at the Danish University of Education. She has within her research taken a special interest in developing a theoretical perspective on organizational learning inspired by American Pragmatism. In addition to her role as Editor-in-Chief of *Management Learning*, Bente Elkjaer is also the Head of the Doctoral School of Organizational Learning (DOCSOL) at the university. elkjaer@dpu.dk

Per-Erik Ellström is a Professor of Education at Linköping University, Sweden. He is also Director of the Centre for Studies of Humans, Technology and Organization (CMTO) at the same university. His research interests includes studies of learning and development processes in work groups and organizations, the interplay between formal and informal learning at the workplace, interactive research, leadership and organization development. perel@ibv.liu.se

Claus Elmholdt is Assistant Professor in the Department of Psychology at the University of Aarhus, Denmark. He is interested in workplace learning, particularly practice-based approaches, learning as social practice, power, identity, and learning in and across communities of practice. claus@psy.au.dk

Tali Freed, Ph.D. is Assistant Professor of Industrial and Manufacturing Engineering, California Polytechnic State University, San Luis Obispo. Her areas of interest include supply chain management, radio frequency identification (RFID), production planning and scheduling, design and improvement of production systems, development of information systems, production costing models, and organization design for effectiveness. tfreed@calpoly.edu

Victor J. Friedman is Senior Lecturer in organizational behaviour at the Emek Yezreel College in Israel. He received his Ed.D. in Counseling, Consulting, and Community Psychology from Harvard University. His work focuses on integrating learning into professional practice, particularly in contexts characterized by uniqueness, uncertainty, conflict and/or instability. He has worked with a wide variety of groups and organizations and has published papers dealing with action science, organizational learning, evaluation, and overcoming social exclusion. victorf@yvc.ac.il

Silvia Gherardi is full professor at the Dipartimento di Sociologia e Ricerca Sociale of the University of Trento, where she teaches Sociology of Organization. She has published numerous books and articles on the following topics:

organizational decision-making, organizational learning, the temporal dimension in organization studies, organizational cultures and symbolism, gender and organizational life. silvia.gherardi@soc.unitn.it

Steen Høyrup is Associate Professor at The Danish University of Education and Director of the University's Research Program for competence development for youth and adults. Fields of interest are research in learning, competence development and organizational learning in the perspective of social psychology and theories of reflection. shp@dpu.dk

Tony Huzzard, Ph.D. in Business Administration, is currently a senior lecturer at the Department of Business Administration, Lund University and a Research Fellow at the National Institute for Working Life in Malmö. His research interests are organizational learning and change as well as critical perspectives on management and organizing. His research activities have included organizational development and the quality of working life in a regional health authority as well as studies of social partnership and European Works Councils. tony.huzzard @fek.lu.se or tony.huzzard@niwl.se

Barry Nyhan, Ph.D. is a senior researcher in Cedefop (European Centre for the Development of Vocational Training) in Thessaloniki, Greece, where he leads research activities dealing with learning and knowledge development. Prior to joining Cedefop in 1998, he was Visiting Professor in the College of Europe in Bruges. He has written and/or contributed to numerous books and journals and has lectured widely throughout Europe. bn@cedefop.eu.int

Barbara Poggio is a researcher at the Dipartimento di Sociologia e Ricerca Sociale of the University of Trento. She has published books and articles on gender and organizations and on narrative analysis. bpoggio@unitn.it

Andrew Schenkel, Ph.D. in economics, is an Assistant Professor at the Stockholm School of Economics. His research focuses on the relationship between learning and social networks and the development of new capabilities and competitive advantage. He teaches in several MBA and EMBA programs as well as conducting executive education. Andrew.Schenkel@hhs.se

A. B. (Rami) Shani is Professor in Organizational Behaviour and Change at California Polytechnic State University and is visiting research professor at the Fenix program at the Stockholm School of Economics. His research interests include organizational design and change, action research methodologies in the pursuit of actionable knowledge creation, creating sustainable work systems, and learning organizations. ashani@calpoly.edu

Michael Stebbins is Professor of Organizational Design at California Polytechnic State University. His research interests include the use of information and communications technology, the design of product development processes, the development of sustainable work systems, and change management. mstebbin@calpoly.edu

Acknowledgements

This book has been written within the international research project 'Productive Reflection at Work', a project initiated and financed by the Swedish SALTSA research programme on 'Working Life Developments in Europe from a Union Perspective'. This programme was launched in 1997 in co-operation between the National Institute for Working Life, a government agency for the conduct of research, development and educational work on work life issues, together with the three central union organizations in Sweden, the Swedish Trade Union Confederation (LO), the Swedish Confederation of Professional Employees (TCO) and the Swedish Confederation of Professional Associations (SACO). The 'Productive Reflection' project group is an international network of 21 researchers from nine countries. The network has met roughly twice a year from 2002 to 2004. The authors would like to thank SALTSA for its support in financing the essential conditions for the network's work in producing the book, such as the network meetings and the preparation of the book. The authors wish to thank the SALTSA Work Organisation working group, Renée Andersson, P.O. Bergström, Monica Brejdensjö, Peter Docherty, Mats Essemyr, Charlotta Krafft, and Elisabeth Sundin for their active support and interest in the project.

The authors wish to thank Frank Blackler, Davide Nicolini and Lennart Svensson, their colleagues in the network who have participated in the work of the project, including the meetings, but who have not participated as authors in the book.

This project has been a part of the research programme on 'Sustainable Work Systems', a joint co-operation between members of the Department for Labour Market and Work Organisation Studies at the National Institute for Working Life, Stockholm and, members of the Work Science group at Institute for Industrial Economics and Management (INDEK) at the Royal Institute of Technology, Stockholm. We also wish to thank other colleagues in the department and the publisher's three anonymous reviewers of our book proposal and sample chapters for their very constructive comments on our work. The programme on 'Sustainable Work Systems' is partially financed by the Swedish Board for Innovation Systems. We wish to thank them for their support.

We would also like to thank those whose professional efforts have resulted in the book manuscript being completed. Anna Seth and Ulla Bogren, NIWL, have taken care of the economic administration. Anita Söderberg-Carlsson, IMIT, has been our copy editor. Our warmest thanks to you all.

Finally deepest thanks to our families, and especially our partners for understanding, if not quite accepting, that our work situation was, as ever, 'rather intensive just now'.

David Boud, Peter Cressey and Peter Docherty
Stockholm, February 2005

Part I
Introduction

1 Setting the scene for productive reflection

David Boud, Peter Cressey and Peter Docherty

Is reflection just a self-regarding activity that distracts from work and separates individuals from their colleagues? Or, is it an integral part of good work? We want to suggest in this book that reflection is far from being an isolating act of solely personal benefit, it is a key to learning to improve production and to making life at work more satisfying. However, for it to fulfil this promise, reflection must be re-thought and re-contextualized so that it can fit more appropriately within group settings. It must also shift from its origins in concerns about individuals learning to learning within organizations.

This book takes the idea of reflection, places it in a new context and examines the implications of it for work and organizations. In doing so it builds on the traditions of reflection in education and professional practice and deploys them to new ends for work groups and organizations. It also contributes to debates about the re-design of work simultaneously to meet the needs of productivity and the quality of working life and to the agenda that discusses the construction of better jobs.

Many people have regarded meeting such different demands as a zero-sum game; in this, the dual goals of productivity and quality of working life appear incompatible. For them, improved production conjures up images of downsizing, work-intensification and treating humans merely as resources, whereas quality of working life has implied the opposite. However, existing changes in work have made possible new ways of thinking about this. The productivity-driven trends to de-layer and remove direct supervision giving responsibilities to work-groups to meet targets has created a context in which more decisions about the immediate environment and the organization of work are often made possible at the local level than in a traditional workplace. As workers have become more invested in their work and identify with it, they, not unproblematically, see that improvements both in their conditions and in production can be made by them, not as individuals but by a collective unit. It is not necessary to assume in this that work is organized in the form of semi-autonomous work groups: almost any unit of activity has features of these conditions that can be deployed to a greater or lesser extent.

Why choose reflection as the focus of this rethinking? The main influence on learning and change is our experience of the world and how we construe it. For work, our experience of it is the dominating feature. Reflection is a key human mechanism in understanding our experience and drawing lessons from it. This has been known for a long time and reflective practice is now a key component of courses for many professions and occupations. While it has been used in training programs, reflection has hitherto been neglected in the context of making sense of work experience for those in work, as distinct from those preparing for work. This neglect is a function of the dominance, in discussions about reflection, of those in the world of education who are concerned about promoting individual learning. This is now shifting and there has been increasing recognition of reflection for work. In a similar way that reflection on educational experiences was designed to lead to enhanced educational outcomes, reflection on work experience is becoming a key to fostering work outcomes, not least of which is sustainable and satisfying work itself.

The location and purpose of the book

How is the book situated? On what assumptions is it based? The book as a whole adopts the following viewpoint although its various contributors take up some positions that challenge these. Firstly, sustainable development for organizations demands that management balance the needs and ambitions of key stakeholders: customers, investors and personnel. Management's efforts to achieve this must address not only static efficiency and effectiveness, such as productivity, profitability and competitiveness, but also dynamic efficiency and effectiveness, such as learning, competence development, creativity and innovation. While faced with growing complexity and unpredictability, many current management strategies and methods, such as lean production, lead to increased intensity in the workplace and decreased opportunities for learning and development and thus adverse long-term consequences.

Secondly, effective learning at the individual, group and organizational levels is achieved not through conventional programs but through acknowledging the learning potential of work and integrating learning activities in the workplace. This is not to deny a role for formal programs, but to acknowledge their limitations. An essential element in this learning is reflection in and on the work being carried out. This is what we term productive reflection. The book presents concepts, models, methods and concrete cases for effective reflection and learning, primarily in the social interaction between personnel in different contexts, such as teams, projects and cross-functional and cross-level forums.

More generally, the book is located at an interesting conjunction in the development of work. A number of megatrends such as globalization and radical changes in information and communication technology have led to increased complexity and unpredictability in the world of organizations. Many in management have met this challenge through increased rationalization and outsourcing to achieve more flexibility and reduce the responsibility of personnel. Two common names for this trend are neo-Taylorism and 'the low road' in which investments in personnel in terms of manning, skill and responsibility levels are kept to a minimum (Docherty *et al.* 2002). In many European countries workers experienced marked increases in work intensity during the nineties. This manifested in decreased control over their work and reduced opportunities for learning and reflection. This in turn means that essential learning must now take place at much faster rate. These changes are also leading to a blurring in the boundaries between work and 'life outside work', both in terms of where and when work and learning is carried out.

A parallel trend known as 'the high road' is characterized by a human resource intensive strategy with higher skill and discretion levels for personnel. This strategy gives priority to the development of individuals and groups with learning integrated in the workplace. This implies an increasing need for what we call 'productive reflection' at work. *Productive reflection* brings changes in work practice to enhance productivity together with changes to enhance personal engagement and meaning in work. These work changes include the greater decentralization of management and the flattening of hierarchies within organizations. This leads to the potential widening of employee capacity and competences. Allied with this is the need for employees to take on greater responsibility for the production of goods and services, to be critically engaged in quality enhancement, the timing of their creation and oversight of methods and processes. What this 'high road' trend spells out, however, is the impact that production changes are having across the whole gamut of occupations, from the shop assistant to the manager, from the shop floor to the designer. On the one hand, introducing the necessity of change towards greater work organization involvement and, on the other, new demands for work to be more meaningful and manageable by the worker. Productive reflection places the thinking and active subject as central to work organization today.

At the same time as these changes were happening there has been a parallel transformation in education practices for professionals, technicians and lower skilled employees. There has been a shift from the formal to the informal, from the classroom to experiential learning in the workplace. In part this parallels the need to develop in employees new skills and competences, but also to prepare them for open-ended learning processes and practices that can encourage reflection. Yesterday's trainees in vocational education and training must now become life-long learners with greater emphasis upon problem-solving, interpersonal skills and contextual understanding and capacity for reflexivity.

The above trends have also been apparent in recent debates about the centrality of learning at work. The explosion of literature about learning organizations is a testament to this with its appreciation of the need to deal with organizational complexity through the inauguration of individual, group and organizational learning structures. Allied with this is the critical contribution of productive reflection to organizational effectiveness and development and employee sense-making and development, in conditions of complexity. Productive reflection is a key to unlocking vital creative forces in employees (a new productive force) and at the same time a way of engaging workers in the creation of new identities, meanings and communities inside work (a new form of engagement), all of these are powerful intangible resources for the organization.

A further rationale for the book is provided by the growing recognition that forms of productive reflection are necessary for the longer-term sustainability of organizational outcomes. In this sense, the Taylorist use of human resources was instrumental and short term in its thinking. The exclusion of the active, thinking, reflecting subject has consolidated poor expectations, practices and productive outcomes. Productive reflection focuses the need to bring the active subject to the centre of work practices, to underline the importance of continuing learning and the necessity to prioritize personnel's quality of life issues if the organization is to be sustainable in the long run. Hence the debate is not simply about new ways to improve workplace learning, it extends to the question of how to achieve better sustainability and renewal of organizational resources. That is, how can we improve the productive forces within organizations at the same time as we lay the basis for a more human and whole-hearted engagement?

The focus of the book

The book is part of a new wave of interest to address issues of reflection in the context of work. While there has been previous work on reflection in educational settings and reflective practice in the context of the work of individual professionals, none deals with the challenges faced by reflection in organizations and in a variety of work groups. The book joins *Organizing Reflection* (Reynolds and Vince 2004), that was published as we were going to press, as representing a move towards seeing reflection as a valuable perspective on organizational concerns. More importantly, this book and our own represent ways of bringing together insights from the often divided fields of adult and organizational learning to deal with pressing matters in the world of work.

A key innovation of our book is that it emphasizes the social collective aspects of reflection – people reflecting together in the workplace. Previously, reflection had been regarded as a way of fostering learning through focusing on personal experience. It may have been conducted with the help of other people, but it was essentially about individual learning; others were only involved to facilitate the process. The book repositions the discourse of reflection away from this individual focus towards one that places reflection of groups in organizations as central. This shift from the individual to the collective here marks an important new development.

Reflection is seen as an integral component of work, a necessary element in evaluation, sense-making, learning and decision-making processes in the workplace. It is through a focus on reflection, we suggest, that the needs of production can be reconciled with the needs of employees to have satisfying engagement with their work. As the identity of worker shifts to worker–learner in new forms of production, so reflection is a key element in working with the challenges to identity that are also involved.

The book consists of contributions from diverse range of international authorities in the areas of management (human resource management, organizational behaviour, organizational development and management systems) and education (adult and vocational learning, experiential learning) as well as organizational psychology and sociology. A particular feature of the book is that it crosses the boundaries of different disciplines and draws together different views of reflection to enable a secure grounding in academic thinking and working practice.

The contributors draw on their own research in organizations as well as their experience and scholarship to ground discussion of reflection in concrete settings and provide useful conceptual frameworks. They also link earlier conceptions of reflection to the ways in which it is being used today and apply it to different sites of practice: networks, teams, work groups and training programs.

How did the book arise?

The book was constructed from an international collaboration of researchers and scholars. They were brought together as part of a joint program for working life research in Europe. This program, named SALTSA from the initials of the collaborating organizations, is a joint activity of the Swedish trade unions and the National Institute for Work Life in Stockholm. As part of a regular cycle of collaborative research a group from SALTSA identified a number of key themes in contemporary working life. One of these themes related to the problem of not having time to think at work and the ways in which this inhibited learning and effective working. This was a theme that crossed sectors, types of work and the levels of training of employees. Work intensification had started to reach the stage at which it was inhibiting the conduct of work itself and was taking a toll on employees. We considered the questions: What could be done to address this problem? Was it an inevitable consequence of demands for increasing productivity?

An initial two-day workshop of researchers from different countries was convened to explore the nature of the problem. The researchers were drawn from a diversity of disciplines and orientations. In particular it drew on those with a background in adult learning and its application in work as well as those with a primarily organizational perspective. Following the workshop they, and others identified at the first meeting, met twice a year over a two-year period as an expert-working group. Countries eventually represented were Australia, Denmark, Germany, Greece, Israel, Italy, Sweden, the United Kingdom and the United States. Members of the group explored ways in which reflection can be used in work settings for the benefits of production and the quality of working life of those involved.

Having considered whether we should cooperate on seeking research funding or on writing, it was decided that a lot of relevant work had already been conducted and that a useful task would be to bring this together in a form that could stimulate wider debate. This led to the present book. Chapters were proposed and discussed and conceptualizations were debated. It was agreed that the aims of the book would be:

1 to provide an understanding of the roles and purposes of productive reflection in work and organizations;
2 to build upon earlier perspectives and analyse ways in which these have been challenged and extended;

3   to provide a rich empirical grounding for reflective practices in a diversity of organizations;
4   to explore ways in which different kinds of reflective activity can be used for different purposes;
5   to locate reflection in the felt experience of work; and
6   to link discussions of reflection with current debates about sustainable work organizations, identity and learning at work.

Organization of the book

The book is structured in five sections. The first section, Introduction, includes the framing of the book by the editors and a discussion of the idea of productive reflection, why it is important for organizations today and the different ways in which it is manifest. Chapter 2 The Emergence of Productive Reflection, takes up the idea of productive reflection sketched in the first chapter. In it the editors locate the development of productive reflection in changing views of work and work organization to show how it is a necessary response to the circumstances of work life at the turn of the twenty-first century. The notion of productive reflection is unpacked and the key features outlined.

The second section, Underpinning Themes and Ideas, consists of two chapters which provide foundations for productive reflection firstly as part of a tradition emerging from reflection in educational settings and secondly as part of reflection as part of everyday work. Steen Høyrup and Bente Elkjær in Chapter 3 set the productive reflection project within the context of earlier conceptions of reflection. Through taking an historical perspective, based originally on the work of John Dewey, the foundations of ideas of reflection are traced. The chapter explores four perspectives on reflection: the individual, the critical, the social relations and the organizational view as precursors for the orientation of productive reflection. Per-Erik Ellström in Chapter 4, The Meaning and Role of Reflection in Informal Learning at Work, suggests that learning at work, just like learning in formal educational settings, is a matter of design, not evolution. It is a matter of organizing the workplace, not only for production, but also for supporting learning at work. In Chapter 5, The Evolution of Collective Reflection, Peter Cressey considers the issue of collective, productive reflection in the workplace and the changing forms that it takes. He concentrates on the development of employee participation as a form of collective reflection, taking as its starting-point the hypothesis that there are many forms of collective reflection inside workplaces that are not recognized as such.

The five chapters in the third section, Differing Contexts and Practices, move discussion of the underpinning ideas to practices in specific organizations. In keeping with the continuing theme that productive reflection is a perspective rather than a set of operational practices, the examples range very widely across types of organization and reflective practices. Not all of the studies used reflection as the organizing concept at the time.

In the first of the explorations of contexts and practices of productive reflection

Andrew Schenkel in Chapter 6, Disciplined Reflection or Communities of Practice, focuses on the context of a large production project and the use of a quality assurance framework. He explores the limitations of such a framework for learning and the necessity of being responsive to new situations that arise when a predetermined framework is not sufficient to deal with all eventualities. He points to the limitations of formally disciplining reflection and the need for acknowledgement of emerging communities of practice in dealing with challenges of production. In Chapter 7, Mike Stebbins, Rami Shani, Tali Freed and Ken Doerr present a collaborative study of what was to be a radical organizational change in a company in the defence industry. In such critical situations, the change process tends to get more attention than the parallel learning process. The realization of opportunities for collective reflection in this case was hindered by such factors as the social distance and absence of dialogue between top and middle management, the professional and organizational culture of the company that rarely considered the needs of employees and the absence of sound structural mechanisms. The secrecy culture regulating the flow of information on a 'need-to-know' basis was also an obstacle to collective reflection.

Ambiguity is a major cause of feelings of intensity at work. Dealing with ambiguity requires social interaction in a joint or collective sense-making process. This process is highly dependent on the character of the communication or dialogue. In Chapter 8 Monica Bjerlöv and Peter Docherty present a model of work-based dialogues that focuses on the processes of differentiation and decentration that play key roles in generating shared understanding. They illustrate these processes with examples that also indicate organizational prerequisites for facilitating these processes. In the final chapter in this section, Chapter 9, Mike Stebbins, Rami Shani and Peter Docherty present a collaborative study of the promotion and facilitation of collective reflection in a turn-around process in a business crisis. Such processes are usually tightly controlled by top management and immediate operational changes take priority over learning both in the short and the long term. Although the initial strategic decisions and development guidelines were taken by top management, successive stages in the change process gave growing scope for personnel involvement as well as the judicious use of different cognitive, structural and procedural learning mechanisms to support collective learning. However, in this particular case, these measures did not apply for all stakeholders and many learning opportunities were not utilized.

The fourth section, Complexities and Challenges, adds to the range of contexts and practices being considered, but also raises some more problematic issues that need to be faced. In Chapter 11, An Ethical 'Community of Practice' Perspective on Reflection, Barry Nyhan argues that the capacity for 'ethical reflection', understood as deliberation and decision making about how to contribute to the excellence of a community of practice, is intrinsic to collective reflection. Thus, an 'excellent' community of practice is also an 'ethical community of practice' which is concerned with achieving shared goals and goods of the community.

The perspectives of trade unions are introduced in Chapter 12, in which Monica Breidensjö and Tony Huzzard reflect on workplace change. They explore the tensions between the pervasive move towards organization leanness and learning. Using two examples they look at the possibilities unions have for supplying new 'learning spaces', with the emphasis being on collective reflection. They show that specific forms of collective reflection can open up new opportunities for learning and also enable unions to draw on new bases of legitimacy and influence in labour processes. A different view of collective reflection is taken by David Boud in Chapter 13, Informal learning: Creating the Space for Reflection at Work. Using experience of a study of informal learning in workplaces he discusses the ways in which workers take the initiative to find ways of reflecting and learning among and despite the formal processes of work and learning available to them. He points to the resilience of members of work groups in finding spaces within and between work to reflect and to the dangers of relying on structured interventions which may inhibit reflection in an attempt to systematize it.

An important way of examining organizations and learning is through discursive practices. In Chapter 14, Discursive Practices at Work: Constituting the Reflective Learner, Claus Elmholdt and Svend Brinkmann draw attention to the ways in which the discourse of reflection is used to create a culture of self-disciplining workers. This makes them compliant to new forms of work organization while simultaneously fostering an illusion of them taking responsibility for what they do. It provides a salutary analysis of the traps in any kind of reflective discourse. In the last contribution to this section, another broad analytical perspective, feminism, is deployed. In Chapter 15, Feminist Challenges to Mainstream Leadership through Collective Reflection and Narrative. Silvia Gherardi and Barbara Poggio point to the need to recognize that there are many perspectives on work and its organization and that we unawarely view leadership through a set of male-oriented assumptions and practices. They argue that an awareness of gender issues is required and that feminist approaches provide ideas and resources needed to allow leadership of all to flourish. They provide an illustration of a narrative approach to the development of reflective leadership that challenges the taken-for-granted assumptions of conventional practice.

The final section of the book consists of a single chapter, Key Issues for Practice and Development. There the editors consider the issues raised by the previous contributions and identify an agenda for the development of productive reflection at work. They point to what has been achieved and to what more is required.

References

Docherty, P., Forslin, J. and Shani, A.B. (Rami) (eds) (2002) *Creating Sustainable Work Systems: Emerging Perspectives and Practice*, London: Routledge.

Reynolds, M. and Vince, R. (eds) (2004) *Organizing Reflection*, Aldershot: Ashgate.

2 The emergence of productive reflection

Peter Cressey, David Boud and Peter Docherty

Why is it that productive reflection has emerged now? This chapter traces the background to the rise of productive reflection and examines its characteristics. In the first part of the chapter it locates an explanation in the changing face of work and production practices. The discussion focuses on the movements from stable to fluid occupation groupings, the strains that this places upon vocational training and the more active role of learning inside organizations. It situates productive reflection as part of the thinking that has followed from critiques of the learning organization movement of the late twentieth century. Rather than focus on the organizational level, it addresses the tensions between the needs of production and development of workers.

The second part of the chapter examines features of what is productive reflection. It describes six key characteristics, but emphasizes that these provide an agenda for the development of productive reflection, not a prescription for practice. Finally, in order to clarify the position taken here, productive reflection is discussed in terms of what it is not.

Locating productive reflection in changing conditions of work

The past 20 to 30 years has witnessed a gradual but profound shift in the treatment of learning and reflection at work. Previously the area had, in the main, been the province of vocational training practitioners and discussed in terms of the training of individuals in the workforce. The issue of competence development was discussed in national terms, in relations to systems of training that had highly regulated and relatively stable formal components. As such the issue of workplace learning, and indeed any training beyond initial qualifications, was considered marginal to a larger debate about learning for actual work and the concept of informal learning was similarly left to discussions amongst academic educators or industrial sociologists (see Marsick and Watkins 1990; Nyhan *et al.* 2003). However, this situation is now somewhat reversed and the relationship between what has been termed formal and informal aspects of learning is seen as vitally important, as is the development of organizational learning that has at its core the aim of embedding critical reflection inside organizations. The idea of training being individually undertaken via external qualifications is increasingly eroded as issues of competence development cannot now be seen as separated from organizational and workplace practice.

Debates about the learning organization were initiated by March and Olsen (1979) and subsequently popularized by Senge (1990) and Pedler (1991) amongst others. These debates stressed the active role of learning and reflection at the workplace level that went beyond the individual to encompass group and organizational mechanisms to look to the future functioning of the organization. Employees needed to go beyond formal training in order to learn a range of vocational, interpersonal and organizational skills that were not part of previous job demands. Learning as distinct from training was taken up as a broader and richer concept. One that implies both a *receptive process* – the receiving, understanding and application of tasks and knowledge – and at the same time a *constitutive process*, one that can initiate, shape and adapt those tasks and knowledge to embrace different situations. Learning, whether individual or collective, meant 'going beyond' rules and procedures or as expressed in learning organization debates, breaking out of the 'single loop' cycle prevalent in most enterprises to question the policies and objectives that previously were taken for granted. To engage in 'double loop' learning (Argyris and Schön 1974) is, as we are suggesting here, to engage in acts of productive reflection. That is, not simply to focus on errors experienced and the positive lessons to be drawn, but also on the process and methodology of learning and work itself, on how innovation can occur and how new organizational knowledge is constituted. Such an approach struck a deep chord in the management world struggling as it was from fundamental changes in product markets and processes.

Essentially the valuing of productive reflection at work is both constituted by and reflects deeper structural changes in production paradigms that lead to greater flexibility in work organizations and active knowledge management. Subsequent chapters in this volume contrast these production paradigms and in so doing trace a shift in people's working lives from the dominance of the physical economy to the dominance of the knowledge economy (Breidensjö and Huzzard, this volume). Whilst the previous century was dominated by mass markets and mass products and an appropriate management mechanism of control, the present day sees the continued existence of such paradigms but also a growth of alternatives based on flexibility, knowledge-intensive products and the need for new forms of responsiveness and learning at work.

From training to reflection in work

Authors such as Piore and Sabel (1984) identify the late twentieth century as the watershed period in work organization when two contrasting models of industrial organization – production systems and managerial approaches – were made visible. The main dividing lines are couched within a Fordist/Post-Fordist opposition where stable markets and mass production are seen to be giving way to more volatile and flexible forms. They describe how such a change spawns longer-term modifications in the organization of work and with it different competency needs and skills. To some extent the new work model that has developed contrasts vast differences in worker skills, autonomy, discretion, as well as a shift from what they call low to high trust employment strategies. In other words this shift heralds a move from a 'mass production era' to the 'flexible specialization' one, described in Figure 2.1.

The analysis presented by Piore and Sabel explains the decay of the stable markets of the post-war world and with it the ending of the stable production systems, key occupational structures and divisions of labour that went with them. Globalization, the need for customized products, the continued penetration of new technology, changing tastes and the new knowledge economy all set a context where change rather than stability is the norm, where skills, competencies and work processes are constantly changed or re-valued and where old verities are continually questioned. The situation does of course remain complex as traces of the 'old model' persist and in some cases develop alongside and complementary to the new models with their need for enhanced multi-skilled and flexible workers.

In management terms the changing context of production and the rebalancing of the labour market that results also entails fundamental changes in management thinking and human resource management. Ezzamel *et al.* (1994) have described the overall picture. They characterized much of the discussion in terms of two contrasting phases; one that describes the old, more Tayloristic, form and approach to management and the emerging phase that operates in the context of change and turbulent markets. Such a contrast was picked up and amplified by numerous authors in the 1980s and 1990s. Walton (1985), for instance, characterized the move in management control strategies as one from 'control to commitment' whilst Auer and Rigler (1990) in their study of Volvo show the development of alternative 'socio-technical' structures based on teamwork and the balancing of social and

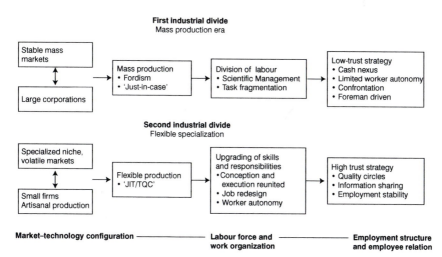

Figure 2.1 The new models of industrial organization. Source: Thomson and McHugh (1990) *Work Organisations*

technical strategies. These studies also show an inexorable move towards greater participative and problem-solving mechanisms inside organizations designed to release employee commitment and creativity. Organizations faced with ambiguity, occupational fluidity and continual change need to amend their development and learning policies in line with that. Walton (1985) described the need for management to gain higher levels of self-activity in problem-solving, self-initiation and the commitment of the workforce. Such change has profound consequences for both workers and management:

> Command is replaced by consent, as the key to corporate success is the develop-
> ment of employees capable of responding, with the minimum of managerial
> direction, to emergent opportunities and threats. ... [A]dvancement comes to
> depend upon the demonstration of skills that empower, energize and support
> staff in continuously producing and refining quality products and services.
>
> (Ezzamel *et al.* 1994: 456)

Hence changes in the context of work and production regimes mean that older bureaucratic 'command and control' structures and the associated forms of management that went with them are now challenged as inappropriate for modern conditions. Ezzamel *et al.* go further and see the contemporary phase as led by flexible production systems, marked by increasing measures of decentralization and the use of multi-functional teams. Together with the greater use of information technology this leads to the development of matrix forms of organization rather than linear ones. Consequently, stable career structures are also threatened as vertical lines of control and career paths are giving way to more complex formations based upon horizontal peer networks where expertise rather than authority holds sway (Hendry and Hope 1994).

Such changes in the organizational environment necessarily substitute 'facilitate and empower' approaches for the 'control' ones of the earlier phases. The 'facilitate and empower' mode demands greater self-discipline and individual responsibility for managing relationships and communications. As mentioned earlier, Senge (1990) and the emergent body of learning organization theory (Dierkes *et al.* 2001) drew on similar analysis when seeking to understand the shift to organizational learning and the needs for management to change their fundamental emphasis away from hierarchy and organizational control structures.

The contrasts in that particular debate are laid out in Table 2.1 below showing how organizations now need to deal with development and creative adaptation rather than stability and law-like repetition. The emphasis is on developmental forms of organizational learning and employee self-activity that can only be facilitated rather than commanded by management. Management becomes a fluid task involving the constant negotiation of job boundaries and competencies, the creation and facilitation of continual learning at the individual, group and organizational level (Nyhan *et al.* 2003). In constantly turbulent markets the products that are needed, the employability of staff and the organizational forms adopted are themselves constantly challenged and re-evaluated. Here we amend the two-

Table 2.1 Transition from training to learning and reflection

	Pre-1990s' emphasis upon	1990s' emphasis upon	2000s' emphasis upon
Approach to learning	TRAINING	ORGANIZATIONAL LEARNING	PRODUCTIVE REFLECTION
Key needs	Rule-governed stability	Appreciation of complexity and ambiguity	Managing of complexity and ambiguity
Approach to competence	Dependent upon stable occupational categories	Dependent upon effective development of human resources	Dependent upon development of distributed and flexible competencies
Approach to problem solving	Fragmented, mechanistic, directed approach to problem solving	Holistic, recursive, participative approach to problem solving	Reflexive, contingent approach to problem solving
Work interaction	Single-function specialists	Multi-functional teams	Predominance of flexible project groups
Work classifications	Job description comprising set tasks and responsibilities	Continuously reviewed and renegotiated assignments	Fluid contracts around complex goals
Learning location	Training/learning largely external	Learning defined within enterprise	Learning contextualized in the workplace

stage transition documented by Ezzamel *et al.*, to take account of the developments subsequent to the learning organization debate. We see a further phase emerging that accords primacy to embedded critical reflection within the workplace rather than training or organizational learning. Such a move means the locating of learning organization theory in workplace practice, where workplace actors take on the role of knowledge processors, producers and practitioners.

In this book, however, it is our contention that the changes discussed by the previous authors in relation to learning organizations do not go far enough. We see emergent changes that in their totality suggest that effective organizational management and practice now depends upon the embedding of *productive reflection*. This means that it is not enough to recognize ambiguity and contingency but to show how organizations can manage the rapid discontinuities and changes they bring with them. Productive reflection must not be seen as an abstract concept or a separable subjective event. Rather it is about new forms of self-management, about how competence is distributed inside companies, about the processes of monitoring and intervention that are constructed. Crucially, it is about the embedding of reflexive approaches to problem solving and change. As Table 2.1 indicates this embedding of *productive reflection* draws upon the creation of contextualized workplace learning that allows and releases the capacity of the workforce, via de-centralized and flexible project groups, the use of multi-functional networks and multiple stakeholder perspectives. The organizational situation is therefore marked by a series of shifts that include the change from individual training to collective reflecting; the irrelevance of hierarchy as a means of designating expertise and useful knowledge; the re-evaluation of expert and lay knowledge and their inter-relationship.

Such awareness leads to the parallel search for conceptions, mechanisms and methodologies that can underpin such change processes. Chapters 7 and 9 of this volume specifically illustrate these points. Hence the need for a process that could enhance practical problem solving, through non-expert involvement, build a methodology based upon a commitment to act and reflect and one that motivated situated learning. Such a search takes us in the direction of more action learning, such as that developed by Revans (1980, 1983) building on Lewin's earlier insights. The precepts of action learning developed by Revans involve a central challenge to conventional sciences' distinction between expert observer and active participant. Placing the need for *questioning insight* before that of *programmed instruction*. For Revans, learning cannot be 'solely the acquisition of freshly programmed knowledge, such as is purveyed by teaching institutions' (1983: 25). It is found in the confrontations of everyday life especially when people, employees or groups are faced with unfamiliar and complex problems for which there is no single solution. This is important for every organization because in the contemporary context of ever-faster change the pace of learning has to match or exceed the rate of change for organizations to survive. Such an approach is premised upon a reflective process whereby long-held assumptions are unfrozen, subject to intense scrutiny through participative experimentation and then (temporarily) refrozen on a new level. To do this entails the creating of problem-solving groups or 'action learning sets' whose role is to solve real problems in an egalitarian manner; meaning the renunciation of mantles of authority. This means that there are no group leaders or even facilitators but that each person needs to act as their own facilitator. It also means that:

> Action learning contains a reflective component. It is not sufficient simply to act. The learning is in the reflection on action and in the renewal that comes from then adapting future actions based on that learning.
>
> (Dilworth 1996: 46)

Apart from Revans' own early work, action learning has mainly been used in the context of management development (Casey 1993). The organizational learning program at MIT lead by Senge was an adaptation of the action learning and action science approaches. This has also been coupled with action research within companies in Europe so that all levels in the organization participate (Coghlan and Brannick 2004; Roth 2002). Gustavsen (1992) in Europe focused on the emancipatory dimension in his methodology for the democratic dialogue including both management and personnel and their unions in joint organizational projects on change and development. Broad national programs were conducted in Norway and Sweden using his framework and methodology. (This 'democratic dialogue' methodology is illustrated in Chapters 5 and 8.) We cannot go into all of the approaches but indicate that they are premised upon methodologies that adopt a critically reflective stance, engaging participants and practitioners in real life issues together with a dialogical approach to problem solving.

Now we want to go on now to explore how we see the process of productive reflection in practice, by looking at key components and its relevance to workplace learning.

What is productive reflection?

The ways we articulate productive reflection here arise from the experience of the contributors to the book in coming together and expressing to each other our different practices. As was described in Chapter 1, the group was formed to explore an issue – enhancing reflection at work – driven by concerns of unions that the contemporary workplace had removed opportunities for reflection. What we realized was that the sense of being time-poor and experiencing life as proceeding at a frenetic pace was not just a phenomenon of work, but was characteristic of most aspects of contemporary society. This has been well represented in Honore's (2004), *In Praise of Slowness*. Honore traces the history of our increasingly rushed relationship with time and explores the consequences of living in what he regards as an accelerated culture of our own creation. Reflection was not seen as a solution to contemporary problems concerning the erosion of time, but it was a response to other dilemmas that were potentially more tractable.

When we focused back on reflection we came to an important realization. While there may be fewer opportunities for some forms of reflection at work, that is, of the kind that allowed development according to the aspirations of the individual worker or groups of occupational colleagues, there was a simultaneous flourishing of other kinds of reflection that placed as central the needs of production and working together. The growing turbulence and change that affected all levels of work and behaviour prompted the upsurge in this. Each of us we realized had been working on different projects in a range of circumstances that contributed to our understanding of both the emergence of new forms of practice and the nature of the practice itself.

Thus the notion of productive reflection we describe here was extracted from these projects and shaped into what we hope is a coherent form. Productive reflection is not theory-driven, but is a response to the conditions of working and learning today. Through surfacing this notion and naming it we hope to make it more accessible and available for wider use. It, of course, encompasses a wide range of interests, not all of which are mutually compatible. Within the notion there is much scope for variation. What we wish to do is not define it in a way that enables someone to say whether they are doing it correctly or not, but in a way that generates practice to explore these issues further. We express a position we consider is fruitful for further development: the success of productive reflection is in the ways in which it is contextualized and embedded in everyday work within organizations.

We have chosen to focus on the term 'productive reflection' in order to capture a number of features. Firstly, it refers to the notion that reflection is something that leads to, rather than concludes, action. In the context of learning and work, reflection is not just an end in itself. Reflection occurs in the context of producing a learning outcome that can be applied to a real situation. Secondly, it refers to a link with whatever is the production that occurs in any given workplace. Productive reflection aims to have an impact on both work products as well as on the wider learning that takes place among participants. Thirdly, productive reflection points to a generative process. It leads not only to particular work outcomes or actions but also to enabling personnel to be active players in work and learning beyond their immediate situation. Productive reflection aims to feed on itself to create a context that fosters learning, knowledge generation and a congenial workplace.

Productive reflection as an idea has emerged from a range of earlier ideas and practices in response to the changed circumstances of work that have been discussed in the previous section. In terms of earlier uses of reflection, it draws on the educational traditions of John Dewey and his followers who have emphasized the key role of reflection of learning of all kinds. It also acknowledges the important influence of Donald Schön (1983) and his work on understanding the context of what professionals do in practice and his notion of the reflective practitioner.

Further, it is also a response to what might be called the 'learning turn' in the organizational world (see also Howard 1990) that we describe in the central column of Table 2.1. This involved recognition of the necessity to consider learning as a fundamental element of work of all kinds. Part of the learning turn has involved viewing organizational effectiveness through the lens of creative adaptation to new and challenging circumstances that demand new responses rather than following an existing pattern. The learning turn has seen the rise of interest in the learning organization as articulated by Coopey (1995). It has encompassed both the new emphases on organizational learning of all kinds coming from the management tradition as well as a focus on workplace learning drawing from vocational educational traditions (Rasmussen and Rauner 1996). Productive reflection is an idea situated in the confluence of these developments, but which plots a new direction to focus on previously inadequately articulated aspects of learning in and for work.

Following from the 'learning turn' we can also identify the later 'reflexive turn' (see column three in Table 2.1). In the 1980s there was an explosion of interest in reflection and its relation both to learning and professional practice. Although not well acknowledged by authors at the time, this was stimulated by the much earlier work of John Dewey. However, this interest in reflection can be seen as part of a widespread development towards a reflexive stance that can be seen in the later work of Schön and also Giddens, and is now being articulated in new ways in the context of lifelong learning (e.g. Edwards *et al.* 2002). That is, a consciousness about consciousness, an awareness about positioning, a turning back to look at oneself and events rather than simply proceeding with action. Reflexivity might indeed be the dominant social and psychological characteristic of the turn of the twenty-first century. Within sociological debates Beck *et al.* (1994), for example, have emphasized the role of *reflexive modernization* as a new form of embedded problem solving. This offers a greater role for an active critical reflection and the necessity of a new rapprochement between expert and lay knowledge systems and, through that, the social construction of knowledge and action. Giddens proposes a model of engagement to mediate between expert and lay knowledge. In his later publications this engagement tends to be presented as a 'dialogic' model within which a cycle of 'reflection-action-evaluation-reflection' is inaugurated (Giddens 1990: 83).

The contention in this book is that the constitution of *productive reflection* in organizations corresponds closely to the processes outlined above inasmuch as it inaugurates a new relationship between expert and lay, new forms of organizational knowledgeability and embedded process of reflection, action and evaluation.

Key elements of productive reflection

What are the key features of productive reflection as represented in this book? What differentiates this idea from earlier conceptions of learning? What connects it to concerns of the changing workplace? It is possible to identify themes that draw the various contributions together. These following elements represent for us the emerging concept of productive reflection.

1 An organizational rather than an individual intent and a collective rather than individual orientation

Previous practices of reflection have emphasized engagement of individual learners or practitioners. Reflection for learning was regarded as being considerably enhanced through working with others, as they were invaluable in pointing out limitations and activities the learner had overlooked or was blind to. It was essentially an act focused on individuals understanding and acting on the basis of their own insights and appreciations. On the other hand, productive reflection as we express it is focused on reflection to lead to action with and for others and for the benefit of the organization as well as the participants in reflective activity. This does not mean that reflection by and for individuals is not important, but that productive reflection is situated in and must incorporate and respond to the intents of the organization.

Of course, the organization may not be a formal entity or the employer of those involved. It could be a part of this or some other collectivity of which those engaged in reflection are part. When referring to organizational learning the organizational unit concerned must be clearly defined. There are different appreciations of what unit is engaged in reflection, both in terms of size and subject position. These can profoundly influence the purpose and form of reflection.

Collective reflection may occur at different levels of the organization, and there are different sets of issues that pertain to each. It might take place, for example, at the level of the workgroup, across workgroups, or across the organization. Groups may not be permanent or fixed; they may come together for different purposes. Any individual can simultaneously be a member of multiple groups. Chapters 5 and 12 discuss differing collective forms of reflection and the variety of forms that those can take.

The collective theme is one that underpins our perspective. It is not just an organizational intent, but an orientation to common interests rather than individual ones that frames collective reflection. The emphasis from an individual and professional orientation is subsumed within a focus on the interests of the group or wider entity.

2 Reflection is necessarily contextualized within work, it connects learning and work

Productive reflection may occur in any location, but it is always contextualized within working activities. Reflective practices cannot be considered apart from the situation and organizational purposes for which they are used. What occurs within one setting might differ radically from that appropriate in another. Work drives reflection and frames what is legitimate. The actual practices used will vary greatly according to the context in which reflection is operating. The need for reflection crosses workplace boundaries and is needed as much for the checkout operator as for the design engineer. Within the working day the former may need to reflect upon strategies to deal with interpersonal issues with customers, workmates or management, in addition to these dealings with new products, processes and problems will also occur.

Contemporary forms of work require employees to be active constructors of their own activities. This necessarily applies to learning, even when others rigidly set production targets and boundaries. Productive reflection connects work and learning and operates in the space between the two. It provides a link between knowing and producing and is a part of change processes. It values workplace knowledge and what has been termed 'work process knowledge' (Boreham *et al.* 2002). Similar to production processes, change processes also involve a parallel learning process. This is exemplified later in Chapters 7 and 9. The manifold use of flexible project groups and active problem solving teams are an expression of the need to tap both the explicit and tacit knowledge lodged in the workplace. Such a need is seen in some of the 'communities of practice' literature referred to in Chapters 4 and 5.

It links with organizational as well as individual action. In productive reflection the emphasis is on acting rather than simply understanding. Reflection leads to interventions into work activity to change what is happening on the basis of insights into what has occurred previously and what might be anticipated. While individuals need to act, it is to organizational or group action that productive reflection is primarily directed.

Building successful reflective practice requires building on the continuities of groups and organizations as well as making an innovative step. Productive reflection needs to be linked to real and significant activities that have importance for those who take part. It also needs in many cases to be institutionally legitimized if the outcomes are to be taken up beyond the group. In other situations institutional policies and politics can inhibit it and destroy the potential it offers.

3 It involves multiple stakeholders and connects players

The processes and outcomes of productive reflection are not confined to one group within an organization. They may be a response to and involve the interests of owners, customers, agents, partners and members of the organization. All or any of these groups may be involved in and contribute to productive reflection. As such, productive reflection taps into the distributed expertise within organizations that is often ignored or determined as dysfunctional (see Orr 1990 or Lave and Wenger 1991).

A feature of productive reflection is that it acts to connect players and not isolate them within their own perspectives. Each person has to take account of other perspectives if an outcome to satisfy all is to be sought. It may not be necessary for all those involved to share all values, but they do need to be prepared to seek to find and operate on common ground. Self-reflection is occurring anyway and productive reflection is an extension of it.

An ongoing danger of collective reflection, like all group processes, is that groupthink may occur (Janis 1972). That is, members of the group subordinate their own thinking to what they take to be the common view of the group. Critical thinking is suspended and inappropriate decisions made. Again, like all group processes, groupthink needs to be considered as a possibility and ways of avoiding it identified.

4 It has a generative rather than instrumental focus

Reflection in educational settings has been much abused through practitioners taking an inappropriately instrumental approach. That is, they assume that reflection as a process can be controlled to lead to pre-determined outcomes. This is neither the case in reflection and reflective practice nor in productive reflection. Attempts will always be made to operationalize reflection in ways that deny its character as exploratory and generative, but such an approach fails to utilize its potential and consigns reflection to just another technique. This is a strategy to undermine what productive reflection can offer and limits its application to yet another mechanism through which employees can be controlled, rather than be given the opportunity to contribute to the development of the organization and themselves. There are limits to the formalizing of reflection and attempts to do so may obliterate productive everyday processes that necessarily exist in all human endeavours. Such an approach indicates the central reflexive and contingent nature of the issue.

5 It has a developmental character

While reflection is used to enhance effective action, it also has a developmental dimension. It is part of a range of organizational practices designed simultaneously to contribute to solving organizational problems of today while equipping members of the organization to be better able to deal with challenges that face them in the future. It does this through building agency among participants, confidence that they can act together in meaningful ways and develop their own repertoire of approaches to meet future challenges. If all it does is address organizational problems, however, and does not nurture the group, it is probably insufficiently sustainable. As pointed to in Table 2.1 the developmental approach also takes account of the growing fluidity of career paths within changing occupational milieus.

6 Reflection is an open, unpredictable process, it is dynamic and changes over time

Productive reflection shares a common characteristic with other forms of reflection; it cannot be predicted in advance where it will lead. It necessarily has unintended consequences. Reflection is needed for sustainability – dealing with ambiguity – which is a vital part of organizational capability. This issue is discussed in Chapter 8. If organizations could know where they were going, then productive reflection might not be needed. Ambiguity cannot be controlled and managed as a routine process, so reflection as an open process that deals with matters that by definition do not have a ready solution or are not clearly formulated is needed. Features such as checklists or 'how-to-do-it' formulas are not appropriate and can be very misleading as they imply a quite different kind of process. Reflection is always in a state of becoming. It is never frozen; it is always in transition or movement. A common trap is that a particular strategy for reflection becomes reified and fixed. Such an approach is antithetical to the notion of reflection.

It also involves a dynamic process that changes over time and over settings. What may be fruitful at one stage becomes a barrier to development later. For it to work well productive reflection needs to be seen as something in continuing renewal, stimulated by some known strategies, but not limited to them. In the same way that outcomes of reflection are not predictable, neither are the timelines. However, most organizational situations have timelines attached, and these de facto define what is possible.

Also, like all human processes, identity and power are inextricably woven within it. Just because a group engages in a process of reflection does not imply that other group processes are suspended. For it to be effective, these other dimensions must be recognized for what they are and worked with as needed.

What is it not?

We are conscious of avoiding the expectation that the book advocates a simple solution – engaging in productive reflection – to what are very difficult issues facing organizations. Reflection is a complex, multifaceted and messy process that is tamed and domesticated at the risk of destroying what it can offer. Reflection is a discursive way of creating a space for focusing on problematic situations and of holding them for consideration without premature rush to judgement. It points to opportunities for groups of people who share a common situation or set of goals to work collaboratively on addressing the situation or goals to their mutual satisfaction. Reflection itself does not specify processes, strategies or methodologies. These will necessarily be many and varied and will radically differ according to the nature of the problem, the character of the group and the context in which they are embedded. There is not a direct correspondence between adoption of productive reflection and the approaches that go with it. These will be determined partly by the purposes being pursued, partly by local traditions and conventions about acceptable strategies and partly through a creative response at the time. It is easier to say what is not compatible with productive reflection than what is.

What is not compatible with productive reflection? The approaches discussed here are not applicable in all circumstances or for addressing all problems. It can help to clarify the idea if we indicate some examples of situations in which productive reflection might *not* be fruitful, i.e. these situations include factors that may seriously hinder the realization of the potential for productive reflection. These include the following:

- Where there is unilateral definition of problems and issues.
- Ownership in the hands of one or a limited number of individuals.
- Decisions are made outside the group that pre-empt most possibilities for action.
- One or more members who know what is the *right* way to proceed.
- Situations in which learning and exploration are not respected.
- Matters that can be dealt with through standard processes and procedures.
- Where there are fundamental barriers to sharing of information within groups.
- Established positions which seek actively or passively to avoid new approaches.

Many all of the case-based chapters in this volume demonstrate the usage of some of these practices with negative results for the organizational actors (see Chapters 6, 7 and 9 particularly). Hence productive reflection has a role to play when the conditions for these are not met. This is often when problems are ambiguous, not within the repertoire of the group or the organization or are part of complex changes that cannot be codified. There are, of course, many problem-solving strategies available when these conditions are found, but it would not be useful to label them as reflection. Regrettably, extending the concept of reflection beyond any reasonable area of applicability has occurred with earlier use of the term. The discourse of reflection has been so seductive (and elusive) that it has been deployed uncritically across contexts in which it was not useful (see, for example, Boud and Walker 1998) as if it were necessarily a 'good thing'. We take the view that it might not be a good thing at all when there are perfectly respectable and useful alternatives to addressing problematic situations.

While in many respects the book paints a positive view of the role of reflection in organizations, it does so cautiously, recognizing that any set of ideas can be used in an inappropriately instrumental fashion that seeks short-term gains without consideration of longer-term effects. It can be put to work at the behest of forces that wish to control and oppress others, set unilateral goals and operate generally in ways that deny the humanity and agency of one or more stakeholders in the process. The discourse of reflection can be used in many ways. For example, as a device to extract more work from 'flexible workers', to gain additional commitment to the organization at the expense of personal, family and community commitments and give participants a false sense of agency in situations where their ideas are not ultimately taken into account. It does this through mobilizing the language of responsibility, of autonomy and control over ones own working. It acts as a seductive mechanism to insinuate itself into the life-world of practitioners who can then believe that they are agents of their own destiny, whether this is the outcome or not.

What follows is a set of chapters that address fundamental issues raised by us here, they do so from a number of angles, some look at the theoretical underpinning whilst others discuss an issue using case study material. All of them take productive reflection at work as their point of focus. The problem of realizing it in workplaces is a strong theme in many of them. We will return to this latter issue of realizing practice in the concluding chapter together with a broader discussion of the way forward for productive reflection.

References

Argyris, C. and Schön, D.A. (1974) *Theory in Practice: Increasing Professional Effectiveness*, San Francisco: Jossey-Bass.

Auer, P. and Rigler, C. (1990) *Post-Taylorism: the Enterprise as a place of Learning Organisational Change*, Stockholm: Arbetsmiljöfonden.

Beck, U., Giddens, A. and Lash, S. (1994) *Reflexive Modernisation: Politics, Traditions and Aesthetics in the Modern Social Order*, Cambridge: Polity Press.

Boreham, N., Samurçay, R. and Fischer, M. (eds) (2002) *Work Process Knowledge*, London: Routledge.

Boud, D. and Walker, D. (1998) 'Promoting Reflection in Professional Courses: The Challenge of Context', *Studies in Higher Education*, 23, 2: 191–206.

Casey, D. (1993) *Managing Learning in Organisations*, Buckingham: Open University Press.

Coghlan, D. and Brannick, T. (2004) *Doing Action Research in Your Own Organisation*, 2nd edn, London: Sage Publications.

Coopey, J. (1995) 'The Learning Organisation: Power, Politics and Ideology', *Management Learning*, 26, 2: 193–213.

Dewey, J. (1933) *How We Think: A Restatement of the Relation of Reflective Thinking to the Educative Process*, Lexington, MA: D.C. Heath.

Dierkes, M., Berthoin Antal, A., Child, J. and Nonaka, I. (eds) (2001) *Handbook of Organizational Learning and Knowledge*, Oxford: Oxford University Press.

Dilworth, R.L. (1996) 'Action learning: bridging academic and workplace domains', *Journal of Workplace Learning*, 8, 6: 45–53.

Edwards, R., Ranson, S. and Strain, M. (2002) 'Reflexivity: towards a theory of lifelong learning', *International Journal of Lifelong Education*, 21, 6: 525–36

Ezzamel, M., Lilley, S. and Willmott, H. (1994) 'The 'New Organisation' and the 'New Managerial Work', *European Management Journal*, 12, 4: 454–61.

Giddens, A. (1990) *The Consequences of Modernity*, Stanford, CA: Stanford University Press.

Gustavsen, B. (1992) *Dialogue and Development*, Assen/Maastricht: Van Gorcum.

Hendry, J. and Hope, V. (1994) 'Cultural Change and Competitive Performance', *European Management Journal*, 12, 4, 401–6.

Honore, C. (2004) *In Praise of Slowness: How A Worldwide Movement Is Challenging the Cult of Speed*, London: Harper Collins.

Howard, R. (ed.) (1990) *The Learning Imperative: Managing People for Continuous Innovation*, Boston: Harvard Business School Press.

Janis, I.L. (1972) *Victims of Groupthink: A Psychological Study of Foreign-Policy Decisions and Fiascos*, Boston, MA: Houghton Mifflin.

Lave, J. and Wenger, E. (1991) *Situated Learning: Legitimate Peripheral Participation*, Cambridge: Cambridge University Press.

March, J. and Olsen, J. (1979) *Ambiguity and Choice in Organizations*, Oslo: Universitetsforlaget.

Marsick, V. J. and Watkins, K. (1990) *Informal and Incidental Learning in the Workplace*, London: Routledge.

Nyhan, B., Cressey, P., Kelleher, M. and Poell, R. (2003) *Facing up to the Learning Organisation Challenge*, Luxembourg: CEDEFOP Publications.

Orr, J. (1990) *Talking about Machines: An Ethnography on a Modern Job*, Ithaca, NY: Cornell University.

Pedler, M., Burgoyne, J. and Boydell, T. (1991) *The Learning Company: A Strategy for Sustainable Development*, London: McGraw-Hill.

Piore, M.J. and Sabel, C.F. (1984) *The Second Industrial Divide: Possibilities for Prosperity*, New York: Basic Books.

Rasmussen, L. (1996) 'Industrial Cultures – Theory and Methods of Cross-National Cimparisons', in Rasmussen, L. and Rauner, F. (eds) London: Industrial Culture and Production.

Revans, R.W. (1980) *The Origins and Growth of Action Learning*, Bromley: Chartwell Bratt.

Revans, R. (1983) *The ABC of Action Learning*, Bromley: Chartwell Bratt.

Roth, J. (2002) *Knowledge Unplugged: An Action Research Approach to Enhancing Knowing in R & D Organizations*, Gothenburg: Chalmers University of Technology, Department of Project Management, Fenix Research Program.

Schön, D.A. (1983) *The Reflective Practitioner*, London: Temple Smith.

Senge, P.M. (1990) *The Fifth Discipline. The Art and Practice of the Learning Organization*, New York: Doubleday.

Thomson, P. and McHugh, D. (1990) *Work Organisations: A Critical Introduction*, London: Macmillan.

Walton, R. (1985) 'From Control to Commitment in the Workplace', *Harvard Business Review*, March/April: 76–84.

Part II

Underpinning themes and ideas

3 Reflection

Taking it beyond the individual

Steen Høyrup and Bente Elkjaer

Today we find a growing interest in the concepts of reflection and reflexivity in many meanings of these terms. In this chapter we relate reflection to workplace learning. Our argument is, that in order to use *reflection* as a fruitful approach to workplace learning, the application of the concepts should not be restricted to an individualized perspective. It is necessary to develop a multifaceted concept that can grasp complex learning as well as organizational processes.

On the practical level, it is obvious that individuals can reflect alone, but always do so in a social context. Individuals may engage in collective reflection, too. From a theoretical perspective, the argument put forward is that individual agency is embodied in social structures and that social structures operate through individuals. As a consequence we should develop a concept of reflection that can encompass both the individual and the social processes that are important for learning at the workplace.

Conceptual grounds

Our use of the notion learning at work, or workplace learning, is to be understood in terms of *everyday learning processes*. This means that learning processes weave into daily work processes. It includes implicit as well as experiential learning (Woerkom 2003:11). In a workplace the most important sources of learning are the challenges of work itself, the organization of work and the social interactions at work.

As a point of departure we define reflection as:

> a complex activity aimed at investigating one's own action in a certain situation and involving a review of the experience, an analysis of causes and effects, and the drawing of conclusions concerning future action, and which results in a changed conceptual perspective.
>
> (after Woerkom 2003: 40)

While this definition seems to underline an individualized perspective, it is important to recognize, however, that the concept of reflection provides meaning at different levels – individual, group or collective and organization.

Our aim is to describe and analyze the concept of reflection from the following perspectives:

- *Individualized*. It is the individual who reflects, in a social context. This is the perspective often used in relation to the notion of 'the reflective practitioner' and problem solving as well as in adult and continuing education.
- *Critical*. The individual reflects on social and political premises.
- *Social relations*. Individuals reflect together in a social context. The process of reflection is collective. Experience – and reflection – can hardly be constituted outside of social relations.
- *Organizational*. This is the perspective of '*organizing reflection*' in which the practice of reflection is directed at organizational learning and change (Vince 2002). The focus is on the implementation of processes and structures for reflection, especially those that move beyond individuals' responsibility to ensure that reflection occurs.

However, before the four perspectives are described, we first present a short history of the concept of reflection.

A short history of reflection

First period: The legacy of John Dewey

Many authors argue that Dewey's thinking constitutes the foundation for the concept of reflection. Dewey conceptualizes reflective thinking as a complex process between individuals' recognition of a problem and its solution (Macintosh 1988). The following elements are important in Dewey's concept of reflection.

The starting-point. The starting-point for reflection is disturbance and uncertainty. Habit does not prompt reflection. When we act in routine ways, we do not reflect. When routine is disturbed, our normal course of action is blocked and a state of uncertainty occurs. The inhibition of action is a necessary precondition for reflection. Inhibition implies 'hesitation and delay', which are the basis for thinking and reflection. In Dewey's terms *reflective thinking* is an active, persistent and careful consideration of any belief or supposed form of knowledge, in the light of the grounds that support it and the further conclusions to which it attends. It includes a conscious and voluntary effort to establish belief upon a firm basis of evidence and rationality (Dewey 1933 [1986]). Thus, for Dewey, reflective thinking arises out of meeting with perplexity, confusion, or doubt in which past experience and relevant knowledge are applied to resolve the uncertain situation. This process may lead to learning experiences, i.e. new ways of understanding and relating to the environment of which we are part.

Another important element is the *definition of the problem*. This means the construction of a tentative hypothesis as to what is the origin and possible solution to the felt uncertainty. The process of reflection begins with the attempt to define what is not working in an uncertain situation. The basis for the exploration of the hypotheses is inquiry into the situation including all elements at work in the felt uncertainty. The definition of the problem impacts on further inquiry and the search for concepts or ideas as guidance for ways that the uncertainty may be resolved.

Formation of guiding concepts or ideas for action. The analysis and definition of the problem of the uncertain situation leads to a working hypothesis formed as a guiding idea for action: a plan.

Elaboration of the meaning of ideas or concepts in relation to each other. The tenacity of the working hypothesis can be tested in experimental thinking in which former experiences may be activated and made use of. For Dewey the heart of reflection is inquiry in which individuals' former experiences may be put to work. In this view, reflection becomes a conscious and voluntary effort to establish connections and continuities in individuals' lived experiences.

Testing of the guiding ideas or concepts in action. Feedback processes. Here the guiding ideas or concepts are tested in action by working the solution out in practice. This is a process of feedback in several ways as the guiding idea or the conceptual grounding is embedded in the practical testing of the solution to the uncertain situation. The testing of the hypothesis makes learning possible as it may create a link between the anticipated consequences of action inherent in the presuppositions and the hypothesis, and the actual changes created by action.

Second period: Research in the mid-1980s

From the mid-1980s it is possible to trace three different approaches to the notion of reflection. In these approaches, reflection is primarily – but not exclusively – connected to *individual* learning. Kolb for instance integrates the term reflection in his notion of individual's experiential learning, Boud develops models of reflection in relation to adult and continuing education and, in Schön's theory of reflection, the core is professionals' thinking in action and professionals' development of skills and knowledge. Although these different approaches involve individuals' interaction with the social environment, the perspective remains primarily individualistic, despite scholars warning against such a restricted view. For example, Boud and Walker in commenting on the use of their perspective say:

> Consideration of the context in which reflective action is engaged is a seriously underdeveloped aspect of the discussion of reflection.
>
> (Boud and Walker 1998: 196)

With this critique in mind, theories of reflection have been moving toward including social processes. We find beginnings of this in this period, but the thinking is most developed in the 1990s and later.

Recent research

Today's writing within the field of reflection represents an integrated period of thinking. We still find an individualistic perspective on reflection in the work of Moon (Moon 1999). However, Reynolds contrasts the concept of reflection with the concept of *critical reflection*. Thus, he argues that critical reflection refers to an examination of the social and political taken-for-granted, both historical and contextual (Reynolds 1998: 187). A social relations perspective is found in Woerkom (2003) and also in Reynolds and Vince's recent work (2004). In the latter, the authors subscribe to the use of reflection as a *social activity* – including the organizational perspective – that might occur within what they call a 'community of participation'. The social and political environment in which collectives are formed and sustained is taking into consideration by these communities, this way underlining the critical perspective too.

The individualized perspective

Although it is not possible here to do justice to the theories and models that form the current perspectives on reflection, the following elaborate the core processes that constitute reflection.

Reflection is primarily prompted by a complex situation involving problems, ambiguity and uncertainty. In a turbulent environment these elements are common conditions at work. Facing a problematic situation, one important process is *defining the problem*, also labelled *framing and re-framing*. Framing refers to how we think about a situation, how we select, name and organize facts to tell a story to ourselves and others about what is going on and what to do in a particular situation (Raelin 2002: 72). Schön argues that in real world practice, problems do not present themselves to the practitioner as givens. They must be constructed from the materials of the problematic situations. Professionals actively convert a problematic situation to a defined problem. When they set or define the problem, they also organize the situation, i.e. they select what they will treat as the 'things' of the problematic situation. They also set the boundaries of attention to the problem and impose upon it a coherence stating what is wrong and in what direction the situation needs to be changed:

> Problem setting is a process in which, interactively, we *name* the things to which we will attend and *frame* the context in which we will attend to them.
> (Schön 1983: 40)

This naming and framing can be understood as making sense of the uncertain situation at hand.

Reflection gains its character and significance by separating thought from action: *Putting experience at a distance enables us to make sense of it* (Malinen 2000: 77). Schön expands the concept of reflection in such a way that a flow of consciousness – reflection-in- action – *occurs at the time of the action*. Professionals respond to problem situations by turning thought back on to the process of knowing implicit in their action. When engaged in problem solving the individual attends to a kind of knowledge embedded in action. This knowledge can be conscious or tacit. Schön's theory involves this intimate relationship between knowing and action. Reflection-in-action is an on-the-spot (as opposed to the retrospect reflection-on-action) process of surfacing, testing and evaluating intuitive understandings – sometimes not conscious – which are intrinsic to experience.

Returning to experience is crucial in Boud's notion of reflection. Returning to experience means that the individual stands back from the immediacy of the experience and reviews it with the leisure of not having to act on it in real time, recalling what has taken place. It is a separation of thinking and action. Returning to experience contributes to learning as wrong perceptions can be detected and the learner can view the experience from other perspectives and have the possibility to look at the event in a wider context than the pressing context in which it was situated. Reflection is here a social process as learners reflect together as they help each other to detect wrong perceptions and create new perspectives on experience. Mezirow states the same point. Reflection is an assessment of *how* or *why* we have perceived, thought, felt, or acted (Mezirow 1990: 6). Reflection enables us to correct distortions in our beliefs and errors in problem solving (Mezirow 1990: 1).

Dewey's conceptualization of reflection is a coherent system of thought and action and this implies that a separation and isolation of thinking processes to some degree violates his theory. It is with this reservation it is done here. To Dewey thinking is conscious and voluntary. Schön includes this kind of thinking in his theory of reflection, but extends the concept of thinking as he argues that reflection-in-action can be unconscious or may be conscious but not in a linguistic codified form.

Dewey identifies four kinds of thinking processes: *Framing*, that is, construction of a tentative hypothesis and solution. *Anticipatory thinking:* thinking ahead and construction of a working hypothesis formed as a guiding idea for action: a plan. *Testing* the guiding idea for action and reasoning about the result of using one of the hypotheses – by imaginative or actual action. *Elaboration* involving a reconstruction of knowledge. In elaboration the meaning of ideas are related to each other, creating a reconstruction of knowledge.

These processes are important in Dewey's and Schön's thinking, and in reality in many theories of reflection. According to Dewey mere action is not enough to create learning. Action is a trying, and it is an experiment with the world to find out what it is like. Generally to experiment means to act in order to see what follows. An important point in Dewey's thinking is that the tenacity of the working hypothesis can be tested in an experiment in thinking and/or in practice, and in this individuals can apply and integrate their former experiences.

Learning is loaded with strong emotions. As learning leads individuals into a field of uncertainty and questioning of established knowledge and beliefs, some degree of anxiety is necessarily associated with it. But learning may also release pride, increased self-esteem and other positive feelings. Boud argues that *attending to feelings* is an important element in reflection (Boud *et al.* 1985). *Attending to feelings* has two aspects: utilizing positive feelings and removing obstructive feelings. Removing obstructive feelings is related to learning in the way that it is a necessary precursor to a rational consideration of events. With negative feelings the individual cannot make a thorough examination of the experience. Awareness of positive feelings is important in learning as they can provide the learner with the impetus to persist in what might be a very challenging situation and they might facilitate the learner's freedom in moving to different perspectives of his experience. On the contrary, the negative feelings can fix the learner to a single perspective.

The process of integration is a core process in reflection. Boud uses the term *re-evaluating experience* and states that this is the most important of the three components of reflection in relation to learning (Boud *et al.* 1985). In reflection, different kinds of experience get in contact with each other, interact, influence and change each other. Learning is *re-learning* and the learning process that reflection supports is a *reconstruction of knowledge*. Malinen gives an interesting account for this encounter between different kinds of experience (Malinen 2000). She conceptualizes two kinds of experience that meet and interact in reflection: *first-order experiences* and *second-order experiences*. Malinen argues:

> The adult's present way of being and seeing the world, others and himself is defined in terms of experiences of this kind. I would term them *first-order experiences. First-order experiences are memory experiences* (Malinen 2000: 67). The total of these first-order experiences – i.e. the adult's unique, autobiographical history – constitute the 'boundary structures' for learning, since they – as a whole – influence the way an adult understands and acts in the world.
>
> (Malinen 2000: 61)

First-order experiences have five fundamental properties:

- They are *past*, 'lived', life experiences.
- They have a *tacit* or *implicit* character.
- They are always *true*, authentic and worthwhile for the adults themselves.
- They are described as *incomplete* and *inadequate* – even distorted (e.g. untested conceptions, more or less articulated ideas, crude and incorrect theories).

In spite of their incompleteness first-order experiences constitute a holistic unity for adults.

Learning in this perspective begins with interplay between first-order experiences and experiences of a different quality: *second-order experiences. Second-order experiences are 'immediate', here-and-now experiences loaded with considerable intensity.* Reflection can be seen as an important mode of this interplay between first- and second-order experiences. *Second-order experiences* have three essential properties:

1 They unlock some part of the subject's first-order experiences, which has suggested appropriate ways in which to see the world, to *doubt* (Malinen 2000: 63).
2 The disturbing or violating second-order experiences usually generates *negative feelings* or *confusion* in adults. The violating second-order experiences are the corner stone of learning: individuals get *a choice*. They can defend the familiar way of seeing and doing, or they can modify it. That is to learn. But how does a second-order experience modify the familiar way of seeing and learning? This is through the third property:

3 *Continuity*. Every second-order experience is seen as interrelated with the totality of first-order experiences, or as even inside this unity (Malinen 2000: 64). A second-order experience provides the clue that one's boundaries can be moved.

Other theories of experience and reflection use other terms, but the very process of integration and reconstructing knowledge is the essence of reflection and learning.

The critical perspective

Michael Reynolds distinguishes between the terms reflection and critical reflection (Reynolds 1998: 183). The crucial distinction in usage is in terms of the questioning of the contextual taken-for-granted – social, cultural and political – which is the hallmark of critical reflection. The contribution of critical reflection is its insistence on asking questions of purpose and on confronting the taken-for-granted that influence individuals' thought and action. In this way the purpose of critical reflection is to examine social processes that mostly have the status of unnoticed or unquestioned certainty. As these taken-for-granted assumptions often give meaning to our lives, some resistance to questioning them is to be expected. Mezirow argues (Mezirow 1990: 1):

> Critical reflection involves a critique of the presuppositions on which our beliefs have been built.

Mezirow presents a fruitful distinction: we can reflect on the *content, process or premise* of problem solving. The latter is critical reflection. In line with this Brookfield argues:

> Critical reflection assumes that adults can engage in an increasingly accurate analysis of the world, coming to greater political clarity and self-awareness. By learning how to surface assumptions and then subject these to critical scrutiny, people can sort out which assumptions are valid and which are distorted, unjust and self-injurious.
>
> (Brookfield 2000: 45)

In Brookfield's terms critical reflection means *hunting assumptions*. Hunting assumptions and posing questions may lead to a more deep kind of learning. In critical reflection we scrutinize important social, organizational and cultural conditions of our life. Reynolds summarizes the principles of critical reflection as follows (Reynolds 1999):

- A commitment to questioning assumptions and the taken-for-granted.
- A perspective that is social rather than individual.
- Paying particular attention to the analyses of power relations.

It should be mentioned that the workplace is not an easy context for critical reflection. Management may see it as ineffective and irrelevant to the bottom line perspective of business. Workers may be afraid to reveal shortcomings or faults. People putting a lot of 'why-questions' may be seen as troublesome and may risk being marginalized. In a way critical reflection bridges an individual and social perspective on learning in recognizing the social and cultural nature of information and knowledge.

The social relations perspective

Raelin associates reflection with learning dialogues. The process of reflection is *collective*; we reflect together with trusted others in the midst of practices:

> Reflection brings to the surface – in the safe presence of trusting peers – the social, political and emotional data that arise from direct experience with one another.
>
> (Raelin 2002: 66)

In the social relations perspective reflection develops into a social practice: Reflective practice is according to Raelin:

> The practice of periodically stepping back to ponder the meaning of, what has recently transpired to us and to others in our immediate environment. It illuminates what the self and others have experienced, providing a basis for future action. In particular, it privileges the process of inquiry, leading to an understanding of experience that may have been overlooked in practice. (...) It typically is concerned with forms of learning that seek to inquire about the most fundamental assumptions and premises behind our practices.
>
> (Raelin 2002: 66)

Reflective practice opens up for public scrutiny our interpretations and evaluations of our plans and actions. We subject our assumptions to the review of others (Raelin 2002: 67). The outcome may be validation of knowledge, assumptions, plans and actions and a development of these through the dialogue implying individual and organizational learning. This approach – people reflecting together in an organizational context – calls attention to the organization as a context for reflective practice. The collective and the organizational perspective are interwoven. In this perspective *disclosure* is an important process. An ideal here is a reflective culture that makes it possible for people to be challenged constantly without fear of retaliation (Raelin 2002: 68). This is a culture that values continuous discovery and experimentation.

What do preconditions and effects of reflection look like in a social relations perspective? The following characteristics are selected from an empirical study (Woerkom 2002: 376):

- *Learning from mistakes.* Reflection leads to consciousness of undesirable matters at the workplace (for example mistakes, problems, lack of motivation). Reflection makes it possible to interpret faults as sources for improvement or learning.
- *Vision sharing.* Individuals express the results of reflection by expressing their vision, asking (critical) questions or suggest improvements. Making vision public is important and constructive for the organization.
- *Sharing knowledge.* Sharing knowledge can be seen as a dimension of non-defensive behaviour, promoting learning (Argyris and Schön 1996). According to Senge (1990) sharing knowledge means that people are not only motivated by protecting their own position but want to be part of something bigger than themselves. If knowledge, insights and visions are not being shared, the organization will not benefit from it, and the individual will be frustrated in his attempts to change work practice (Woerkom 2002: 377). Raelin describes the skill *disclosing*, which becomes crucial when reflection is a process of interaction, an organizational process. As people disclose more about themselves, the group learns more about its membership (Raelin 2002: 73).
- *Challenging groupthink.* Groupthink consists of ideas that a group has accepted as sacrosanct and critical thinkers are people who challenge this. Vince uses the terms *assumption breaking.* He states that assumption breaking is the most arduous of all the steps in the reflection process, because identifying and questioning assumptions goes against the organizational grain (Raelin 2002: 67).
- *Asking for feedback.* Feedback is essential to learn from the consequences of our actions. Some workplaces are structured in ways that do not make feedback processes visible for the actor. Employees operate in a social context and have the need for support for their ideas to make things happen.
- *Experimentation.* In the work context it is important to put ideas into practice.

Our analysis of the first mentioned three perspectives uncover different distinctive processes and characteristics of reflection that seem to be related. To put it simply, we compare only two perspectives, arranging the critical perspective as a row of critical elements in reflection.

Table 3.1 summarizes the main processes in the two perspectives.

The processes involved in the two perspectives should not be conceived of as a polarization. The processes of reflection in the individual perspective can be recognized in the social relations perspective, sometimes with a slightly different meaning and greater complexity. The two perspectives supplement each other.

This is in accordance with the thinking of a number of writers: Boud *et al.* suggest:

> Reflection does not have to be a solitary activity. It can occur in group settings as well as through individual writing and thinking.
>
> (Boud et al., 1985: 16)

Table 3.1 Comparing main processes of reflection from an individual and a social relations perspective

Dimension	Individual perspective	Social relations perspective
Situations that trigger/support reflection	Habits do not work. Complex, ambiguous, uncertain and unique problem situations	A social climate of trust, support, and visibility of feed-back-processes A culture of reflection
Formal/informal aspects	Can be spontaneous or planned	Can be spontaneous or planned
Relationship between cognitive processes and action	Separation of thinking and action. Distance to experience. Stop and think. Reflection interrupts the flow of experience to produce knowledge and learning basic toaction	The practice of periodically stepping back to ponder the meaning of what has recently transpired to ourselves and to others in our immediate environment
Content	Can be private	Disclosure in the group Shared knowledge/ experiences
Cognitive processes in reflection	*Can be* tacit language/not codified language. Intuitive processes as in reflection-in-action. Framing/reframing, labelling of problem Anticipatory thinking Receiving feedback Testing of hypotheses Elaboration. Synthesis of different kinds of experience	Thoughts get converted through interaction into explicit language (codified) Framing/reframing, labelling of problem Asking for and receiving feedback Sharing knowledge Vision sharing Collective planning, analysis and decision making
Elements of action	Inquiry and experiments	Interaction Experimentation Asking for feedback Learning from mistakes
Emotional processes in reflection	Attending to positive feelings Confronting and elaborating negative feelings (anxiety)	Anxiety related to disclosure Making mistakes and threatening common values Positive feelings of belonging to a group, trust etc.
Critical elements of reflection	Hunting assumptions. Questioning of the taken-for-granted	Challenging groupthink Assumption breaking Focus on political, social and cultural processes

Woerkom uses the concept *critical reflective work behaviour*, the meaning of which is close to our concept of reflection:

> We can now define critically reflective work behaviour as a set of connected activities carried out individually or in interaction with others, aimed at optimizing individual or collective practices, or critically analyzing and trying to change organizational or individual values.
>
> (Woerkom 2003: 64)

She sees critical opinion sharing, asking for feedback, challenging groupthink and sharing knowledge as activities carried out in interaction with others. Learning from mistakes is both an individual activity and a social activity when it refers to hiding mistakes from others, and thereby limiting possibilities for oneself and others to learn from them (Woercom 2003: 64). Reflection aimed at problem solving and experimentation can be conceived of as individual activities.

The organizational perspective

Within the organizational perspective the concept of reflection reaches quite another meaning. It differs radically from what has gone before. In the organizational perspective reflection is understood as an *organizing process* in order to create and sustain opportunities for organizational learning and change (Vince 2002: 63). It involves the *use of reflection* to implement structures for 'communities of participation' as identified by Reynolds and Vince (2004: ix). Reflection is a collective action, and Raelin (2002) points to the fact that collective action must be 'heedful' action in order to make people act attentively, conscientiously and critically. For this reason reflection needs to take into consideration data beyond our personal, interpersonal and organizational taken-for granted assumptions (Reynolds and Vince 2004: ix).

Vince suggests that specific practices that contribute to reflection as an organizing process will be informed by three characteristics (Vince 2002: 63):

- The practice should contribute to the collective questioning of assumptions that underpin organizing in order to make power relations visible.
- Reflective practices necessarily provide a 'container' for management of the anxieties raised by making power relations visible.
- Reflective practices contribute towards democracy in the organization.

The first of these seems clearly to refer to concepts of 'hunting assumptions' and challenging groupthink. In this perspective 'assumption breaking' is not something that happens to individuals within an organization. It is questioning collective assumptions. In this perspective assumptions emerge, take shape and institutionalize for important organizational reasons, giving security and coherence to the uncertainties of organizing. Assumptions promote constraint as well as coherence as basic elements of the organization. Therefore assumption breaking is serious and a risk, it makes power relations visible. This way the approach connects to the critical perspective. For Vince, *questioning of assumptions is a practice* that needs to be thought of as integral to organizing rather than the province of individuals. Reflection is a collective capacity to question assumptions.

The second item refers to feelings in reflection, especially anxiety. In the organizational perspective making power relations visible gives rise to individual and *collective anxiety that promotes defensiveness and resistance to organizational learning and change.* In Vince's terms: reflective practices need to offer opportunities for building experience and familiarity in containing anxiety.

The last item aims at developing democracy in the organization. It is Vince's idea that present managerial authority is constructed, justified and enacted as individual responsibility for making decisions. The focal point of authority is the individual manager. Vince contrasts this to the idea of 'management in public' that suggests that managers' authority needs to be based on their ability to 'open leadership and decision-making to the critique and imagination of others' (Vince 2002: 68–9). Authority therefore is in the act of creating *processes of inquiry* involving other stakeholders. Managers can be responsible for creating 'containers' for democratic dialogue and action. *Such inquiry and 'containment' is an example of reflection as an organizing process* (Vince 2002: 68).

In the organizational perspective we can clearly see elements of reflection from the individual, critical and collective approach. It seems that the organizational perspective does not set aside the other approaches but accentuates another aspect of reflection: collective actions and structures that imply organizational learning and change.

The individual and social relations perspective can be seen as integrated in one category compared with the organizational perspective in Table 3.2.

The picture shows us that, although there are obvious similarities, the focus of the two perspectives are quite different. In the organizational perspective focus is very much on implementation of frames, structures, collective actions and organizational matters. The structures have to support processes of reflection conceptualized within the three other perspectives.

Conclusion

It seems possible to ascribe the concept of reflection a more precise meaning by pointing to different distinctive processes that constitute reflection from an individualized-, a critical-, a social relations- and an organizational perspective. It is constructive to include the four perspectives on the concept of reflection to conceptualize the complex processes of learning at work. It seems evident that reflection is incomplete if conceived of as a private individual activity. Further the critical perspective seems to be part of all perspectives. Although we find similarities between the main processes of reflection in all four perspectives, reflection in an organizational perspective seems to involve a quite different theoretical approach to the concept of reflection. In the organizational perspective the focus is primarily on organizational matters and the implementation of structures and collective actions. Still these structures have to support processes of reflection conceptualized within the three other perspectives.

Table 3.2 Comparing the individual and social relations perspective with the organizational perspective

Dimension	Individual and social relations perspective	Organizational perspective
Purpose	Reconstruction of meaning of individual experiences Examination and elaborating of experiences Optimising individual or collective problem solving	To make explicit and share organizational matters and workplace problems and plans in order to make common decisions and influence common actions and change of workplace structures and workplace policy
Nature	A broad range of intra- and interpersonal processes Can be private activities or public social interaction	Social activities. Collective actions Implementation of structures (Creating communities of participation)
Origin	Spontaneous, or planned and structured processes	Planned activities, controlled by management Implementation processes Institutionalized processes
Relation to learning and development	Supports individual learning or learning in teams	Supports organizational learning and development
Critical element	Analysing and trying to change individual or organizational values	Reflection is a collective capacity to question assumptions. Questioning power structures and political and cultural processes in the organization
Language form	Can be tacit, implicit, intuitive, or explicit	Explicit and socially shared and accepted language
Access	Content may be private with access through introspection, or public and shared. Disclosure may be a threat or uncomfortable	Content is common organizational matters and work related items. Can be made transparent at planned meetings etc. Disclosure in relation to organizational values may operate here
Content	A broad range of perceptions, experiences, cognitive and social processes	A narrow focus on power structures, forms of democracy and political and cultural processes influencing organizational life

References

Argyris, C. and Schön, D.A. (1996) *Organisational Learning II. Theory, Method, and Practice*, Reading: Addison-Wesley.

Boud, D. and Walker, D. (1998) 'Promoting Reflection in Professional Courses: The Challenge of Context', *Studies in Higher Education*, 23, 2: 191–206.

Boud, D., Keogh, R. and Walker, D. (eds) (1985) *Reflection: Turning Experience into Learning*, London: Kogan Page.

Brookfield, S.D. (2000) 'The Concept of Critically Reflective Practice', in Wilson (ed.) *Handbook of Adult and Continuing Education*, San Francisco: Jossey-Bass: 33–49.

Dewey, J. (1933 [1986]) 'How We Think: A Restatement of the Relation of Reflective Thinking to the Educative Process', in J.A. Boydston (ed.) *Later Works 8*, Carbondale and Edwardsville: Southern Illinois University Press: 105–352.

Macintosh, C. (1988) 'Reflection: A Flawed Strategy for the Nursing Profession', *Nurse Education Today*, 18: 553–7.

Malinen, A. (2000) *Towards the Essence of Adult Experiential Learning. A reading of the theories of Knowles, Kolb, Mezirow, Revans and Schön*, Jyväskylä: SoPhi, University of Jyväskylä.

Mezirow, J. (1990) *Fostering Critical Reflection in Adulthood. A Guide to Transformative and Emancipatory Learning*, San Francisco: Jossey-Bass.

Moon, J.A. (1999) *Reflection in Learning and Professional Development: Theory and Practice*, London: Kogan Page.

Moon, J.A. (2004) *A Handbook of Reflective and Experimential Learning. Theory and Practice*, London: RoutledgeFalmer.

Raelin, J.A. (2002) ' "Don't Have Time to Think!" versus the Art of Reflective Practice', *Reflections*, 4, 1: 66–79.

Reynolds, M. (1998) 'Reflection and Critical Reflection in Management Learning 1', *Management Learning*, 29, 2: 183–200.

Reynolds, M. (1999) 'Critical Reflection and Management Education: Rehabilitating less hierarchical approaches', *Journal of Management Education*, 23, 5: 537–53.

Reynolds, M. and Vince, R. (eds) (2004) *Organizing Reflection*, Aldershot: Ashgate.

Schön, D.A. (1983) *The Reflective Practitioner. How Professionals Think in Action*, New York: Basic Books.

Senge, P.M. (1990) *The Fifth Discipline. The Art and Practice of the Learning Organization*, New York: Doubleday.

Vince, R. (2002) 'Organizing Reflection', *Management Learning*, 33, 1: 63–78.

Woerkom, M. (2002) 'Critical Reflective Working Behaviour: A survey research', *Journal of European Industrial Training*, 26, 8: 375–83.

Woerkom, M. (2003) *Critical Reflection at Work. Bridging individual and organisational learning*, Enschede: Print Partners Ipskamp.

4 The meaning and role of reflection in informal learning at work

Per-Erik Ellström

Introduction

There is considerable evidence in support of the significance, or even the necessity, of informal learning, not only in work contexts, but also in schools and in the community (Barnett 1999; Coffield 2000). However, at the same time there is also strong evidence indicating the limits of informal learning. As shown by Brehmer (1980) in an influential article, it is very difficult, even at the level of moderately complex tasks, to develop explicit knowledge through experience even if people are given massive amounts of practice. The main reason seems to be that learning from experience presupposes knowledge about the task that can be used by the learning subject to identify and interpret the experiences. Accordingly, there is a Catch-22 for experiential learning in the sense that the knowledge needed to make sense of the experiences cannot be acquired through experience. Furthermore, it is widely recognized that informal learning, not least in working life, often has an adaptive and instrumental character. This is due in part to the continued prevalence of minimal skill requirements in large sectors of the labour market (e.g. Ashton *et al.* 2000).

How, then, are we to understand this seemingly contradictory evidence about the importance of informal learning? As is argued by Ashton *et al.* (2000) on the basis of their extensive study of skills and skill requirements in British workplaces, one key factor is how the employers organize the workplace. In what they call modern organizations, featuring amongst other things, consultation meetings with employees and employee participation in continuous improvement efforts, all groups of employees (skilled and unskilled) were shown to have developed their skills. Of course, this type of workplace was not typical. As might be expected, the majority of the workforce (about two-thirds) did not work under such favourable working conditions (Ashton *et al.* 2000). However, what we can learn from this and similar studies is that learning at work (like learning in formal educational settings) is a matter of design, not evolution (Ellström 2001; Fenwick 2003; Shani and Docherty 2003). That is, it is a matter of organizing the workplace, not only for production, but also for supporting learning at work.

The argument so far implies that more qualified informal learning at work – learning beyond simple adaptation – presupposes a workplace designed to promote learning, as well as employees with sufficient knowledge and skills to be able to

identify and make sense of the experiences and opportunities for learning encountered in relation to the work process. Thus, in accordance with Dewey (1910/1997:
29), it could be argued that informal learning at work requires the cultivation
(through previous learning) of habits of reflection, i.e. 'habits of critical examination
and inquiry'. Such a position would also be in line with the idea that reflection and
reflective practices are important keys to experiential learning – an idea that has
been a salient theme in educational research for some time (Boud *et al.* 1985;
Mezirow 1991).

The purpose of this chapter is to explore the meaning and role of reflection in
relation to informal, everyday learning in work contexts. In this connection a
distinction is made between four levels of action and reflection, which is also used
as a framework for defining informal learning. Furthermore, the space for reflection
and learning at work is discussed in relation to the organization of work processes,
in particular the significance of the time-dimension and the alleged trade-off
between time for production and time for learning.

The concepts of learning and reflection

The focus of this chapter concerns informal learning at the workplace. As used
here, the notion of informal learning refers to learning that occurs in connection
with different kinds of work activity. Such learning may occur without awareness
or intention to learn on the part of the learning subject (implicit learning), or it
may involve a more or less deliberate effort to learn (cf. Eraut 2000). In most cases
the learning subject is assumed to be an individual, but as the concept of learning
is used here, it could also apply to situations where the learning subject is a team
or an organization (for a discussion of the relationship between individual and
organizational learning, see Ellström 2001). An important point of departure for
this chapter is a distinction between two qualitatively different forms or levels of
learning which I prefer to call adaptive (reproductive) and developmental (creative)
learning (Ellström 2001). The notion of adaptive learning has a focus on a subject's
mastery of certain given tasks or situations, on the refinement of task performance
or, for example, of existing routines in an organization. This is in contrast to
developmental learning, where the focus is on individual/collective development,
and/or on more radical transformations of the prevailing situation. Thus, in
developmental learning there is an emphasis on exploring and questioning existing
conditions, solving ambiguous problems and developing new solutions. The notion
of developmental learning used here has links to Dewey's (1910/1997) notion of
reflection, as well as to such different traditions as Engeström's (1987) activity
theory based model of expansive learning and Argyris' *et al.* (1985) model of
investigative organizational learning. The distinction between adaptive and
developmental learning will be further elaborated in section 4 below.

As noted above, the concepts of reflection and reflective practice have been
used for quite some time by various theorists in their attempts to conceptualize
and understand processes of experiential learning (see also Boud, Chapter 13 in
this volume). What then is meant by the concept of reflection as used in this chapter?
Because the concept of reflection will be dealt with more thoroughly in the next

section, it suffices here to give a rough working definition of the concept. This will be done without any attempt to cover the immense literature on the subject, but rather on the basis of a selective review (e.g. Bengtsson 1995; Boud *et al.* 1985; Boud and Walker 1998; Dewey 1910/1997; Mezirow 1991; Schön 1983). Thus, for the purposes of this chapter, the concept of reflection can be broadly defined as a more or less deliberate and conscious process of interpreting and making sense of experience. More specifically, a process of reflection may be described and analyzed as interconnecting cognitive and emotional processes (thinking and feeling), and focusing on the planning, monitoring or evaluation of action, i.e. it can occur before, during or following the action. Furthermore, processes of reflection may be viewed as mental processes or as individual or collective actions (practices). Reflection and reflective practices can have a focus on the content, processes, or premises of certain activities, a focus on ourselves as persons (self-reflection), and/or a focus on political-emancipatory activities. In the next section, an attempt is made to say something more specific about the meaning and role of reflection in relation to practical actions and learning at work.

Four levels of action and reflection

The concept of action as used here has the general meaning of intentional behaviour. More specifically, the concept of action refers to behaviours that are carried out on the basis of implicit or explicit knowledge, rules or standards in order to accomplish a task or reach a goal. As noted by many philosophers (e.g. Searle, 1980) as well as behavioural scientists (e.g. March and Olson 1976), the intentional character of action does not necessarily imply that the actor, consciously or unconsciously, has intentions, motives or goals *before* acting. On the contrary, intentions, motives and goals may be discovered during or after the performance of an action through mechanisms of learning, or as reconstructions that are used in order to justify the action to oneself or others. Furthermore, there are actions that are best described as spontaneous, automatic or routinized behaviour (cf. below). Although actions are intentional, different aspects of the context and its rule systems are assumed to create constraints or opportunities for action (Burns and Flam 1987). Conversely, people are assumed to actively influence and shape the contextual conditions under which they live and work.

How then can the meaning and role of reflection in relation to practical action and learning be understood? As a starting-point for discussion of this issue, a distinction is made here between four levels of action called:

- skill-based (routinized) action (Level I);
- rule-based action (Level II);
- knowledge-based action (Level III);
- reflective action (Level IV).

This typology is based on theory and research within the field of cognitive action theory (e.g. Frese and Zapf 1994; Rasmussen 1986). The assumption is that the different levels of action entail different levels of reflection. Although the different levels of action are assumed to be organized hierarchically, reflection and action on one level do not exclude parallel or integrated activity at other levels. In practice, optimal handling of a certain task may require performance at a specific level of action, or performance at different levels, in sequence or in parallel (Olsen and Rasmussen 1989).

The level of skill-based action

At the skill-based (routinized) level, actions are performed without much conscious attention and control. Generally, the acting subject cannot verbally report the knowledge the actions are based on (cf. Berry and Broadbent 1988). Thus, in this sense we can talk about this level of action as being governed by implicit or tacit knowledge. The actions are typically performed smoothly and with little subjective effort. The information processing is parallel and rapid. Although performance is automatized and governed by implicit knowledge, routinized actions are not performed passively or 'mindlessly'. On the contrary, higher-level control functions are assumed to monitor ongoing actions and to anticipate upcoming problems and demands in the environment (Olsen and Rasmussen 1989). Consistent with this observation, Giddens (1984) talks about the 'reflexive monitoring of action' to indicate the active character of routine actions. In several respects, performance at this level of action corresponds to what Schön (1983) calls knowing-in-action. That is, performance that occurs through smooth 'on-line' anticipations and adjustments in response to variation and changes in contextual conditions.

Performance at the level of skill-based action is, somewhat paradoxically, both a result of and an effective barrier to learning. It is a result of learning in the sense that routinized actions are established through explicit or implicit processes of learning (Anderson 1982, 1983; Berry and Broadbent 1988). However, once established, actions at this level are very difficult to change and 'relearn'. This is especially true if one only, or primarily, relies on intellectual and verbal forms of education and training (Frese and Zapf 1994; Gersick and Hackman 1990), or if reflection is treated as primarily an intellectual exercise (cf. Boud and Walker 1998).

However, routinization of action also means that a person can master many activities without much cognitive effort, and thereby is able to reallocate attention and time from routine tasks to more creative tasks. Besides creating feelings of mastery and self-confidence, this provides the freedom to perform cognitive operations while acting (e.g. to solve problems while performing routine work). In this sense, well-established routines and action patterns may be seen as preconditions for generating the freedom and variation of action that we associate with creativity and developmental learning. Furthermore, the consolidation of thought and action patterns as routines or habits is also a way of coping with the daily flow of events, problem situations and contradictory demands, while maintaining a sense of security and stability in life (Giddens 1984).

People function well at a routinized level of action until problems or surprises of one kind or another, positive or negative, arise. These require, instead, a capacity for rule-based, or even for knowledge-based and/or reflective action. That is, we need to be able to depart from our routine conduct. This is clearly in line with

Dewey's (1910/1997) view of reflection as a process which begins with a felt difficulty or disturbance in the routinized way of handling a certain task or situation (cf. also Schön 1983 and his notion of reflection-in-action). Excessive routinization, however, may easily impede our detection and management of contextual changes or disturbances. As a consequence, we tend in many situations to ignore or misinterpret changes in our surroundings, so as to maintain existing structures and patterns of thought and action.

The level of rule-based action

In contrast to the level of skill-based action, the rule-based level of action is characterized by a greater flexibility and a higher degree of conscious control. At this level of action a subject is assumed to be able to handle familiar situations or problems in accordance with stored and ready-made rules that can usually also be reported (Anderson 1982). Thus, there are stronger demands on a subject's skills to identify and interpret situations and problems that may emerge during action. Furthermore, actions are performed on the basis of a rule or procedure that is based on experiences from previous occasions of a similar character, communications from other people, or that has been developed through a process of problem solving and experimentation in the situation at hand.

The boundary between this level and the level of routinized action is not distinct. Much of the discussion concerning the level of routinized actions is also relevant at the rule-based level. For example, the double function of routinization as being potentially both supportive and restraining for learning and knowledge creation is equally relevant for this level of action. In particular, there is a risk for functional fixation and adherence to rules that are no longer valid due to, for example, changes in the situation or in the task at hand.

Learning at this level of action is linked to the interpretation and application of rules and procedural knowledge ('know-how'). This is far from a simple mechanical process. As argued by Burns and Flam (1987), rules are often adapted and reinterpreted in the actual situations where they are used. This process is critically dependant on the subject's ability to fill in the openness and incompleteness that characterize most rules. In many respects, reflection at this level of action comes close to the way Schön (1983) uses the notion of reflection-in-action: it is driven by unexpected outcomes of actions ('surprises') and it gives rise to experiments in order to revise the rules of thumb or procedures currently in use. However, contrary to Schön's (1983) emphasis on the critical and analytical character of reflection-in-action, experiments conducted at the rule-based level of action appear to be based on observed empirical correlations of successful acts and their outcomes, rather than on an analytical diagnosis of the situation (Olsen and Rasmussen 1989).

The levels of knowledge-based and reflective action

At the knowledge-based level, the actions are consciously controlled, generated and selected on the basis of analyses of tasks and goals, previous experiences and contextual conditions. The knowledge base for action may comprise factual knowledge and/or more general theoretical and explanatory knowledge. This is the level of action that we move to when we encounter novel or unfamiliar situations for which no rules or procedural knowledge (know-how) are available from previous experience. At this level of action, performance is assumed to be controlled by goals and based on explicit knowledge, i.e. knowledge that we are able to report verbally.

At this level of action, there is both the space for and a need for reflective exploration, interpretation and problem solving. In this sense, Schön's (1983) notion of 'reflection-in-action' may be an adequate way to characterize the meaning and role of reflection at this level of action as well. However, in contrast to the rule-based level, there is also space for analytical diagnosis of a situation, and for what Mezirow (1991) calls the critical assessment of the content and processes of activities.

The main difference between the knowledge-based and the reflective levels of action is that the latter level refers to actions based on evaluations and reflections concerning not only the performance and consequences of actions, but also reflections concerning the task and the goals themselves. That is, what Mezirow (1991) calls critical reflection or reflection on the premises of action. One of the crucial elements of this reflection process is to make explicit, and thereby testable, the often implicit and taken for granted premises of our actions. This requires that the actor is able to see the action and its consequences in perspective. However it also requires the ability to consider alternatives and to critically analyze underlying assumptions and other conditions of action. Thus the concept of reflection relevant at this level comes close to Schön's (1983) notion of reflection-on-action. What seems to be essential to such a process is that it is guided by explicit knowledge that can be used in the analysis of the task and goal of action, its underlying assumptions and in interpreting and evaluating the consequences of the action. In this kind of reflective process, logical inconsistencies as well as self-reflection become focal concerns, which also make a reliance on meta-cognitive knowledge necessary, i.e. knowledge about oneself and one's own knowledge, its scope and limits, strengths and weaknesses.

Learning as an interplay between levels of action and reflection

Now, the distinction between adaptive and developmental learning (see section 2 above) can be somewhat elaborated in terms of the model of different levels of action and reflection that was introduced in the previous section. Considering first the process of adaptive learning, it can be conceptualized as a process of learning where the learning subject manages to handle a certain task or situation in a routinized (automatized) way. Adaptive learning thus implies a learning process where the learning subject 'moves' from a reflective or knowledge-based level of action to levels of action founded on experience-based, implicit knowledge (cf. Anderson 1982; Berry and Broadbent 1988), i.e. to a skill-based level of action. However, this process could also begin at the level of rule-based learning, or even directly at the skill-based level. In the latter case, learning occurs through processes of imitation and trial and error (Olsen and Rasmussen 1989). This view of adaptive learning can be related to the well-known stage model for the development of expertise proposed by Dreyfus and Dreyfus (1986). According to this model, it is argued that the level of expertise is characterized, among other things, by a kind of automatic, fluid task performance resembling the kind of automatized actions that are characteristic of the level of skill-based action as defined above.

Contrary to this process of adaptive learning, the process of developmental learning is based on our ability to break our way out of categories and procedures defined in advance, and to design and establish new patterns of thought and action through processes of reflection and problem solving. This could also be described as an 'upward movement' from the level of skill-based (routinized) action to the levels of knowledge-based or reflective action. As argued above, these latter levels require conscious analytical thinking, reflection on previous experience and explicit knowledge of the object and task at hand. This type of learning sequence could be expected if an individual (or group), while working at a routinized level of action, encounters an unfamiliar problem or a new situation for which there is no ready-made rule or solution available. In such a situation, one is forced to seek a solution via problem solving. This idea of adaptive and developmental learning as an interplay between the four levels of action is illustrated in Figure 4.1 above.

To further clarify the distinction between adaptive and developmental learning, two additional points should be made. Firstly, the distinction does not concern two forms of learning that are in some sense mutually exclusive. Rather, they represent two complementary forms of learning, where one form or the other can be dominant or relatively inconspicuous, depending on which conditions prevail in the specific situation. Secondly, both forms of learning are needed. Although adaptive learning might be perceived as having mainly negative connotations, for example, focusing on people adjusting themselves to a perhaps aversive reality, the significance of this kind of learning should not be underestimated. Newcomers' socialization to a new workplace and their attempts to master existing norms, cultural practices and routines can be mentioned as examples of the importance of adaptive learning (Fenwick 2003). Conversely, developmental or creative learning, although the connotations are positive, may nevertheless entail negative aspects. For example, a too strong emphasis on flexibility, transformation of prevailing practices, and the creation of new solutions might create negative stress and feelings of anxiety and insecurity. Under favourable conditions, however, developmental learning might be a driving force for change and innovation in an organization (Brown and Duguid 1991). In addition, studies of expertise in different areas (e.g. Olsen and Rasmussen 1989) attest to the importance of being able to deal alternately with well-known, routine problems and new or unknown problematic situations and, thereby, being able to alternate between an adaptive and a developmental mode of learning.

Promoting reflection and learning at work

As indicated above, it is important for an individual (and for the organization that he or she is part of) to maintain a balance between adaptive and developmental learning. One of the difficulties in doing this is that these two forms of learning

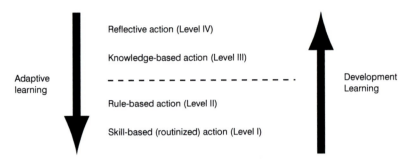

Figure 4.1 Adaptive and developmental learning as an interplay between the four levels of action and reflection

seem to require different conditions (Ellström 2001). Another difficulty has to do with the above noted tendency present in many workplaces to 'make invisible' the existence and significance of developmental learning in the actual carrying out of work. This type of learning is not paid attention to and is thus not included in formal, official job descriptions, i.e. in what Brown and Duguid (1991) call the canonical practice.

How should these difficulties be dealt with? As was touched upon in the introductory section, more qualified informal learning at work presupposes a workplace designed to promote learning. Of course this does not imply a view of work-based learning as an automatic process that may be 'triggered' simply by arranging 'objective' working conditions in a way that is likely to facilitate learning. On the contrary, in order to be able to identify and use potential opportunities for reflection and learning at work, employees need to have access to different kinds of learning resources, including not only 'objective' factors such as space and time for learning, but equally important, a range of subjective factors. Such subjective factors would include a subject's knowledge and understanding of the task at hand (Brehmer 1980), awareness of learning opportunities and self-awareness of how one has dealt with such opportunities in the past (Fenwick 2003), as well as a number of emotional and social factors. The latter would include motivation, self-efficacy, personal and occupational identities. Taken together, these subjective factors constitute important components of what might be called a learning readiness (Ellström 2001). Of course, such a learning readiness is itself the result of previous learning.

This argument can be further illustrated and developed by relating it to the issue of time and other resources as preconditions for reflection and learning at work, and the view that there is a trade-off between time for routine activity (production) and time for learning. In line with this view, there is ample evidence indicating that developmental learning actually requires specific resources ('slack') so as not to be driven out by the demands of routine activities (March 1991; March and Simon 1958). Furthermore, the relevance of the time-dimension to discussions of reflection and learning at work is also clearly shown by Eraut (1995, 2002) in his criticism of Schön's (1983) notion of reflection-in-action. As argued by Eraut from data on teaching activities in classroom settings, time-pressure in a classroom limits the scope for deliberative thinking, and thereby also the scope for reflection-in-action in the sense used by Schön (1983). This conclusion is also supported by data from studies of naturalistic decision-making (e.g. Klein *et al.*, 1993). As shown in several studies within this tradition, time-pressure tends to create a situation that favours the kind of intuitive, non-analytic decision-making processes typical of a skill-based level of action (cf. the notion of knowing-in-action as distinct from reflection-in-action as proposed by Schön 1983). More deliberative and reflective activities focusing on the content, processes and outcomes of actions require time – time to observe, time to think and time to exchange ideas with others (Ellström 2002; Eraut 2002).

Of course, this view does not imply that simply providing time for reflection and learning would mean that this time will be used for reflective activities. Thus, even if time is a necessary condition for reflection, it is hardly sufficient. The crucial condition is of course how the time is used. To handle this issue, it might be useful to move from a focus on the allocation of 'clock-time' between different activities (e.g. an allocation of time between time for production and time for reflection), to a focus on peoples' temporal structuring of their work (cf. Antona-copoulou and Tsoukas 2002; Hassard 2002). In this latter perspective, time is defined by organizational members and is the product of prevailing beliefs and cultural practices in the organization. By implication, a change in the use of time in an organization would be viewed as a result of collective learning processes, rather than a consequence of a management decision to change the allocation of time.

In fact, such a view is supported by the findings of Fenwick (2003) cited above. According to her results, an increased subjective awareness of the learning opportunities encountered in daily work, and how these learning opportunities were handled, proved more important than the allocation of 'objective' learning time for the promotion of learning from everyday activity. Thus, these subjects appeared to 'learn how to learn' from their own practice and, thereby, also how to find the time for this learning. From this perspective, then, the first priority of management should not be to allocate time for learning which is separate from everyday practice. Rather, the focus should be on putting development and learning issues on the agenda, and ensuring that the organizational members have the necessary knowledge and skills to be able to identify and deal with these issues as an integral part of ongoing activities.

In line with such a view, a number of studies have shown that there is, in practice, substantial creativity and possibly also space for reflective activities in many kinds of work processes (e.g. Barley and Kunda 2001; Brown and Duguid 1991; Hirschorn 1984). However, as also shown by these studies there are tendencies in many organizations to drive out reflective activities from the organization's official arena and into the 'shadow system' of the organization, or perhaps to outside the workplace. Seeking a better understanding of how reflection and developmental learning takes place in practice is therefore a key research task. Another key research task is to seek a better understanding of how reflective practices can be supported by, for example, being made 'visible' and a part of the official language and agenda in working life.

52   *Per-Erik Ellström*

References

Anderson, J.R. (1982) 'The acquisition of cognitive skill', *Psychological Review*, 89: 369–406.

Anderson, J.R. (1983) *The Architecture of Cognition*, Cambridge, MA: Harvard University Press.

Antonacopoulou, E. and Tsoukas, H. (2002) 'Time and reflexivity in organization studies: an introduction', *Organization Studies*, 23, 6: 857–62.

Argyris, C., Putnam, R. and McLain Smith, D. (1985) *Action Science. Concepts. Methods, and Skills for Research and Intervention*, San Francisco: Jossey-Bass.

Ashton, D., Felstead, A. and Green, F. (2000) 'Skills in the British workplace', in F. Coffield (ed.) *Differing visions of a Learning Society*, Bristol: The Policy Press.

Barley, S.R. and Kunda, G. (2001) 'Bringing work back in', *Organization Science*, 12, 1: 76–95.

Barnett, R. (1999) 'Learning to work and working to learn', in D. Boud and J. Garrick (eds) *Understanding Learning at War*, London: Routledge.

Bengtsson, J. (1995) 'What is reflection? On reflection in the teaching profession and teacher education', *Teachers and Teaching*, 1, 1: 23–32.

Berry, D.C. and Broadbent, D.E. (1988) 'Interactive tasks and the implicit–explicit distinction', *British Journal of Psychology*, 79: 251–72.

Boud, D. and Walker, D. (1998) 'Promoting reflection in professional courses: the challenge of context', *Studies in Higher Education*, 23, 2: 191–206.

Boud, D., Keogh, R. and Walter, D. (eds) (1985) *Reflection: Turning Experience into Learning*, London: Kogan Page.

Brehmer, B. (1980) 'In one word: not from experience', *Acta Psychologica*, 45: 223–41.

Brown, J.S. and Duguid, P. (1991) 'Organizational learning and communities of practice. Towards a unified view of working, learning, and innovation', *Organization Science*, 2: 40–57.

Burns, T.R. and Flam, H. (1987) *The Shaping of Social Organization. Social Rule System Theory with Applications*, Beverly Hills: Sage Publications.

Coffield, F. (ed.) (2000) *The Necessity of Informal Learning*, Bristol: The Policy Press.

Dewey, J. (1910/1997) *How We Think. A Restatement of the Relation of Reflective Thinking to the Educative Process*, Mineola, NY: Dover Publications Inc.

Dreyfus, S.E. and Dreyfus, H.L. (1986) *Mind over Machine*, Oxford: Basil Blackwell.

Ellström, P.-E. (2001) 'Integrating learning and work: conceptual issues and critical conditions', *Human Resource Development Quarterly*, 12, 4.

Ellström, P.-E. (2002) 'Time and the logics of learning', *Lifelong Learning in Europe*, 2: 86–93.

Engeström, Y. (1987) *Learning by Expanding: An Activity Theoretical Approach to Development Research*, Helsinki, Finland: Orienta Konsultit Oy.

Eraut, M. (1995) 'Schön shock: a case for reframing reflection-in-action?', *Teachers and Teaching*, 1, 1: 9–22.

Eraut, M. (2000) 'Non-formal learning, implicit learning and tacit knowledge in professional work', in F. Coffield (ed.) (2000) *The Necessity of Informal Learning*, Bristol: Policy Press.

Eraut, M. (2002) 'Menus for choosy diners', *Teachers and Teaching*, 8, 3/4: 371–9.

Fenwick, T.J. (2003) 'Professional growth plans: possibilities and limitations of an organization-wide employee development strategy', *Human Resource Development Quarterly*, 14, 1: 59–77.

Frese, M. and Zapf, D. (1994) 'Action as the core of work psychology. A German approach', in H.C. Triandis, M.D. Dunnette and L.M. Hough (eds) *Handbook of Industrial and Organizational Psychology*, Palo Alto, CA: Consulting Psychologists Press.

Gersick, C.J.G. and Hackman, J.R. (1990) 'Habitual routines in task-performing groups', *Organizational Behavior and Human Decision Processes*, 47: 65–97.

Giddens, A. (1984) *The Constitution of Society*, Berkeley: University of California Press.

Hassard, J. (2002) 'Organizational time: modern, symbolic, and postmodern reflections', *Organization Studies*, 23, 6: 885–92.

Hirschhorn, L. (1984) *Beyond Mechanization: Work and Technology in a Postindustrial Age*, Cambridge, MA: The MIT Press.

Klein, G.A., Orasanu, J., Calderwood, R. and Zsambok, C. (eds) (1993) *Decision Making in Action: Models and Method*, Norwood, NJ: Ablex Publishing.

March, J.G. (1991) 'Exploration and Exploitation in Organizational Learning', *Organizational Science*, 2: 71–87.

March, J.G. and Olsen, J.P. (1976) *Ambiguity and Choice in Organizations*, Bergen: Universitetsforlaget.

March, J.G. and Simon, H.A. (1958) *Organizations*, New York: Wiley.

Mezirow, J. (1991) *Transformative Dimensions of Adult Learning*, San Francisco: Jossey-Bass.

Olsen, S.E. and Rasmussen, J. (1989) 'The reflective expert and the prenovice', in L. Bainbridge and S.A. Ruiz Quintanilla (eds) (1989) *Developing Skills with Information Technology*, Chichester: John Wiley and Sons.

Rasmussen, J. (1986) *Information Processing and Human Machine Interaction. An Approach to Cognitive Engineering*, New York: North Holland.

Schön, D.A. (1983) *The Reflective Practitioner: How Professionals Think in Action*, New York: Basic Books.

Searle, J.R. (1980) 'The intentionality of intention and action', *Cognitive Science*, 4: 47–70.

Shani, A.B. (Rami) and Docherty, P. (2003) *Learning by Design: Building Sustainable Organizations*, Oxford: Blackwell.

5 Collective reflection and learning

From formal to reflective participation

Peter Cressey

Introduction

In this chapter I want to look at the issue of the growth of collective productive reflection in the workplace and the changing forms that it takes. I will be concentrating on the development of employee participation as a form of collective reflection, taking as my starting-point the hypothesis that there are many forms of collective reflection inside workplaces that are not recognized as such. Indeed the notion of productive reflection has no central academic core in a singular discip-linary approach but takes a position that crosses accepted academic boundaries. Because of this it is an unsettling concept and the journey leads writers into unfamiliar territories whose correspondence may not at first glance seem obvious. However, the growing importance of the issue does seem to be manifest and comes from an observation that similar long-term trends or phenomena are being observed from the very different areas of industrial relations, education, sociology and management science. These centre upon growing moves to the decentralization of problem-solving, the greater role for critical reflection, the questioning of expert knowledge systems and the need for a methodology/ies sensitive to the embedded function of knowledge and action.

The debate about collective reflection is important in the action research and workplace learning arenas but has not found as much resonance in the industrial relations or human resources field. In these latter areas the issues are instead re-represented in terms of employee voice – how employees can get involved in enterprise decision-making, consultation structures or problem-solving at an operational level. Because of this, in industrial relations/industrial sociology much of the emphasis is upon the centrality of power and how it is brokered inside organizations – what determines the strength of employee voice rather than its active or constitutive parts. For the HR theorists employee participation is again characterized in terms of employee voice and their related institutional forms – but more in terms of their functional fit in terms of communications and corporate performance. Moreover, reflection and learning interactions have historically been framed in terms of vocational training separable and largely outside the remit of the workplace, hence the added disciplinary dimension that educationalists would bring is similarly problematic.

In this chapter I want to review the issue of employee participation from the perspective of collective refection looking at the ways and forms that employee intervention can and does take. I also want to look at the way researchers have characterized the collective contributions employees make and, finally, the methodologies best suited to allowing active and reflective contributions within the context of differing institutions and differing interests. The chapter describes three key phases of employee participation drawing upon European research evidence that indicates a move from formalistic through functional to reflective participation. Taking as its starting-point the wide ranging changes in production and organizational structures described in Chapter 2, it illustrates the growing necessity for productive collective reflection at the workplace. The movement to more decentralized and collective reflection formats is not, however, straightforward and the current situation sees both potential and problems in its enactment inside organizations and workplaces.

Three phases of participation

The long-term changes in production regimes mentioned in Chapter 2 have been emerging strongly in the past three decades. These have been exerting a correspondingly strong influence upon workplace practices in the spheres of employee involvement, problem solving and knowledge creating practice. Here I want to draw out how these changes be described using evidence regarding changes in the level, format and content of employee involvement to suggest that there are three overlapping phases evident, I have named them the *formal*, the *functional* and the *embedded* phases of collective reflection.

Formal reflection

As mentioned earlier most of the post-war period's discussions regarding the role of employee participation/dialogue has tended to be pitched at an institutional level. As such this was an issue for the social partners drawn from the industrial relations arena. The perspective on worker inputs into decision-making is framed by the institutional formats and traditions of various countries, their national representational formats and the social and political milieus (Poole 1986). Hence key social actors met at various levels of the economy and workers' interests were represented there; this overlapping format is well-illustrated in Europe by the concept of the Social Dialogue. Such institutions were additional to the nationally dictated forms of employee representation and rule-creating mechanisms found at state and enterprise levels. In this realm the key words that inform the notions of employee involvement were those associated with processes of institutionalization – formality, committee based, exchange based upon consultation, legitimacy based upon membership numbers rather than job-based competence, indirect representation that led to an indirect form of workplace intervention that was not necessarily based upon the fruits of collective worker reflection.

The post-war history of trade union attempts for extending worker influence over enterprise decision-making show them pursuing a '*rights-based*' approach where workers or, more likely, their representatives can redress the power imbalance in enterprises. In this perspective participation as a democratic force in industry is uppermost (Cressey and Williams 1990). The major form of participation is one that has a concern for the creation and guarding of procedures that cede rights to the parties. Often such rights were relatively distant from the workplace allowing for worker representation (whether unionized or not) to sit on boards of directors (West Germany), Works Councils (Netherlands, West Germany, Belgium) or to make national agreements that were supplementary to national bargaining (Denmark, Sweden). Non-statutory formats such as the latter could also be supplemented by enterprise and company specific formats for consultation (UK and many others) again that took the idea of involvement to be one based upon separated representation, with parallel forms of separated reflection from workplace concerns.

The result of this is was a privileging of rights-based influence rather than active and thoughtful interventions in the work organization that addressed specific workplace problems. Greater importance was attached to the guarding of the perimeter of employment conditions, union representation and redundancy and, above all else, the continuation of stable structures for agreements. This is not a criticism – it represents an approach that stresses stability and protection rather than change and intervention as the mark of workplace/union activity. However, in our terms it does represent a form of *reductive reflection* that lessened the ability of the workforce to engage in and actively change important and immediate issues. Quite often the workers who did do so were treated with suspicion – for instance those involved in early forms of quality circles were seen as infringing union action and entering managerially defined agendas.

This approach was not only frustrating for workplace members but also for senior trade unionists who could see that situations of change and turbulence in corporate affairs demanded forms of employee and union involvement of a qualitatively different order. A point made forcibly by trade union representatives in a Leonardo study is that in the face of production system changes and the reorientation of basic functions new social mechanisms for agreement and feedback have to be inaugurated. The existence of a committee, a works council or a formally organized joint consultation structure does *not* signal the existence of trade union influence or real and vital participation anymore. As the intellectual content of jobs grows, as the demands for greater social skills increase and as the importance of active problem solving develops, the need for active rather than passive involvement particularly in human resource issues grows. A thread running through most of the cases signaled here are the active and self-responsible involvement strategies on behalf of the trade unions and employees. To quote Cressey *et al.* (1999: 30):

> The dialogue is increasingly inside the strategies of management, involved in elaborating future needs, helping the transmission of greater awareness of corporate developments and actively assisting the implementation of change.

This last element can be painful for the unions when it involves job reductions and restructuring, but here as the cases show the unions have not flinched from involvement providing there is a quid pro quo. This has usually meant a call for *real* partnership – being involved before the issue at hand is cut and dried, being involved in the elaboration process, implementation and evaluation – not as outsiders but in tandem.

The question that this poses is how can unions get an active role and be involved? In Europe since 1976 one has seen the demise of national rights-based formats (IDE Group, 1993), only the EU has promoted a statutory approach based on Directives enhancing employee rights to information and consultation. In contrast as we will see below, the enterprise has increasingly become the focus for participative initiatives.

Functional reflection

The role for what becomes known as direct dialogue and participation by the worker was not the central issue in the previous approach. Research in the past three decades, however, has looked at how more direct representative approaches, where the frameworks of interaction and participation, are built up both in terms of active groupwork as well as networks of action inside enterprises that can encourage forms of critical reflection (EPOC 1997; Purcell 1995). In part these emphasize a more functional contribution that participation can make to making the enterprise more productive and hence secure for all of its workforce. For enterprise management worker participation can be a '*productive force*' aiding the efficient use of enterprise resources that might best be described as positive-sum force in industry. Participation and employee inputs are valued for the joint benefits that they provide for management and the workforce, allowing for improvements in the industrial relations atmosphere, the securing of high trust relationships and the setting up of procedures through which productivity and innovation improvements can be reached.

Evidence from European case studies of participative firms shows a complicated picture inside enterprises where many formats can exist that are both direct and indirect in character. German firms, for instance may have at the same time, statutory worker directors, works councils, joint decision-making forums on health and safety, consultative arrangements, teamwork, quality circles, direct communication programs and collectively agreed company agreements. Other European countries may equal such provisions or have different mixtures of these formats operable in enterprises at the same time. There are then variations in format, a number of key models of participation and these importantly will vary in the form and nature of participation that they contain, in the degree of influence in the decision-making process secured and in the ability to reflect upon and get inside a range of issues.

A dominant trend in the period since the mid-1970s has been a distinct move away from those institutional forms portrayed above, and a move towards more direct involvement and problem-solving. In both Europe and America the same pattern is repeated where direct versions of employee voice are replacing the more representative or negotiating kind (Purcell 1995; Kaufman 2001; Brown *et al.* 1998). The predominance of the direct and informal approach across Europe (EPOC 1997) have reinforced this and supported claims made by Purcell (1995) about the possible 'de-institutionalization of industrial relations'.

Alongside this has been the growth in importance of team structures that demand high inputs by team members into the production processes and the implementation of new strategies and technology. From the early 1980s Sundstrom *et al.* (1990) and later Mueller (1994) indicate that team formats vary in the kind of productive function that they perform. The taxonomy created by Sundstrom *et al.* shows four distinct formats – firstly advice and involvement teams that are restricted in decision making scope and activity, such as quality circles that get involved in detailed suggestions as to how products and processes might be improved. The second form is production and service teams that create or generate given products or services, an example of this could be semi/autonomous workgroups such as those developed by socio-technical experiments. A third form is projects and development team with much more involvement in the design and collaboration over product outcomes bringing in diverse employees, often, but not solely, white collar or professional, within design teams. Finally, action and negotiation teams are distinguished that can comprise highly skilled specialists often directly tied to specific performance events, for instance flight crew and surgery teams. What the analysis shows is the greater emphasis placed upon how teams participate in task design, in mission clarity with autonomy to challenge the given truths, and how they use collective knowledge to achieve and improve tasks and performance feedback.

However, as discussed in Chapters 6 and 12 in this volume not all team structures offer participative or reflective opportunities. The lean production variant reflects the restricted form of teamwork as Roth (1997) found out in looking at the effect of lean production in German industry. He identified the teamwork model used in lean production as a distinct turn away from what he calls the 'qualified teamwork' format used by the Swedish company Volvo. In the Lean Production system, although teamwork is at the centre of changes, Roth (1997) sees the main aim as 'rationalization'. So rather than seek learning or developmental outcomes the main thrust of teams is:

> to get clear productivity gains, to enable Kaizen to work, to strengthen cost-centre awareness, to extend worker responsibilities over areas that individuals would refuse to accede to and to enable a consensus to be formed that limits worker autonomy whilst increasing management control.

The importation of Japanese-style teamwork as a form of rationalization, according to Roth, actually increases stressful working, worsens working conditions, does little for worker skills and attempts to separate workers from their trade unions. The areas of productive reflection in these revolve around being given additional responsibilities for intervening to maintain quality, maintenance and job continuity.

For continuous improvement (*Kaizen*) to operate one has to have the ability to collect data, monitor problems and propose solutions.

So the process of decentralization of reflection is occurring but here within a highly structured and intensive format. This alerts us to the two-sided potentiality for exploiting decentralized forms of collective reflection. Much of the debate about this has been carried on inside the high performance workgroup/systems (HPWS) discussion. On the positive side High-Performance Work Practices can improve the knowledge, skills and abilities of employees and also increase their motivation, reduce shirking and enhance the retention of quality employees. Proponents of HPWS theory claim that they are characterized by a common desire to raise employee skills, motivation and empowerment through various ways including enhanced problem solving (Appelbaum *et al.* 2000). However, Ramsay *et al.* (2000) recognize the systemic trend in capitalism towards the intensification of work, which means that managers are driven constantly to find ways to make employees work longer or even harder as a means to maximize labour input and this includes the intensification of both the physical and mental elements of work.

Embedded collective reflection

We have seen above how different phases of participation have moved from a rights based agenda to one that centres upon production and problem solving. Here another phase is described where the issue of collective reflection is placed at the core of workplace practice. With the growth of 'learning organization' philosophies that centre upon individual, team and corporate structures for reflection we can see a corresponding change in the form of employee participation (Nyhan *et al.* 2003). As Tranfield *et al.* (1998: 378) have noted:

> The main function of social organization is argued to have changed from being concerned with standardization, coordination and control, to being concerned with the delivery of creativity and innovation. The prime function (of management and supervision is) supporting the new technologies by creating problem-solving non-standard transactions which cannot be easily handled by the information technology operating an automated 'corporate algorithm'.

The need identified here is for a workforce input that can critically challenge systems thinking rather than celebrate it, for non-formal networks of *dialogue* and *reflection* that operate outside enclosed system loops. To see the issue of employee involvement from this perspective then means a re-alignment of issues around how best to use expertise, how to engage people in specific processes of reflection and dialogue and a finer appreciation of the createdness of enterprise added value – the importance to this of the social constructedness of workplace practices and processes. Such trends also raise larger questions for future employee participatory forums and what the balance between institutionalization and active intervention of workers as individuals should be. It also brings into question the union role in encouraging direct participation and reflection in a way that does not contradict collectivism and representation (see Breidensjö and Huzzard, Chapter 12 in this volume). The issue pulls unions into considering how they can best represent their members in issues previously thought to be outside their accepted sphere of activity: issues of creativity, strategy, internal dialogue that enable active intervention in design and practice. It also has to confront the nature of entrenched interests and the barriers that these impose in real-life situations, these can be referred to as accretions of practices and expectations that have grown up over decades and cannot be eliminated overnight.

So for now we can see how there is a trend in employee participation that detects a change in the institutional form and level of involvement. However in that debate more emphasis is placed upon the empirical extent of institutionalism and its format rather than the constituents of that involvement in terms of reflection, learning if any creative difference is made. For this we need to look elsewhere at debates that go a little outside the industrial relations and human resource disciplinary approaches, bringing in an action research perspective and a social constructivist one.

The application of alternative social science techniques that enhance workforce collaboration and increased efficiency was pioneered by Kurt Lewin. He undertook path-breaking action research into the positive functions of worker participation in improving work conditions and increasing productivity (Lewin 1946; Weisbord 1987; Gustavsen 1992). Lewin sought to bridge the gap between theory and practice by extending experimental methods into the factory so as to allow social science to make real changes to organizational mileux. His pioneering experimental work with groups was later taken up by Coch and French (1948). They devised experimental projects to test the impact of worker participation inside enterprises. What they did was to create groups with different forms and degrees of participation in the changes. After monitoring the changes, the researchers came to the conclusion that the group who were involved directly in the change processes without mediation through representation reached the highest levels of productivity, leading them to conclude that:

> The more participation the better the ability to cope with change and utilize it for productivity purposes.
>
> (Gustavsen 1992: 12)

This perspective shifts the focus away from the institutional participation alluded to earlier, towards understanding the active and constitutive role of participants in change processes. There are many exemplars of the action research approach and all of them take the debate about employee participation into a concern with the process and methodology of that participation. Gustavsen (1992) gives a good account of many of the programs of action research since Lewin and privileges one form of action research that he entitles 'democratic dialogue'. This format emerges from the Swedish research program – LOM (Leadership, Organization and Co-determination) that operationalized the concept of democratic dialogue.

(See Gustavsen 1992: 7–9 for a fuller description of the program's aims and methodology.) He claims the development of democratic dialogue went beyond the notion of limited participation in experimental problem-solving to a more consistently interactive and reflective process.

An author who builds on this analysis is Romme (2003). He advocates collective reflection within a design-oriented methodology of intervention. His work was carried out in a Dutch enterprise that sought to go beyond the limited form of institutional participation. Its CEO wished to transcend the conflicts of interest often generated through the works council structure. He put forward an alternative based on a *circular organizational design* aimed at the creation of learning ability by active participation at the organizational level as well as at the group and individual levels. The actual ground rules and methodology in essence illustrate some of the key elements of the design model:

> The circular methodology acknowledges the ill-defined and embedded nature of organizational problems. Moreover this methodology appears to focus upon finding solutions, rather than on extensive analysis of the current situation. It also emphasizes and enables participation by people involved.
>
> (Romme 2003: 566)

This circular organizational design process is now legitimated by the Dutch government so that an enterprise adopting this model is not subject to the legal provisions of the Works Councils requirements (Romme 2003: 566).

The literature on situated learning and communities of practice is clearly relevant to forms of reflective engagement in the workplace. The seminal work has been conducted by Lave and Wenger (1991) and Wenger (1998). They use cross-disciplinary sources to underpin their work. Their main concepts are learning and practice in situated contexts. Learning is described as being at the confluence of four different processes entailing the construction of:

- identity (learning as becoming);
- meaning (learning as experience);
- community (learning as belonging);
- practice (learning as doing) (Wenger 1998: 5).

The essence of this approach is the self-formation of sub-cultures and identities. Employees in their everyday life confront with codified and explicit knowledge, in collaboration with the wider institution and in collaboration with each other. The notion of collective reflection is instilled in the ways people acquire, challenge and sustain their actions, the way they reify processes and reformulate them. Learning in practice for Wenger (1998: 85) means processes for:

- Evolving forms of mutual engagement for example mutual relationships.
- *Understanding and tuning their enterprise* – the definition and reconciliation of interests, accountability.

- *Developing their repertoire, styles and discourses* – meanings, artifacts, stories and the creating and breaking of routines.

There are a number of detailed studies that support Lave and Wenger's analysis, for example, Seeley Brown and Duguid (1991), Orr (1990, 1996) and Bechky (2003). These studies give life to the analytical concepts stated above and display the active and generative processes of reflection and collective action that go to sustain and crucially change workplace practice. The communities of practice exist within constraints such as with customer demands, financial budgets, work organizational forms and managerial regimes of control. The studies provide us with rich ethnographic accounts of the createdness of practice and the importance of community within that. For me reflection is intimately bound up with the social learning theory described in Chapter 3, one that takes us away from the cognitive and discursive theories that are in common usage:

> to focus attention directly upon learning as a pervasive embodied activity involving the acquisition, maintenance and transformation of knowledge through the process of interaction.
>
> (Contu and Willmott 2003: 285)

Discussion

The argument I put forward presents these movements and notes their identification of common trends. We have seen above how different phases or forms of participation have stressed a rights-based agenda, a production-based and a problem-solving agenda. The other theme described how the issue of collective reflection is placed at the core of workplace practice. One thing should be made clear here, the phases or forms do not supersede each other. All three variants of collective reflection are to be found in organizations in most European countries. In addition direct formats are not seen as means to bypass trade-union represent-ation. The employee participation alternatives offer rather different forms of collective reflection.

The further important question is: to what extent they are being inaugurated in organizations and workplaces? Much of the evidence of research indicates that whilst managers are aware of the necessity of employee involvement and the tapping of lay/tacit knowledge it is hard to find much depth in organizational practice where this is done in a continuous fashion. Much of the research on employee participation, undertaken by the British Department of Employment, by the European Foundation and by the European Commission, notes the consistent gap between aspirations and reality (EPOC 1997; Cressey and Williams 1990). In a similar fashion Contu and Willmott (2003) show how management often interpret much organizational research in a biased way, which often entails a conservative reading of Lave and Wenger that elevates the functionalist, at the expense of the radical interpretation. Contu and Willmott (2003) show how issues of power and interest are largely effaced meaning that the contradictory elements, the matters that unsettle, refute or challenge deep-seated managerialist principles are avoided. Addressing the issue of power and the representation of interests, there is no simple correspondence between efficacy and adoption of particular forms of participation. Indeed, much of what has been promoted in all three forms of participation – the formal, the functional and the embedded – threaten existing managerial cultures, systems and narratives.

Collective reflection unleashed in the three participative forms potentially *disrupt* the prevailing hierarchy and rules of procedure: profound questioning and critical reflection have to *unsettle* the consensus as it exists, and entail a potential loss of control for management. The issue now is the extent to which organizational actors have to and can live with uncertainty and ambiguity. Similarly in relation to the communities of practice Orr's (1990) account of the copier technicians also demonstrates how management, when faced with non-standard practice in terms of learning, reflection and action, stepped in to stop or obstruct the communal processes, the informal troubleshooting regimes and the learning by story-telling, demanding instead strict adherence to the official repairs manual.

The question of suitable forms for participation presents managers with the same dilemmas as in other areas in industrial sociology – how to unlock the creative forces of collective participation and reflection whilst at the same time retaining control over work procedures, learning processes, performance and output. (Cressey and MacInnes 1980.) The mantle of authority is difficult for management to discard. In retaining such processes of control they also retain a comfort zone that they know gives adequate but not necessarily good performance.

At the same time as the urge to re-impose control occurs, management recognizes that control per se does not generate the added value, the intangible assets of which learning and reflection are keys. In this sense management may have the authority to speak and decide but not necessarily to be right (Cunliffe 2003: 999) as the very processes of reflection imply a lack of certainty, the avoidance of self-referring systems, the need to countenance otherness and contradiction. The nub of the analysis points out that stakeholders, including trade unions and management, increasingly find themselves in situations of uncertainty, contradiction and ambiguity. This leads to doubts about whose expertise to privilege, to questions regarding how to mobilize organizational resources and how to deal with both the formal and embedded structures of collective reflection. In such ambiguity how does one manage? This highlights the need for precisely that new form of participation, listening, speaking and dialoguing – to enable active reflective as an on-going process.

Conclusion

There have been three forms described here in relation to employee collective reflection. Each form describes trends and processes that I contend are interconnected and point to a growing decentralization of problem-solving in the enterprise. Within that we see the need for egalitarian and democratic structures of engagement, the need also for active reflection processes that challenge and confront existing forms of knowledge, and the need for methodologies of appropriation and action that are sensitive to flux, ambiguity and social createdness. These movements may be described differently but one of the central ones seems to be from institutionalized participation to dialogue. Parallel to that movement is a reinvigoration of an action learning approach that sees less emphasis upon the reception of knowledge and more emphasis upon reflection and the creation of new knowledge. The chapter highlights that, among national and organizational diversity, there is a growing agreement regarding the greater role for critical and collective reflection due to the necessity of having to operate in complex situations of change involving multiple interests and stakeholders.

Creating processes, structures and institutions for collective reflection will not be easy, and the move to embedded reflection will not be generally achieved, given the constraints and complexities identified. What it does mean is a challenge to the stakeholders inside enterprises and workplaces to be open to a more experimental approach. To give recognition to lay knowledge based on experience married to experiment within a problem-oriented context. It also challenges both managers and trade union representatives to recognize the contribution and added value that flows from collective reflection outside the institutional forums. Above all it calls for the creation of a usable methodology for decentralized and collective reflection based in collaborative design processes.

References

Appelbaum, E., Bailey, T., Berg, P. and Kallenberg, A.L. (2000) *Why High Performance Work Systems Pay Off*, Ithaca. NY: Cornell University Press.

Bechky, B. (2003) 'Shared Meaning across Occupational Communities: The Transformation of Understanding on a Production Floor', *Organizational Science*, 14, 3: 312–30.

Brown, W., Deakin, S., Hudson, M., Pratten, C. and Ryan, P. (1998) 'The Individualisation of Employment Contracts in Britain', *Employment Relations Research Series*, 4, London: DTI.

Coch, L. and French, J.R.P. (1948) 'Overcoming Resistance to Change', *Human Relations*, 1: 512–32.

Contu, A. and Willmott, H. (2003) 'Re-embedding Situatedness: The Importance of Power Relations in Learning Theory', *Organizational Science*, 14, 3: 283–96.

Cressey, P., Della Rossa, G., Docherty, P., Kelleher, M., Kuhn, M., Reimann, D. and Ullstad, C. (1999) *Partnership and Investment in Europe: The Role of the Social Dialogue in Human Resource Development*, Consolidated report, Brussels: EC Leonardo project EUR/96/2/1071/EA/III.2.a/FPC.

Cressey, P. and MacInnes, J. (1980) 'Voting For Ford: Authority and Democracy in Industry', *Capital & Class*, 11.

Cressey, P. and Williams, R. (1990) *Participating in Change. New Technology and the Role of Employee Involvement*, Dublin: European Foundation.

Cunliffe, A. (2003) 'Reflexive Enquiry in Organisational Research: Questions and Possibilities', *Human Relations*, 56, 8: 983–1003.

EPOC Research Group (1997) 'New Forms of Work Organisation', *Can Europe Realise its Potential*, Dublin: European Foundation.

Gustavsen, B. (1992) *Dialogue and Development*, Assen/Maastricht: Van Gorcum.

Industrial Democracy Europe Group (1993) *Industrial Democracy in Europe Revisited*, Oxford: Oxford University Press.

Kaufman, B. (2001) 'HR and IR: Commonalities and Differences', *Human Resource Management Review*, 4: 339–75.

Lave, J. and Wenger, E. (1991) *Situated Learning: Legitimate Peripheral Participation*, Cambridge: Cambridge University Press.

Lewin, K. (1946) 'Action Research and Minority Problems', *Journal of Social Issues*, 1946: 34–6.

Mueller, F. (1994) 'Teams Between Hierarchy and Commitment: Change Strategies and the "Internal Environment" ', *Journal of Management Studies*, 31, 3: 383–403.

Nyhan, B., Cressey, P., Kelleher, M. and Poell, R. (2003) *Learning Organisations: European perspectives, theories and practices*, Vol. 1 and 2, Luxemburg: CEDEFOP Imprint, Publication Office of the EU.

Orr, J. (1990) 'Sharing Knowledge, Celebrating Identity: Community Memory in a Service Culture', in D. Middleton, and D. Edwards (eds) *Collective Remembering*, London: Sage.

Orr, J. (1996) *Talking about Machines: An Ethnography of a Modern Job*. Ithaca, NY: ILR Press.

Poole, M. (1986) *Towards a New Industrial Democracy: Workers Participation in Industry*, London: RKP.

Purcell, J. (1995) 'Ideology and the End of Institutional Industrial Relations: Evidence from the UK', in C. Crouch and F. Traxler (eds) *Organised Industrial Relations in Europe: What Future?* Aldershot: Avebury: 101–19.

Ramsay, H., Scholarios, D. and Harley, B. (2000) 'Employees and High-Performance Work Systems: Testing Inside the Black Box', *British Journal of Industrial Relations*, 38, 4: 501–31.

Romme, G. (2003) 'Making a Difference: Organisation as Design', *Organisational Science*, 14, 5: 558–73.

Roth, S. (1997) 'Germany: Labor's Perspective on Lean Production', in T. Kochan, *et al.* (eds) *After Lean Production: Evolving Employment Practices in the World Auto Industry*, Ithaca: Cornell University Press.

Seeley Brown, J. and Duguid, P. (1991) 'Organizational Learning and Communities-of-Practice: Toward a Unified View of Working, Learning and Innovation', *Organization Science*, 2, 1: 40–57.

Sundstrom, E., De Meuse, K.P. and Futrell, D. (1990) 'Work Teams: Applications and Effectiveness', *American Psychologist*, 45: 120–33.

Tranfield, D., Parry, I., Wilson, S., Smith, S. and Morris, F. (1998) 'Teamworked Organisational Engineering: Getting the Most out of Teamworking', *Management Decision*, 36, 6: 378–84.

Wenger, E. (1998) *Communities of Practice: Learning, Meaning, and Identity*, Cambridge and New York: Cambridge University Press.

Wiesbord, M. (1987) *Productive Workplaces: Organizing and Managing for Dignity, Meaning and Community*, San Francisco: Jossey-Bass.

Part III

Productive reflection

Differing contexts and practices

6 Disciplined reflection or communities of practice?

Andrew Schenkel

During the construction of the multi-billion dollar bridge between Sweden and Denmark, Tom, a 28-year-old civil engineer, conducted a routine control of a concrete support beam called a girder. The control procedure was conducted in accordance with the ISO 9000 quality standard, which was used to check that requirements were met and working processes followed. To his surprise, during the checklist-based inspection Tom found a deviation from requirements in the form of a 'rat-hole', or area where there was no concrete. Tom knew that this deviation was not desirable; it meant that customer requirements were not met, it could delay the overall project, and it could have cost implications. Management had made it clear on numerous occasions that the success of the project depended upon meeting the prescribed schedule.

As the Quality Controller for the girder section, one of Tom's formal duties in managing this deviation was to complete a one-page 'Non-Conformity Report'. This report described the deviation, identified its causes and suggested actions to prevent it from recurring. However, in filling out the report, Tom could not establish what should be changed in the current working methods in order to prevent the deviation from recurring. Tom therefore consulted his colleague, Jan, a supervisor with over 30 years of experience in the construction industry. But Jan could not assist him. Tom then turned to his formal manager for advice. The manager's recommendation was that Tom followed the prescribed procedure and consulted the Technical Department. Soon after being contacted, the head of the Concrete Section at the Technical Department went to the girder-production area to inspect the deviation – the 'rat-hole'. Tom described the inspection and ensuing interaction as follows: 'The members of the technical department go down and look at the deviation and make a decision. They are the concrete experts, the ones who know a lot about it.' After the inspection, the 'expert' modified working methods. Tom continued with a new working method in mind.

The above description of Tom's management of a deviation is illustrative of how a quality standard can influence reflection and the quality of learning that takes place. In particular, it illustrates how a quality system in one-off project with time constraints and specific work practices is used. At the core of the ISO standard is what Argyris and Schön (1995) described as type 1 learning. That is, the detection and correction of errors with errors involving a mismatch between expected outcomes and actual ones. While the very design of ISO 9000 facilitates type 1 learning, it can also lead to Argyris and Schön's type 2 learning, if it is designed in such a manner. Type 2 learning denotes not only the detection and correction of errors, but also more importantly, an according change in values. As such Type 2 learning is often associated with reflection since it is through reflection that changes in underlying values, the defining difference between type 1 and type 2 learning, is obtained. Reflection in this context thus involves exploring why the problem occurred and, in conjunction with this, correcting the underlying problem.

Reflection has often been viewed as an individual action in which a person ponders over the situation at large and tries to seek some deeper meaning of their personal experience. However, the very nature of the problems that people encounter in large complex projects means that often one person cannot solve the problem due to inherent cognitive limitations. Accordingly, this suggests that collective reflection is needed. This represents a marked shift from the traditional view of reflection as an individual focused activity to one that is group centred. In turn, this suggests that type 2 learning is associated with collective reflection.

As a group activity, reflection can occur formally or informally. Formal group reflection can be purposefully designed as part of the quality standard or be emergent. In the case of the 'rat-hole', formal procedures encouraging collective reflection were absent as shown by Tom going directly to the technical department for advice and the very nature of the advice given. However, reflection can also occur through informal problems solving groups or groups of people informally and contextually bound in a work situation who are applying a common competence in the pursuit of a common enterprise (Brown and Duguid 1991; Lave and Wenger 1991; Wenger 1998; Teigland 2000). Communities of practice form in the context of solving problems because of the inherent complexity of problems and cognitive limitations of individuals. At the same time there can exist barriers to reflection and by extension the formation of such communities of practice. For example, communities of practice presuppose that that there are not obstructions in terms of geographical separation and time constraints as these would inhibit mutual engagement in the community. An alternative barrier could be institutional biases towards technical rationality – taking action – as opposing to reflecting with the actions taken being of a 'satisficing' character. Perhaps even the presence of a bureaucratic inspired quality system such as ISO 9000 could act as an impediment toward reflection.

In terms of effective problem solving or problem prevention in complex projects it would seem that collective reflection would be qualitatively beneficial unless there were barriers which obstructed its formation. Thus, in terms of effective problem solving it would have seemed quite natural for Tom to seek out help in solving the problem in other parts of the organization outside of his own group and that this problem solving network may have displayed characteristics of a community of practice. However, this was apparently not the case.

Thus, the question arises as to why communities of practice were not developed further in this setting. Why did Tom not seek advice from colleagues in another group who were dealing with similar problems? Can the answer to why reflection in informal groups – communities of practice – did not take place be found in ISO 9000 itself?

The purpose of this chapter is twofold: firstly, to explain the influence that a quality standard such as ISO 9000 has on the formation of communities of practice; secondly, to explain how it influences reflection. It begins by providing background information about communities of practice and some of their main processes. Thereafter, Foucault's concepts of discipline and surveillance are introduced and described. The purpose of this section is to provide a lens in which to understand facilitators and barriers to the formation of communities of practice. Thereafter, some features of the research methods used are discussed and this is followed by an analysis of the emergent advice network with the purpose of understanding whether the project was a community of practice and if it was not what type of structural characteristics it displayed. Once the characteristics of the network are ascertained, the question explored is why did the network take on the shape that it did and to answer this question the concepts of discipline and surveillance are used. The chapter concludes with a discussion around reflection in communities of practice.

Communities of practice

The concept of communities of practice received attention in the early 1990s, when it was observed that learning takes place through informal social interaction anchored in the context of problem solving (Brown and Duguid 1991). It was proposed that the inflexibility of formal routines leads to the development of informal groups to solve problems (Lave and Wenger 1991 and Brown and Duguid 1991).

A *community of practice* is a particular type of informal group in which practice is founded on and manifested in everyday work. The basis for any community of practice, according Wenger (1998), consists of a *joint enterprise, a shared repertoire* and *mutual engagement. Joint enterprise* is the common purpose that binds the group (Wenger 1998) and guides the development of the community's common means of conducting work. A *shared repertoire* consists of the community's common way of doing things, gestures, artefacts, vocabulary and causal maps (Wenger 1998) to this extent it represents the accumulated tacit and explicit knowledge of the community. The shared repertoire can be viewed as the glue that binds communities of practice and distinguishes them from other types of groups (Boland and Tenkasi 1995; Teigland 2000). Brown and Duguid (1991) noted that primarily through three communication-based processes – *narration, collaboration* and *social construction* – a shared repertoire is formed, maintained and reproduced. Further, it was suggested that it is through narration, collaboration and social construction that group reflection takes place.

Narration describes how people create and tell stories in order to improve their understanding of problem situations. In contrast to formal manuals, which are inflexible, stories are flexible as well as rich and can therefore be customized to each particular situation. As these interpretations become part of the community's shared repertoire; they are used to interpret future situations. *Collaboration* refers to the involvement of both storytellers and listeners in the stories that are told. As a consequence, insights gained belong not only to the individual, but also to the community. Through collaboration it becomes unnecessary for individuals to know all that is required to solve a problem since they can rely on the cumulative knowledge of the community (Wenger 1999). *Social construction* describes how people in a dialogue negotiate meanings that become accepted as knowledge by the community (Berger and Luckman 1966).

The development of a community's joint enterprise and shared repertoire are dependent upon *mutual engagement* in terms of the ability of community members to interact. The amount and pattern of interactions is commonly referred to as the structure. Building upon concepts from social network analysis, Schenkel *et al.* (2002)[1] proposed that the social network concept of connectedness capture the concept of mutual engagement. *Connectedness* denotes the degree to which individuals mutually engage with each other and is of importance since the extent to which a network is connected affects the degree to which the community's shared repertoire, one of the defining characteristics of a community of practice, is developed, disseminated and reproduced. Through mutually engaging with other community members, individuals learn the community's shared repertoire and can thus be identified as members of the community (Lave and Wenger 1991; Schenkel *et al.* 2002).

This section has described and outlined the main characteristics of communities of practice. It is proposed that *joint enterprise and a shared repertoire* provide the context for reflection while *mutual engagement* the process for reflection. While engagement is both a process as well as characteristic of communities of practice it is also the means through which collective reflection can occur as well as a sign of it. To this extent engagement represents both a process as well as an outcome. Without engagement it is difficult for communities or practice to form and function as well as for collective reflection to take place.

Discipline and surveillance

The discussion so far has focused on communities of practice; however, informal organizations do not exist in isolation, but are affected by formal organizations. Formalization in the context of ISO 9000 means that customer requirements are formulated and explicit procedures to control and evaluate that targets are met are articulated in manuals. Further, when deviations from targets are identified there are explicit procedures for how these should be managed with the purpose of fulfilling customer requirements.

One of the ways in which scholars have noted that the formal organization can affect the informal organization in quality systems is through the peer discipline that emanates from surveillance (Sewell and Wilkinson 1992). The concepts of discipline and surveillance emanate from Foucault's (1977) book *Discipline and Punish*. This volume describes how a penal system went from inflicting physical punishment on the body to breaking down and rearranging both body and mind in order to bring about desired behaviour. This change meant that behaviour and thinking were perceived as independent of the individual and appropriate for manipulation. Disciplining thus took on a strategic dimension since it could be used to achieve a particular end. Normality was judged in terms of this end, and all other ways of thinking and behaviour were viewed as deviant.

The principal techniques on which disciplining is based are *active* and *passive* surveillance. Foucault discusses in some detail Bentham's Panopticon, a type of *passive* surveillance system. The panopticon, the basis of a model prison, is an architectural structure comprising a central watchtower surrounded by a ring of cells. From the watchtower, an unseen observer can view prisoner's cells, positions, rooms and beds. Whether prisoners are actually monitored or not is unimportant. Unable to see into the tower and thus to know whether they are being watched, they assume that they are constantly monitored.

While the panopticon is the basis for passive surveillance, *active* surveillance requires a 'disciplinary gaze' in the form of constant physical monitoring. Passive surveillance can be discontinuous because prisoners do not know whether they are being monitored, but active surveillance needs visible agents to exercise control in order to be credible. To be effective, active surveillance is conducted through hierarchical relationships in which selected group members watch over others. Thus, active surveillance is based on physical presence with the potential threat of punishment to normalize behaviour.

Whether surveillance takes place passively through the panopticon or actively in the hierarchy, the disciplining effect of surveillance in producing normalized behaviour can lead to *self-regulation* by individuals, who start to correct their own actions. As this process advances, the robustness and credibility of the surveillance systems become less important since disciplining is increasingly passive and independent of the individual. Therefore, once self-regulation has been established, the threat of punishment is no longer necessary.

Disciplining requires not only active and passive surveillance, but *individualization* as well, since individualization permits identification of deviant behaviour. Through making the invisible visible it becomes possible to detect and normalize deviant behaviour – reports and files are one means of rendering people visible. Individuals and groups that are visible become 'unique' objects, which can be disciplined (Foucault 1977).

In sum, this section has laid the groundwork for formal processes through which the formal organization may influence the formation of communities of practice as well as reflection. In terms of facilitating reflection, discipline and surveillance need not to be considered as negative until the effects that it has on communities of practice and reflection are considered. In other words, discipline and surveillance can be positive if they contribute to the development of communities of practice and reflection.

The research study

The international contracting consortium, Sundlink Contractors, which designed and constructed the 7.8 kilometer Øresund Bridge connecting Denmark and

Sweden, provided the research site of this study. Sundlink Contractors utilized a formal quality system standard based upon ISO 9000. Organizationally, Sundlink is functionally divided into two main groups: operational and support departments.

The empirical data for this chapter comes from nine small case studies as well as questionnaire focused on understanding how reported deviations from prescribed procedures or products were managed. The second data used in this study comes from the Sundlink's manuals which describe ISO 9000 related procedures.

Analyzing the advice network

The initial example in the beginning of the chapter is one indication that informal organizations as conceptualized by communities of practice were not widespread at Sundlink. By extension, this might suggest that conditions for facilitating reflection were not encouraged. This section explores the extent to which the structure of the project's emergent advice network fulfils the structural requirements of a 'well functioning' and in this way a reflecting community of practice.

Figure 6.1 portrays a map of the informal network of who seeks help from whom among the members of the project. It was created from questionnaire data provided by participants. It illustrates the degrees of connectedness between individuals.

Of the 120 project members, there were only five isolates, or individuals not connected to any other member in the network. All other members were connected with at least one other person. Although this network is connected, one of the defining properties of a well functioning community of practice, it is not sufficiently well connected to be considered a community of practice – there are, for example,

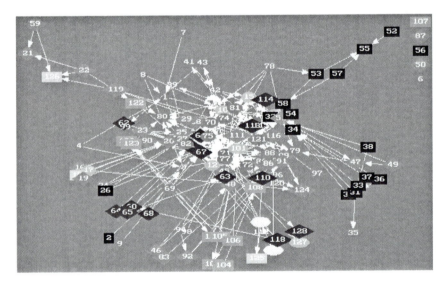

Figure 6.1 Informal network of help-seeking among all project members (node shape indicates section membership)

too many one-way, unilateral connections. In a community of practice, one would expect many more multi-directional connections between pairs of individuals in order to encourage reflection through enabling multiple understandings as well as being indicative of a reflecting community of practice.

What network characteristics did the emergent network exhibit?

As noted, the informal advice network was not sufficiently connected to provide the conditions for mutual engagement and as such it was not considered as a well functioning community of practice. As engagement is also a precondition for collective reflection, the analysis also suggests that this was not a group that could collectively reflect over errors. Given that it was not a reflecting community of practice, what were its structural characteristics? This question was investigated through comparing the informal advice network with the formal advice network as prescribed by Sundlink's manuals which describe ISO 9000 related procedures and in particular the one used for managing deviations from prescribed norms.

What was this procedure? It began with the initial reporting of the deviation to the Quality Controller, a specific actor responsible for quality issues, and specifically for completing a Non-Conformity Report that documented the deviation. This report consisted of four parts: (1) a description of the deviation; (2) an explanation for its occurrence; (3) proposed remedial action, or action focused on remedying the situation on hand; and (4) proposed corrective action, or action to prevent the deviation from recurring. If unable to complete the report for lack of relevant knowledge, the Quality Controller was to contact the Support (Technical) department on technical matters and the Support (Quality) department for advice on contractual issues. For example, the Quality Controller might not know what remedial or corrective actions should be taken and would turn to the Support (Technical) department for assistance. Once completed, the report was to be signed by the department manager and sent to the Support (Quality) department for approval and further processing. Thus, in terms of interactions, the formal procedure prescribes that the Quality Controller should be contacting the support departments in deviation situations.

Through a statistical technique called the quadratic assignment procedure (Hubert and Golledge 1981; Baker and Hubert 1981), we can establish the degree to which the emergent advice network as ascertained by questionnaire data is correlated with the formal advice network as prescribed by the Sundlink's formal procedure for managing deviations. The analysis showed that the two networks overlapped and were significantly correlated at 71.4% (p < .0001), suggesting that interactions as prescribed by the formal procedures were followed. In turn, this finding can be taken to indicate that the formal procedures influenced the informal advice network to the extent that well functioning communities of practice did not form at a project level. One consequence of the formal procedures was that the Support (Technical) department became core in the inter-organizational advice network as shown by Figure 6.2.

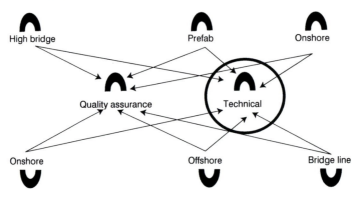

Figure 6.2 Network of inter-department relations

The qualitative data also indicated that people in operational departments at this project felt compelled to contact the Support (Technical) department for assistance. The alternative to seeking advice from this department would have been contacting members of other operative departments or even people outside of this project. However, this was seemingly not the case. One person in the Support (Quality) department described his contacts in the following manner: 'When a deviation occurs, the Support (Technical) expert *must* be quickly informed. I call the Support (Technical) department and describe what type of problem we have. We then go around, look, and come up with a solution.' Another person in the Support (Quality) department, who said, 'I contacted Support (Technical) department's expert, expressed a similar view. But, it was because of the discussion that I had with my section head and my predecessor. They recommended that we ask the Support (Technical) department's expert whether *we could* repair the deviation on the spot or wait.' Finally, an operative supervisor commented about the key role of the Support (Technical) department as follows: 'When we have damages that *we have to* discuss we usually contact the Support (Technical) department's expert. He usually comes down and then we discuss corrective action.'

A closer examination of the network data reveals that the Quality Controller from the Support (Quality) played a central role in the management of deviations according to the prescribed procedure. The Quality Controller was the most contacted person in deviation or problem situations and was more contacted then the section head or other managers. Interestingly, the person most often contacted in deviation situations, the Quality Controller, also had the least experience. In a deviation situation, one would expect that more experienced personnel, rather than a relative newcomer to the industry, would be consulted. When asked why the relatively young and inexperienced Quality Controller was contacted in this particular situation, the section manager referred to the role of the formal organization, commenting, '(He) is the person responsible for the girder handling.'

The Quality Controller confirmed the influence of the formal organization on the informal advice network when he said, 'As soon as there is a non-conformity (deviation) at the work site, it is reported. If I do not see it myself, then the workers or supervisors report it to me. Then it is my responsibility to take care of it. Partly to inspect it with the supervisors and section head, and then we develop a decision as to what we should do. As soon as there is a non-conformity (deviation), I should immediately make a report.' Thus, the formal procedures as prescribed by ISO 9000 affect the structure of the informal advice network to the extent that communities of practice are not more pronounced.

Is the advice network a community of discipline?

In the previous section it was suggested that there was a strong relationship between the informal and formal advice networks, indicating that prescribed procedures were followed. To explain how a formalized system like ISO 9000 can influence the development of a community of practice, and thereby learning and reflection, the concepts of discipline and surveillance provide a lens to understand this. This section argues that surveillance through an extensive system of actors and systems embedded in control procedures based on ISO 9000 impeded the formation of communities and the possibilities for collective reflection between groups experiencing similar problems.

Surveillance at Sundlink was carried out by Quality Controllers who were officially responsible for ensuring that working methods and procedures were followed and for conducting spot checks on a regular basis. The operations manual describes the responsibilities of the Quality Controller as follows: 'Quality Controllers have the responsibility for the compilation of Quality Records and Inspection Reports. The Quality Controller shall also perform spot checks on inspection routines to ensure the correct preparation of inspection records.'

It is proposed that this type of surveillance comprised an active surveillance system embedded in the hierarchy. The Quality Controller was immediately subordinate to the Department Manager and also reported directly to the managers of the support departments. One department manager commented about the reporting obligations of the Quality Controller as follows: 'We have a Quality Controller that reports to me. His duty is see that the system is working and that the papers are flowing.'

However, the Quality Controller was not the only actor charged with surveillance; a manager in the Support (Quality) department as well as the client conducted formal audits. In the context of ISO 9000, these audits consisted of examining the procedures and accompanying paperwork by examining whether Non-Conformity Reports (deviation reports), checklists and inspection lists were in order. These audits were normally conducted on a quarterly basis.

An effective surveillance system requires that deviations be visibly segregated. For this purpose, checklists/inspection reports were used to judge whether work was normal or deviant and this had the effect of segregating deviations and making them visible. As one operative supervisor commented, 'I am responsible for this caisson and all the concrete in it. So when we take off the forms, we do a visual check of it and discover any damage. I perform this check and fill out what type of damage it is. Then I leave it to the Quality Controller.'

Through this type of detailed record keeping, the Quality Controller discovered the deviation described in the beginning of this chapter. Record keeping specifically involves checking that prescribed working methods are followed and confirming that the final product meets prescribed targets. In making deviations visible, a system of classifying deviations emerged. One operative supervisor exemplified it as follows, 'There are two areas of damage on the eastern wall up there along the long wall. Honeycombs Type 1 because it is not a visible wall. If you had seen the reinforcement, it would have been Type 2 damage.'

Once deviations are identified, they are further segregated and made through procedures. This procedure stipulated that in conjunction with each identified deviation a 'Non-conformity Report' is filled out. In this standardized report information such as the section where the deviation occurred as well as its causes and proposed actions to prevent it from reoccurring are filled in. Once the report was completed it was sent to the Quality Assurance Department where it received a unique identification number. Initially, reports were classified according to operative section as well as deviation type. This allowed for trends within and between sections to be made. Thus, through a comprehensive set of checklists and procedures for the management of deviations, a comprehensive surveillance system was constituted to ensure normalization in the form of following work methods and attaining targets.

The analysis has suggested that surveillance and discipline influenced normality in terms of adhering to procedures. These procedures meant that contact between different actors experiencing similar problems was largely excluded and at the same time the relative strict adherence to procedures impeded the formation of communities of practice as well as conditions for collective reflection.

Conclusion

ISO 9000 is used in organizations for the purpose of ensuring quality. It is supposed to be designed to offer opportunities for learning in the form of communities of practice and reflection. However, as shown here, the quality standard as designed at Sundlink did not offer this possibility and these possibilities were limited because of the surveillance and disciplining processes that formed the pillar of ISO as enacted at Sundlink. Thus there was an inherent tension between following systematic quality procedures and collective reflection, with surveillance being the impediment to reflection. This surveillance system was based on reinforcing dominant formal procedures at the expense of developing informal communities of practice in which reflection played a key role. Formal procedures – that did not include group reflection – reinforced by surveillance and discipline, proved to be an unhappy combination in terms of facilitating reflection and the development of communities of practice. In other words, both formal as well as informal collective reflection was impeded by direct or indirect design.

From a learning and reflection perspective, a number of important issues are raised. First, there is a need to balance learning and reflection with control and surveillance. In other words, how much should reflection and learning be taking place formally and how much informally. The formal aspect of reflection and learning provides an opportunity to institutionalize what is learned as well as providing legitimacy for reflection. However, in the case examined while the formalized procedures made a legitimate claim on how problems should be handled they also directly impacted on the ability of people to reflect and learn. For some departments such as the technical department this claim facilitated learning and reflection, but for many other in the project learning was impeded. This suggests that control issues focused on ensuring quality need to be balanced to facilitate informal reflection as well as existential questions such as who is knowledgeable examined. This means that knowledge, reflection, learning and power are very closely intertwined with each other.

The conclusions drawn in this discussion need to be put into the context that ISO 9000 is a flexible standard and thus concepts of surveillance and discipline can be used as a means to design productive reflection and learning into work. In other words, the baby should not be thrown out with bathwater. At the end of the day the question is what type of organization does one want to create – a reflecting one which gets at the root of problems or one that fixes errors but not their source.

Notes

1 This section as well as the analysis of the network data builds upon Schenkel *et al.* (2002) as well as summarizing some of their key findings.

References

Argyris, C. and Schön, D. (1996) *Organizational Learning II: Theory, Method and Practice*, Reading, MA: Addison Wesley.

Baker, F. and Hubert, L. (1981) 'The Analysis of Social Interaction', *Sociological Methods and Research*, 9: 339–61.

Berger, P. and Luckman, T. (1966) *The Social Construction of Reality: A Treatise in the Sociology of Knowledge*, London: Penguin Publishers.

Boland, R.J. and Tenkasi, R.V. (1995) 'Perspective Making and Perspective Taking in Communities of Knowing', *Organisation Science*, 6: 350–72.

Brown, J.S. and Duguid, P. (1991) 'Organizational Learning and Communities of Practice. Towards a Unified View of Working, Learning, and Innovation', *Organization Science*, 2: 40–57.

Hubert, L. and Golledge, G. (1981) 'A Heuristic Method for the Comparison of Related Structures', *Journal of Mathematical Sociology*, 23: 214–26.

Foucault, M. (1977) *Discipline and Punish: The Birth of the Prison*, London: Penguin Press.

Lave, J. and Wenger, E. (1991) *Situated Learning: Legitimate Peripheral Participation*, Cambridge: Cambridge University Press.

Schenkel, A., Teigland R. and Borgatti, S. (2002) 'Theorizing Structural Dimensions of Communities of Practice: A Social Network Approach', in Schenkel, A. *Communities of Practice or Communities of Discipline: Managing Deviations at the Øresund Bridge*, Stockholm: The Economic Research Institute, Stockholm School of Economics.

Sewell, G. and Wilkinson, G. (1992) 'Someone to Watch Over Me: Surveillance in a Total Quality Organisation', *Sociology*, 26: 271–89.

Teigland, R. (2000) 'Communities of practice in a high technology firm', in J. Birkinshaw and P. Hagström (eds) *The Flexible Firm: Capability Management in Network Organizations*, Oxford: Oxford University Press, pp. 126–46.

Wenger, E. (1998) *Communities of Practice: Learning, Meaning, and Identity*, Cambridge: Cambridge University Press.

7 The limits of reflexive design in a secrecy-based organization

Michael Stebbins, Tali Freed, A.B. 'Rami' Shani and Kenneth H. Doerr

Organizational redesign processes can take many forms from the simple implementation of an 'off-the-peg' standard solution to a 'carefully tailored' solution characterized by many iterations of experimentation, evaluation and collective reflection by various stakeholders. Two key contextual factors affecting such processes are culture and decision-making authority. These variables are complex in themselves and their influence on the redesign process can be moderated by specific factors. This chapter presents a case which illustrates how efforts to accommodate collective reflection within an organizational redesign program were affected by organizational culture and centralized decision-making and how these effects were heightened by a 'secrecy factor'.

One of the most promising topics to explore in contemporary knowledge-based organizations concerns productive reflection and learning that takes place during significant organization restructuring. Reflexive design incorporates aspects of action research, appreciative inquiry, socio-technical systems and self-design. It provides unique insights concerning the redesign process and the management of system wide change (Stebbins and Shani 2002). However, the extent to which reflexive design might be applied under extreme organizational conditions is unknown. This chapter investigates the limits of productive reflection and learning under conditions of secrecy. We will provide a brief overview of ideal reflexive design and then demonstrate significant gaps between theory and practice through the examination of the PrimeOptics case. Finally, we will provide observations about the case and implications for productive reflection in similar organizations.

Organization design

Relatively few theories provide comprehensive frameworks that can shed light on the chaotic process of redesign (Beer 2001). *Design* is thought to be a blend of theory, knowledge embedded in the particular industry/sector and work situation and the contributions of those who participate in the redesign process (Mackenzie 1986). The process is both technical and political, and involves purposeful effort to design the organization as an integrated system. Moreover, design is treated as a complex task that aligns the people, resources and work. In today's environment, the list of participants in redesign projects may include all key stakeholders, owners, personnel, customers and suppliers. However little is known about the impact of including or excluding specific stakeholders. For example how does the exclusion of non-managerial employees affect redesign outcomes? Will the new design be less sustainable? In complex organizations, elaborate structural learning mechanisms are often created to guide the change program and to foster sound communications, reflection and learning during all program phases (see for example, Chapter 9). In contrast, what are the helpful processes, and what are the outcomes of redesigning work when it is conducted by a few people having similar backgrounds, making decisions in secret? What are the appropriate types of involvement, dialogue and reflection, under conditions of secrecy in the change process?

Reflexive design, reflection and learning

Certain common values have emerged regarding idealized reflexive design. These values relate to the context for initiating change, the change process and the desired outcomes. For example, a strong value is dual emphasis on quality of work life and competitive organizational performance. Both are addressed throughout the change process through critical evaluation of new designs and their impacts on different stakeholders. Design is conceived as *a reflexive methodology of intervention – a type of enlightened, self-critical process that accepts differences in science and practice.* By definition, reflexive design means to mirror or direct back the redesign work. Since the dictionary definitions are so similar, in this chapter we will freely use the words reflective and reflexive. Collective reflection *is the ability to uncover and make explicit what was planned, observed, or achieved in practice; therefore it is concerned with the reconstruction of meaning and results in work-based learning* (Raelin 2000). In the context of a change program, some new types of reflection and learning are evident. They might include:

- Participants explore vision and goals as well as alternative redesign frameworks. The stakeholders investigate and choose among redesign approaches that fit their unique situation (see Figure 7.1).
- Participants' self-apply theory, methods and practices. In keeping with self-design values, organizational members take ownership of the change process through high involvement at all stages. In a spirit of inquiry, all parties including consultants consider both theory and practice, and deliberate on ways to link them.
- Participants are encouraged to identify and explore the meanings and implications of possible dilemmas – for example that team-centred designs might suppress individual creativity.
- Design activities are iterative. Deliberations among stakeholders occur through-out the process to assure that redesign produces the desired balanced outcomes. Self-design and learning from experience are facilitated (Figure 7.1).

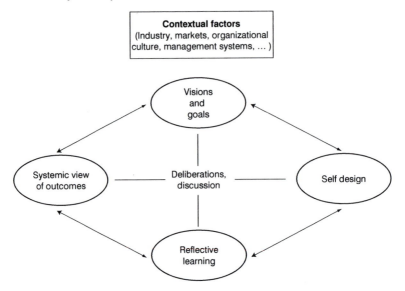

Figure 7.1 Reflective design: a conceptual roadmap

Secrecy as an impropitious culture and context for collective reflection

As is illustrated in Chapters 8 and 9 in this volume, the constraints on redesign and learning can stem from the existing management, culture and organizational configuration. For example, organization theory suggests that a matrix organization carries a certain culture of openness, ongoing clash of perspectives, full use of knowledge worker talents and problem-solving on behalf of customers (Galbraith 1994). However, a defense industry firm with a matrix structure may not have these characteristics (Landau 2003). Instead, secrecy and competitive pressures across defense contractors may lead the firm to adopt unique internal processes that do not encourage workplace learning and knowledge transfer beyond somewhat isolated work units (cf. Schenkel, Chapter 6 in this volume).

Secrecy is a contextual variable as well as a cultural variable. Organizational culture is usually defined in terms of persistent shared values and behavioural norms (e.g., Mitroff and Kilmann 1984). Aspects of the culture (e.g. secrecy, in terms of doing business on a 'need-to-know' basis) are likely to conflict with principles of ideal reflexive design. We need to explore how learning in general and productive reflection in particular are advanced under a culture that emphasizes secrecy.

Vision, goals and criteria

Reflexive design theory advocates local control of design processes and high participant involvement in the creation of goals and design criteria. Thus this approach is more of a bottom-up approach to change. The question of how goals and design criteria are developed during redesign programs is an interesting issue, especially under conditions of secrecy. *Design criteria* are statements that describe, in ideal terms, what the organization design should accomplish. Design criteria usually have an action verb; they state that the design should *facilitate, promote, encourage, provide for, or motivate* (Nadler and Tushman 1988). Design criteria reflect the values of the different stakeholders and are written in response to competitive conditions, the tasks to be executed, the collective sense of current problems and perceived cause of problems, and other constraints. Design criteria drive the entire decision-making process and provide links to strategy, technology integration and the development process that occurs in design cycles. The advantages and limits of design criteria are explored in the case to follow.

Collaborative design

The design process must consider individual and team capacity to cope with a changing work. One of the most compelling aspects of reflexive design is the emphasis on personal support to employees and learning. Successful redesign work requires the active involvement of those who must live with the changes as well as social support mechanisms (Shani and Docherty 2003). During operational redesign, individual experimentation takes place within the context of group work and inter-group relationships. Accordingly, reflexive design can be characterized as 'collaborative design', entailing collaboration among members of the units directly concerned and also among concerned stakeholders.

Collective reflection

Reflexive design processes must provide space and time for learning and developing competence in work. This includes providing forums for structured deliberation within the normal project stages as well as time for spontaneous and unplanned learning and reflection. The process of change centres on the knowledge and experience of those who are closest to the work at hand. Learning, coping capacity and other individual competencies support people as they experiment with new roles, relationships and work activities (Raelin 2000). Successful transformation depends upon effort, individual capabilities and sound facilitation of the overall reflexive design process. The above characteristics are associated with the ideal process of reflexive design. The redesign process led by managers of PrimeOptics is captured next. It is used here to highlight aspects of *good reflexive design* as well as *major flaws* that do not promote productive reflection and learning.

The PrimeOptics case

PrimeOptics is a division of one of the largest defense and aerospace systems contractors in the United States. With billions of dollars in annual sales this defense contractor employs many thousands of employees worldwide. The company is known for its high standards of technological innovation and customer relations, as well as for its relatively low employee turnover rates. Despite these positive factors, at the outset of the case the PrimeOptics division suffered from declining sales and a lower market share. A customer survey conducted in early 2002 indicated that PrimeOptics was not considered cost-competitive. 'We love your technology; it's needed to save lives; we wish we could afford it' was the typical response from PrimeOptics' customers.

PrimeOptics devoted considerable resources to customer relations and responsiveness. It had strong program management offices for customer interfaces and a full spectrum of engineering personnel assigned to the various programs. Each program was responsible for a family of technologically related products, throughout their life cycles. Due to the secretive nature of the industry, programs were developed for specific customers. Program autonomy and internal company barriers led to non-uniform production and business processes. As a result, the company was often too slow and expensive in moving from prototypes to efficient manufacturing.

To address the perceived threat to the company success and survival, an overall change program was designed, aimed at reducing cycle times, reducing cost of engineering support, improving the transition from product development work to production work, and positioning the company to compete in new markets. To accomplish this, six taskforces were created, one of which is focused here – the Production Execution group. The group's task was to restructure production operations and to significantly reduce manufacturing costs. It was expected that financial and productivity gains would come through a reorganization of engineering support groups and a breaking up of the PrimeOptics matrix organization. The explicit intent was to cut engineering support costs by 50%.

PrimeOptics had an embedded matrix structure (see Figure 7.2), in which the engineering support groups reported to both production and program management. There were certain inefficiencies associated with having dozens of mutually exclusive programs. For example, there were problems connected with allocating engineering staff in periods of peak and low demands. But PrimeOptics had not developed cross-program managerial processes to address these and other issues. The PrimeOptics organization seemed to have all the problems and very few of the benefits normally associated with matrix structures.

Staffing the taskforce

The vision for the change program called for a shift in decision-making authority and control from program offices to the factories. Accordingly, management staffed the production execution taskforce with factory managers and supervisors, and excluded program offices and engineering support personnel. It was very evident from the taskforce staffing that management did not want to save the matrix. While most of the managers on the taskforce were former engineers, only two of the 10 taskforce members had program office or customer contact experience from prior jobs. Due to the organizational culture, participation in the taskforce was secret and few people outside the taskforce knew that it existed or what it was doing.

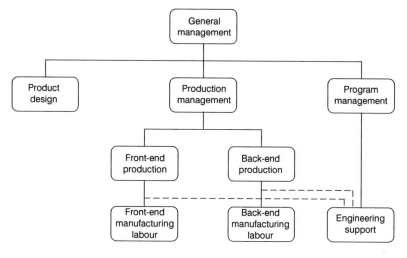

Figure 7.2 Organization chart with embedded matrix structure

Time line

The taskforce was created in February 2002. Since some taskforce members were aware of organization designs in other divisions of the company, they used their contacts to investigate design innovations that might be adapted to the PrimeOptics situation. They identified six manufacturing designs that were thought to be successful elsewhere and seemed to match the vision. They then began to elaborate them and provide definitions that would allow comparisons. The taskforce met biweekly, and conducted data gathering between sessions. Reflecting on this phase of the taskforce work, team members later observed that the pace was almost frantic, even though they worked to a self-imposed deadline. The taskforce proposed a new strategic design in June 2002. However, after this point there were many delays in feedback and directives from management and taskforce members became impatient with the lack of action. The management decision was announced in November, and the cutover to the new design began in January 2003.

The researchers' role

In late March 2002 the taskforce leader brought in a team of two university researchers to assist the taskforce and to provide independent opinions and information on 'state-of-the-art' practice. One researcher was an expert on industrial engineering, and the other was an expert on organization design. The researchers began their work by linking the taskforce deliberations to alternative design theories including reflective design. The idea was to place the taskforce work into a larger perspective so that the group could consider a wider and more robust set of options. For example, the researchers felt that work in progress most closely matched the Nadler and Tushman (1988) redesign process. They guided the group through the various steps in the Nadler and Tushman process to educate members on comprehensive design and to allow some critique and reflection on what had been accomplished and what had not been accomplished. This type of comparison and discussion among consultants and clients is a key feature of reflective design.

The researchers also helped the group identify issues that would have to be addressed in the coming design and development stages. They provided the platform for the taskforce leaders' reflection about both the design process and substantive issues, and provided their own expert assessment. They also encouraged management to bring in more stakeholders, but this advice was not acted on. Consistent with PrimeOptics culture and values, managers stated that the project was kept secret 'to allow the taskforce maximum freedom in generating alternative designs, and to avoid rumors'. Accordingly, most other PrimeOptics managers, supervisors and employees remained in the dark on the redesign process both before and after recommendations were made.

The organization design process performed by the taskforce

During the period from late March to May, the taskforce developed six alternative organizational designs. The researchers were unable to participate in all the face-to-face discussions due to distance and time limitations. But they were able to bombard the group with questions via phone calls and email messages. Based on the desired future capabilities, the taskforce developed a list of 10 criteria that could be used to evaluate the six options. It is noteworthy that design criteria were created by the taskforce members in relative isolation.

The researchers pointed out that 'people issues' were seldom directly included in construction of criteria. For example, the 'ability of designs to promote career paths' criterion was assigned a 3.4% decision weight. The taskforce norm was to avoid people and emotional considerations in favour of criteria that emphasized costs and technical solutions. The PrimeOptics culture, values and norms stressed engineering objectivity. After the project was completed, several members indicated that this inhibited frank discussion. On reflection, they indicated that structures were being created that would benefit specific members of the taskforce, but that this was deliberately not discussed during meetings. Team members could clearly see their potential new roles in the different options being considered but did not discuss their personal likes and dislikes 'in order to stay objective'.

By the time that the taskforce began deliberations on the best choices, the researchers were again on the scene. Consistent with the original objectives, the group focused on two alternative designs that decentralized engineering and program office activities to the factory, breaking up the matrix. At this critical stage the researchers raised several issues for collective reflection:

- Are the leading alternatives significantly different from each other?
- Would either of the models facilitate the expressed needs of other taskforces?
- How would the models perform under scrutiny of other stakeholders?
- How risky are these models to the company's main strengths – innovation and customer responsiveness?

The taskforce members welcomed these points being raised, but they did not feel that time or additional resources could be spent on questions raised by the researchers. Keeping a self-imposed deadline for presenting their final design seemed more important than following a reflexive design process that might take several more weeks of work. Instead, taskforce members combined the best elements of the two models and submitted one design to top management.

Top management took four months to design their own solution retaining key features of the matrix organization (Figure 7.3). This was surprising to all parties given the initial overwhelming management sentiment against the matrix. The taskforce leader was especially shocked because he had informal contacts with other taskforces and was not at all aware of top management intentions. He felt that the redesign was significant in the sense of new factory authority over certain engineering support groups, but he did not understand why other elements of the proposed design were rejected. The matrix would be retained, with little hope for achieving major cost reductions. Much of the past sense of urgency and crisis faded away. With a return to company profitability, top management expected to make few cuts in staffing.

In January 2003 the taskforce leaders and researchers took stock of the situation. It was apparent that top management had abandoned the vision, values and rationale behind the change program. Taskforce members did not know why the new design was selected or how it might be justified. That is, without the crisis of high support costs and need for downsizing, what would management and the taskforce members communicate to the workforce as the reason behind the significant changes in organization design?

The transition process and dynamics

The researchers, hoping to broaden participation and to foster a spirit of reflection and learning, proposed an elaborate structural learning mechanism. This mechanism would tightly link in human resources, training, information systems and other support services commonly required in the cutover to new designs (see Chapters 8 and 9). However, the newly appointed production executive chose instead a simple implementation group of four sub-team leaders (all managers) and an overall transition team leader. Since some of the newly appointed transition team members had not been involved in the prior process, the group took time to revisit earlier taskforce decisions. With a better understanding of past options considered as well as top management's strategic design, the group began to alter the operational design of the factories. This activity was 'design on the fly'. New work emerged from collective reflection on the current situation and experiences, a feature of reflexive design. The transition group had freedom to redesign work on the shop floor, and selectively began to involve work teams in experimentation with new work methods and production processes. Compared to the prior taskforce the team did not have to worry about approvals as it had authority to put changes in place immediately. The researchers observed that this type of collaboration and involvement with employees had seldom been seen earlier in the change program. As the transition team conducted its work, they encountered some obstacles to

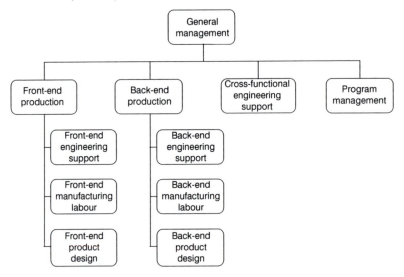

Figure 7.3 New modified matrix following redesign

innovation and efficiency. The transition team felt that the new design could not achieve full potential until dedicated engineering staff members were physically co-located in the factories. However, there simply was not enough space in the factories for engineering staff, and the transition team had to alter this important aspect of the operational design.

Discussion

Reflections on the case and the scope of the redesign process

Reflexive design theory is a useful framework for analysis of the PrimeOptics case. According to theory, the quality of deliberations and discussion at all stages of redesign work is crucial to achievement of balanced results. Moreover, the reflexive design approach calls for high involvement from all parties and self-application of theory, methods and practices. In the PrimeOptics case, important stakeholders were left out from the start. This had serious implications for the construction of the vision and goals, self-design activities, the scope and time for reflective learning, and managerial capacity to adopt a systemic view of outcomes. In the larger change program, learning and reflection were not perceived as important elements in the change process. Leaders and members of the various taskforces did not regularly meet to share progress and discuss problems, and were not aware of potential impacts of their own activities on others. The top manager kept abreast of taskforce activities but missed opportunities for synergy and reflective learning at all management and employee levels. Thus the various taskforces had a restricted view of the internal environment and shifting priorities. This was demonstrated most dramatically by the rejection of the production execution taskforce recommendations. Top management decided not to cut engineering support costs by 50%, and decided to retain basic elements of the matrix organization. Overall, the decision-making was top-down, except for the generation of taskforce recommendations. Lack of dialogue up and down the hierarchy seriously limited productive reflection, learning and commitment to the strategic design.

At the taskforce level, conditions were much better. Considering our earlier list of new types of reflection and learning (see 'Reflexive design, reflection and learning', p. 81), some aspects of reflexive design were handled quite well. Taskforce participants explored goals, alternative redesign models and developed design criteria. The group clearly adopted an approach in agreement with PrimeOptics' unique culture and situation. Taskforce members were able to self-apply theory, methods and practices and assumed strong ownership of the change process. However, they also set unrealistic deadlines and sacrificed opportunities for collective reflection to meet self-imposed project milestones. Management and the taskforce did not regard design work as iterative, or that it should receive attention beyond the rather 'closed' taskforce membership. The redesign taskforce did not check their work with top management or any other group and thus left themselves open for criticism and the eventual surprise of seeing their suggestion replaced by a new design passed down from top management.

It is noteworthy that the taskforce simply passed on its recommendations, and did not seriously engage in discussions with top management. This continued the group's pattern of avoiding conflict, discussions of differences and consideration of emotional or non-technical issues. In retrospect, taskforce members reflected that a great deal of time was wasted on development of design criteria, quantitative ratings of the alternative designs, and merging the two leading models. These considerations had little to do with the design created by top management. They felt that the time might have been devoted to conversations with the top manager so that the final strategic design could reflect their knowledge of conditions in the factory and how the design might be implemented. Both the PrimeOptics culture and locus of decision making seemed to block meaningful dialogue.

Reflective design processes include time for learning and development of new competencies. This includes deliberations within normal project stages as well as time for spontaneous and unplanned learning and reflection (Stebbins and Shani 2002). This is especially important as redesign shifts toward implementation and people need support experimenting with new roles, relationships and work activities. As noted in the case, management did not see the need to create a transition support infrastructure that would support experimentation, training and learning at operating levels. Implementation was left to a small management team. Production process changes were initiated with selected work teams, and the implementation group modified the strategic design to account for various obstacles and factory realities. These initiatives produced the kinds of collaborative design, productive reflection and learning that researchers hoped to see during the overall program.

Reflexive design authors and consultants promote a systemic view of values-based outcomes. Dual emphasis on quality of work life and competitive organizational performance is a core value (Docherty *et al.* 2002). PrimeOptics, however, rarely considered the intellectual, emotional or physical needs of employees as it established a vision and goals, conducted self-design activities and implemented the new design. Low involvement of employees, customers and other stakeholders led to myopia, sub-optimization and considerable wasted effort during the strategic design stages. In this respect, the PrimeOptics case is an example of how *not* to carry out reflexive design.

Reflective practice during redesign

Reflexive design theory is in part based on Self-Design thinking (Mohrman and Cummings 1989; Weick 1977) and it is a design process characterized by multiple iterations. As different stakeholders enter the picture, goals, design criteria and new designs are subjected to continuous scrutiny and modification. Design work often cycles back to earlier stages, incorporating new values, ideas and information. This occurred when the researchers entered the picture and led a comprehensive review of design approaches and ideal theory compared to taskforce activities. It also occurred later, as the new transition team members studied earlier design work and made operational design changes at implementation. Despite these limited connections to reflexive design theory, it can be concluded that the PrimeOptics redesign process had serious flaws in leaving out the principal stakeholder, top management. It is not clear that additional redesign cycles involving other stakeholders would have been productive, since management rejected most ideas proposed by the taskforce. There was time available for productive reflection and learning with other stakeholders, but the real opportunity existed between the taskforce and top management.

In the absence of sound structural learning mechanisms to stimulate new conversations, what can be tried to trigger learning in a secrecy-based organization? The case suggests that researchers/consultants can create ad hoc or temporary forums, different from the client's typical style of running meetings and conducting the design process. This was accomplished when the researchers presented and led discussions about alternative design theories, and when they asked difficult questions about the value of proposed designs. Therefore, educational interventions and expert consulting, if co-operatively sponsored by both researchers and clients, show high promise for stimulating productive reflection and learning in secretive organizations.

Reflective design under secrecy conditions

We viewed secrecy as both a contextual and organization culture variable. The challenges encountered in the effort reported in this chapter were magnified by the embedded phenomenon of secrecy or the 'need-to-know' culture. As we said earlier, collective reflection is the ability to uncover and make explicit what one has planned, observed or achieved in practice – therefore it is concerned with the creation of collective meaning. Thus, by its very nature, reflexive design requirements emphasize the need for high involvement of all the stakeholders in the reflection process, in the exploration of alternative solutions and in the creation of shared meaning. Thus 'secretive' culture significantly limits the ability to fully engage in reflective or reflexive design.

We discovered in this study that the challenge is even greater when the secrecy-based culture is coupled with an organizational configuration that is more like machine bureaucracy than adhocracy or matrix. PrimeOptics relied on the hierarchy to get things done and did not have many of the characteristics associated with matrix culture and problem-solving processes. Many limits to productive reflection and learning were identified and addressed in this chapter. We observed low involvement of employees and other stakeholders in decision making and restricted communications between sub-units and levels. The organization as a whole was not used to experimenting with opposite ways of relating and working. However, on a local level, the taskforce manager took steps to open up the redesign process by welcoming outside researchers and modifying deliberations when researchers were present. Some reflexive design was possible at the taskforce level in this secrecy-based company, even without an umbrella of support from top management. We can conclude from our case example that advancement of reflexive design in a secrecy-based organization requires greater involvement of top managers and other stakeholders in the process and willingness to explore both technical and social considerations during redesign.

References

Beer, M., (2001) 'How to Develop an Organization Capable of Sustained High Performance: Embrace the Drive for Results-Capability Development Paradox', *Organizational Dynamics*, 29, 4: 233–47.

Docherty, P., Forslin, J. and Shani, A.B. (Rami) (eds) (2002) *Creating Sustainable Work Systems: Emerging Perspectives and Practice*, London: Routledge.

Docherty, P., Forslin, J., Shani, A.B. (Rami) and Kira, M. (2002) 'Emerging Work Systems: From Intensive to Sustainable', in P. Docherty, J. Forslin and A.B. (Rami) Shani (eds) (2002) *Creating Sustainable Work Systems: Emerging Perspectives and Practice*, London: Routledge, 2–14.

Galbraith, J.R. (1994) *Competing With Flexible Lateral Organizations*, Boston, MA: Addison Wesley.

Landau, D. (2003) 'Dynamics of Organizational Vision During Change: The Case of a Defense R&D Organization', Doctoral Dissertation, Tel-Aviv University Faculty of Management.

Mitroff, I.I. and Kilmann, R.H. (1984) *Corporate Tragedies: Product Tampering, Sabotage and other Catastrophes*, New York: Praeger.

Mohrman, S.A. and Cummings, T.G. (1989) *Self-Designing Organizations: Learning How to Create High Performance*, Boston, MA: Addison-Wesley.

Mackenzie, K.D. (1986) *Organization Design: The Organizational Audit and Analysis Technology*, New York: Ablex.

Nadler, D.A. and Tushman, M.L. (1988) *Strategic Organization Design: Concepts, Tools, and Processes*, New York: Harper Collins.

Raelin, J.A. (2000) *Work-Based Learning: The New Frontier of Management Development*, PH OD Series, Englewood Cliff, NJ: Prentice-Hall.

Shani, A.B. (Rami) and Docherty, P. (2003) *Learning by Design: Building Sustainable Organizations*, Oxford: Blackwell Publishers.

Stebbins, M.W. and Shani, A.B. (Rami) (2002) 'Eclectic Design for Change', in P. Docherty, J. Forslin and A.B. (Rami) Shani (eds) *Creating Sustainable Work Systems: Emerging Perspectives and Practice*, London: Routledge, 201–12.

Weick, K.E. (1977) 'Organization Design: Organizations and Self-Designing Systems', *Organizational Dynamics*, 6: 30–46.

8 Collective reflection under ambiguity

Monica Bjerlöv and Peter Docherty

Throughout the 1990s indicators of workers' perceptions of work have demonstrated growing experience of work intensity, no doubt reflecting management's efforts to improve performance through rationalization and reducing costs. In many countries, this has been especially the case in the public sector. As pointed out earlier, people feel they do not have the time to think or reflect. The growing complexity in the worlds of business and work would make this more difficult in all events. Recent studies have shown, however, that perceived sources of intensity are not so much related to physical exertion or the pace of work, but rather socio-psychological factors such as people's difficulties in understanding and managing their work situation and communicating with others (Antonovsky 1987). Difficulties in understanding are rooted in such factors as ambiguity, uncertainty and equiv-ocality. Stress arises from the frustrating efforts to make sense of what different parties in the work situation – colleagues, superiors, customers, suppliers – mean, intend, value and prioritize in their interactions with each other. Weick (1995) calls this sense making 'a process of committed interpretation'. It entails remembering, reflecting and constructing meaning through linking received cues to existing configurative structures. It is a process that seeks to introduce stability into an equivocal flow of events by means of justifications that increase social order.

In most situations, ambiguity cannot be reduced by individual reflection. Reducing ambiguity requires interaction, either directly with those who are the source of the ambiguity (senior managers, board members, politicians, customers or suppliers), their representatives (immediate superiors, sales or purchasing people) or colleagues (team-mates and fellow workers). However, many modern playwrights, such as Harold Pinter in the UK and Lars Norén in Sweden, have brilliantly illustrated the mundane difficulties of social communication: conversations as situations where many are speaking, but few are listening or fewer understanding. In this chapter we present a model of the communication process that is aimed at heightening the efficiency and effectiveness of listening and, thereby, sense-making, developing a deep, shared understanding of the complexities and varied meanings of a common work situation. This model is illustrated with several examples drawn from our on-going research on organizational development. We conclude with some comments on the organizational facilitation of the development of work-based dialogues, joint speaking and listening.

A communicative learning process

The description of collective reflection both within and on work is that of a developing sense-making process. Dialogue produces both the development of local practice and learning to learn. Understanding work, the job design, the organization and its activities depends upon the possibility of comparing one's own perceptions and experiences with those of others. Logically, the starting-point should be shared experiences and shared everyday contexts.

The work-based dialogue illustrated in Figure 8.1 takes as its point of departure an issue or event, that provides a practical link between the individual and the group, the collective level (see e.g. Bjerlöv 2002; Gustavsen 2001; Shotter and Gustavsen 1999). Dialogue takes place in a context of ambiguity: there is a lack of clarity or consistency regarding such factors as values, goals, intentions, resources, limits and domains, authority and discretion. It may entail uncertainty and difficulties in assigning interpretations, priorities, dependencies, probabilities, causality and difficulties in understanding how a system or one's work situation functions and one's own and others' positions in it (March 1994).

Making sense in an ambiguous situation is a search for context within which small details fit together and can be understood. It is about people interacting to flesh out hunches. It is a 'continuous alternation between particulars and explanations, with each cycle giving added form and substance to the other' (Weick 1995: 13).

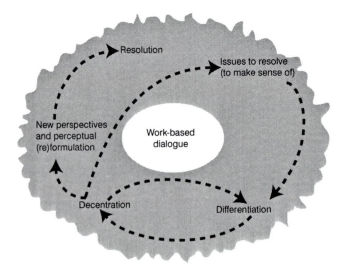

Figure 8.1 A communicative learning process

The two processes that we regard as central in the communication and sense-making process are differentiation and decentering. The group communication process takes its point of departure in an issue of concern to the group. Piaget (1962) found that differentiation precedes decentration. *Differentiation* is the process whereby people distance themselves from their own subjectivity by experience, based on the identification of differences and diversity between their own way of understanding something from other ways, or other people's ways, of understanding the same thing.

Decentration is a process whereby people critically validate their own assumptions to enable the perceptual reformulation of a previous point of view, shifting the given cognitive perspective. This process, first broached by Piaget (1962: 3–5), concerns the issue of shifting one's focus, enabling one to view the differences and diversity, perceived through interaction with others, as being other possible solutions or interpretations. What we are dealing with here is an insight about 'how', not merely 'what'. Furthermore decentring entails the ability to differentiate between one's own point of view and other possible points of view, and from there, to *act* according to the assumption that 'the way I understand a phenomenon is as true for me as other people's understanding is for them'.

Differentiation and decentration are processes built on a continuously on-going cognitive movement. The process depends on a switching process between several different perspectives on separate features of the issue. The iterations of differentiation and decentration will lead to further attempts to resolve the issue or to perceptual (re) formulation. *Perceptual (re) formulation* is a transformation from one taken-for-granted cognitive perspective to another. It is based on the individual having been able to incorporate increasingly larger parts of a context of immediate importance, such as a workplace, and having drawn on that so as to formulate new knowledge and experience: a change in understanding (Piaget 1962).

These concepts are a way of explaining the phenomenon of the co-creation of knowledge. To extend the idea somewhat, this co-creating of knowledge can be used in various processes of organising work. The model presented in Figure 8.1 is a starting-point for a theoretical framework for ongoing sense-making processes and the parallel process of organising work. Using this framework, workplaces and organizations can construct a suitable local, practical model of working for continuous organizational development.

Illustrations

The handling of ambiguity through collective reflection in dialogue arises in many types of situations, such as meeting changes in work arising from market or institutional developments, the initiation of development activities regarding new products, services or work processes and the introduction of new concepts, models or methods in work. Different parties and individuals will experience uncertainty and ambiguity at different points and in different ways. We present three examples as illustrations taken from on-going collaborative research projects dealing with organizational development. The examples concern general issues often associated with high ambiguity:

- Following a major political development – new membership of the European Community – senior management changed the structure and 'rules of the game' in the business radically, assigning us a new role. How do we give this role meaning and communicate it to others?
- Following a corporate restructuring, a new division has been formed and its operational multi-professional centres must be developed. How, where and with what do we start that development and what conflicts are to be expected between the different professions represented?
- As a proactive move to meet new national and international competition, the company introduced a new business strategy and management system. How do different levels and functions in the organization perceive these changes? To what extent does there exist a 'shared understanding' of key concepts and issues?

Illustration I: Giving a new professional role content and meaning. Coaches in local pharmacies in a state-owned pharmacy company

A few years ago, the state-owned pharmaceutical distribution monopoly made a series of radical changes in its organization and its way of doing business in order to meet the potential changes in the market place following Sweden's entry into the European Community. These changes included its organization, business and functional strategies and management system. Non-hospital pharmacies were organized in a 'Health' division, which was organized in regions covering the whole country. Regions were organized in districts, each of which contained a number of pharmacies of varying size. Districts were allowed considerable flexibility in organising their business. The district in this illustration consisted of five pharmacies. The district manager made the pharmacies semi-autonomous and self-designing, removing the position of pharmacy manager. Each pharmacy was organized according to 'product areas' with some staff responsible, for example, for competence development. Ex-pharmacy managers became 'pharmacy coaches'. The district had a 'virtual' matrix structure; those responsible for the product areas and special functions in each pharmacy met regularly at the district level. Thus the ex-managers, now coaches, met together every other week.

One of the purposes of this new organization was to increase the participation of staff members in operations and management. As a step in realising this, all groups were given the task of formulating a business plan for their own pharmacy, and for the entire district. These plans are evaluated and revised four times per year. The functional groups were given responsibility for the development of their fields of activity. Planning and follow-up meetings were held regularly at both the pharmacy and district level. A pilot interview study with the combined coaches and competence administrators' group was carried out regarding the experience of this 'organization through communication'. This provided examples of how meetings functioned as arenas for collective reflection for sense making and how they can function in the everyday ambiguity of pharmacy workplaces.

The specific ambiguity issue here is: How do we find a new way of working in new roles with the same actors? This was the primary challenge facing the combined group of ex-managers who had been appointed coaches and the line staff who had been made responsible for competence development. This was to be an example of the idea that 'the way we talk will transform into the way we work'. The individual cognitive processes and the shared social one both constitute examples of social constructs. Ambiguity in the coach group was related to the breadth and diffuseness of its assignment that was almost seen as 'build a new world of work' – they had 'no compass', little support and were poorly motivated until they decided to grapple with a specific issue.

The pilot interviews took place about a year after the new organization had been introduced. All those interviewed agreed that the group still had to define its task and function. The ex-managers had considerable difficulty in making sense of their role as coaches and thereafter altering their behaviour to that role. It was not, however, just the tasks and role that changed. It was necessary for the group members themselves to develop their own ways of working. Everyone was used to working in a traditional hierarchy that did not provide much freedom of action, and did not therefore demand from staff members the kind of independence and initiative, which were essential requirements in the new organization.

The interviews indicate that the launching of this new organization with important and demanding new tasks and, above all, completely new methods of working, has been an arduous and slow process, demanding patience of both staff and management, in different roles and at different levels. At the same time, many employees expressed the view that being left to evolve their own ways of working meant that they have learnt new things that they could not have anticipated initially.

How did the coach and competence developer group find a way in this new way of working in new roles? We asked the eight interviewed about the importance and function of their meetings. They referred to their meetings as a space for reflection that was highly appreciated. This was evident from such comments as 'The meetings are necessary, especially for the development of the new role of the coach.' Also, the meaningfulness of the meetings is illustrated as a context for differentiation. For example '…it becomes meaningful as you draw on different points of view. For example, when I want to decide on formal educational activities, and someone else tells me that the staff members themselves are capable of making their own evaluations. Then that is an instance of insight for me, and I'll think, "Right, you are! of course they can".'

Another example demonstrates the value of differentiation, seeing and understanding the differences, as well as decentering, understanding that there are other legitimate ways of viewing the matter, 'When you ask something at a meeting and someone describes how others are doing things, or their way of reasoning, then I see that things will work out fine. Because the way it works is that once you have formulated a question, there is a break, and you think the matter through once more, while you're waiting for the other person's answer. You expand your way of thinking by listening to others.' The quote illustrates how the scope for reflection appears to be perceived and how it can manifest itself. As they hear themselves formulate and put forward a point of view to other people, a scope for intellectual decentering on a social basis is provided. Making one's experience and insights public means making one's knowledge accessible to others. We are here dealing with shared as well as individual learning. This can be developed into a method of working in itself.

The fact that the members themselves can identify that they are here dealing with sense-making processes is illustrated in the following: 'The meetings allow for scope for understanding the task and the fields of activities. Things are brought out into the open. I have to think together with other individuals.' Another person says 'We look for issues to set out from, and, at the same time, we perfect the ability of seeing the fields of activities in such a way that no important issue is lost as we move along.' This is a phase of identifying issues to resolve. It is also an indication of participants perfecting their ability of seeing increasingly larger parts of the organization and its activities, to broaden and expand their organizational knowledge.

Discussions in the coach group lacked a sense of direction until they managed to focus on a concrete issue, personnel evaluation and compensation revision. This changed the way they worked, especially regarding their communication with each other in the group. Interview comments included: 'Now we have figured out what we should do and also how to achieve that. We discovered the issue of the setting of salary levels within the pharmacy region.' 'The setting of salary levels made the work tangible, and helped us make progress in developing the group's area of responsibility and its communication.' 'People are not used to co-operating this way in groups. Some bickering and conflicts have resulted from this.' 'But we are getting better and better at this.'

This illustrates how the members together found a first issue to resolve in order to get further into making sense of the new way of work with new roles and old experiences. They had to differentiate and decentre not only between individual perceptions but also between old, collective, 'taken-for-granted' knowledge and experiences to formulate new perspectives. The group meetings develop into a communicative context in which members become more efficient, at a conscious level perfecting differentiation and decentering, and thereby reflect and open up for collective learning.

Illustration II: Defining a development agenda: integration or local autonomy? A start conference in an organizational development project

A new division in a nationalized company responsible for the rail traffic management had decided to conduct a major development project regarding the management and control of rail traffic operations. The focus of the project was the regional traffic control centres (TCCs). Two key issues were to be addressed: firstly, the management relations between the head office and the TCCs, and, secondly, the development of the role of traffic controllers in the TCCs. One important point of departure in the project was the promotion of learning between different levels and functions in the organization.

The staff represented different professional categories: traffic controllers, track maintenance supervisors, public traffic information officers and managers. Each category deals with a part of the system essential for the smooth running of traffic in the region. The work system is based on all employee categories working together around the clock, in a three-shift system over a 10-to-14-week period.

The project started at one TCC with a *start conference* which included a cross-section of the different personnel categories in the workplace, staff representatives from the head office responsible for the development project, the researchers involved and representatives from senior management. The start conference provided a one-day opportunity to achieve a shared view of the organization and its activities, and to identify the need for development and improvements. Eighteen staff members from the TCC, four representatives from the head office and two researchers, participated. *The ambiguity issue was: what kinds of changes are needed now to better utilize the competence and knowledge in the organization?*

Key issues were to be discussed that needed to be implemented within the next two years. The 18 staff members were grouped into five groups at the beginning of the day. Each group was asked to describe what the organization and its activities should look like in two years' time, and to formulate a vision for the future to be used to identify those issues to be given priority. In a second meeting, the groups were asked to identify obstacles for carrying out these necessary changes. In a third meeting, the groups formulated strategies that would make it possible to overcome the obstacles and to preserve the visions they had formulated. Finally, the participants formulated a concrete action plan to be carried out in the coming three weeks. One or two named participants were assigned responsibility for each one of these tasks. The central theme running through all four meetings (visions, obstacles, strategy and course of action) was the need to improve the technical system and its supporting informational structures.

These initial dialogues on a vision were lively and focused. The various professional categories had, in part, different perspectives and experiences. In fact their initial expectations were that their different professional perspectives might well give rise to misunderstandings between them. The dialogue entailed investigating those differences. In the process, they found that they had more or less the same perceptions regarding the relevance of different problems. Their differences concerned perceptions of *why* change was needed in a specific area, rather than in the perceived need for change itself. That is precisely why the areas that were defined were considered important. Different perspectives on and interpretations of the problems and their causes emerged – there were several different ways of understanding one single phenomenon.

Time was required for participants to familiarize themselves with a way of thinking that is based on evaluation, and to view others' comments as insights, critical validations, which perhaps made them understand that problems, and their causes, could be defined in several 'possible' ways. On coming as far as that, a decentering process was achieved in the groups (see Figure 8.1). The individuals' description of experiences resulting in the perception of, for example, the limits of the railway traffic operations system, was put forward, and were made public and accessible to all participants. The participants worked actively and concentrated on investigating differences and similarities, and were thereby able to move the dialogue further in sense making and the process of knowledge formation into a phase of resolution. The courses of action resulting from the start conference were the outcome of differentiation and decentration. This process went further into perceptual formulation and resolution. The specific content evolved and emerged out of the participants' desire to develop their own jobs. The need for change was formulated as follows: 'If the traffic system is to function satisfactorily, the traffic control system must operate perfectly.'

All the participants were agreed that the various subsystems making up the total system were not fully and reliably synchronized, so that the total system was not working entirely satisfactorily. Organising the flow of information, especially between shifts, was mentioned as being unwieldy. When starting their shift, people usually faced large backlogs of emails about important traffic disruptions and work on the tracks (e.g. shut offs). All too often this was a far too large an unsorted volume of information to be dealt with at an individual level. The staff members had many suggestions to improvements in communications to improve sense-making. Their discussion of the issues clearly illustrated the processes of differentiation and decentration. By the end of the workshop the participants had formulated plans of action, a kind of perceptual formulation to use in the resolution phase (see Figure 8.1).

Illustration III: Do we have a shared understanding of what our services strategy means for our work? Discussions in a cross-level forum in a state-owned pharmacy company

The Development Forum was the name originally given to the advisory group in the pharmacy company mentioned in our first illustration. It was formed to follow the developments in the various research projects we were conducting in the company. The group was made up of a vertical slice through the hierarchy from the top management group to the high street pharmacy. Its members were the assistant managing director, a manager at the divisional, regional and district levels and a pharmaceutical assistant from a pharmacy, plus an HRD staff expert at divisional level.

The issue of ambiguity in this illustration arose from the insight that the shared understanding in common basic concepts in the business idea were in fact not shared. In discussing developments in the projects the members of the forum soon became aware that many of the aspects of the business that they had taken for granted as being shared understandings were in fact not shared. The new strategies, policies and management systems that had been introduced so smoothly, were in fact different things to different people in different roles in different parts of the company. Their ambiguity could well be re-named 'ignorance'. The members of the forum had not initially been aware of the extent and character of their individual understanding of key concepts. The feedback from the on-going research projects provided the basis for learning and productive reflection through the work-based dialogue. The forum added a second task to its assignment: to attain a deeper understanding of a key aspect of the new strategy, namely '*customer focus*', by discussing the individual members' presentations of their interpretations of the concept: one person's interpretation was presented at each meeting.

The learning elements in this situation as well as the dialogue and reflection processes are closely linked to the processes of differentiation and decentration and perceptual formulation or reformulation. What we are getting at is the process of distancing ourselves from taken-for-granted assumptions primarily to create possibilities for critical validation and to catch sight of other possible perspectives. Summing up and interpreting participants' activity at the meeting contributes to our making sense of the organization.

The assistant managing director was newly employed and did not make a presentation. The divisional manager's interpretation of 'customer focus' high-lighted the development of products and services and on promoting learning within the organization as well as increasing its market share. She experienced less ambig-uity about the organization than others did and her contributions to the discussions were often formulated as interpretations of the meaning and consequences of what others had said. She admitted, 'This forum constitutes my space for reflection regarding the organization and its activities. Here issues and ideas linked to the organization and its activities have been raised that I'd otherwise never have had the chance of knowing about them. This forum constitutes an actual place for reflection with immediate relevance to the ability and possibilities for me and others to efficiently continue the work of developing the pharmacy's activities.'

The regional manager did not focus on the customer as such, but expressed some uncertainty, questioning how the organization was functioning and managers were acting, as distinct from identifying business preconditions. The district manager had recently been appointed to a new type of position, being responsible for five pharmacies. She had introduced several innovations in their organization and management and was mainly focused on acquiring feedback on the impact of these innovations on performance and on management's reactions to and support for her ideas. She experienced unchanged ambiguity regarding the limits to and the conditions for innovation. The representative from the high street pharmacy was responsible for competence and learning and was interested in understanding how the new strategies contained possibilities for developing her colleagues' competencies and careers. She was inclined to 'think aloud' interpreting both herself and others and felt that she had got a better understanding of the company and reduced ambiguity.

In a series of six bi-monthly half-day meetings, customer focus was discussed in terms that ranged from operationalized statistics of 'number of customers served per day per employee' in the local pharmacy, to how leadership should be developed at different levels in middle and higher management levels in the organization. All the experiences related put the participants' subjective knowledge and assumptions in a new broader light – a light that forced dialogue into a process of differentiation and, to greater or lesser extent to a process of decentering and perceptual re-formulation. Nevertheless this became a context of perceptual formulation that was new to the participants.

The development of shared understanding in the Development Forum required a process of deconstruction to occur, in the sense that the participants dismantled and investigated the experience that had been expressed and compared it with their own. The reflective conversation or discussion evolves into an investigation that consists of looking for differences and similarities in order to grasp the experience and place it next to one's own. Also, in this context a differentiation and decentration process occurred. Something that can be called an interactive investigation pushed this process forward. This process lead to the creation of shared perceptions.

What is revealed in the comments above does not necessarily form entirely new knowledge. On the contrary, perhaps we are here confronted with such matters that are on many people's minds, i.e., their perceptions and experiences concerning work and activities within the group of companies. But it is the accessibility to one another's perceptions, the process of turning the problem over in one's mind, so as to grasp the problem and all of its aspects that brings about new knowledge, which possibly results in new ways of doing things. It is the interaction between different representatives from various levels of the organization that produces a kind of internal public accessibility. This means that more and more have access to increasingly larger parts of the activities, resulting in the making sense of the organization and the business.

Discussion transforms to dialogue

In each of the illustrations, the individuals and the groups enter an arena for collective reflection and sense making. They work their way through interplay of episodes of differentiation and decentration, cognitive as well as social. Table 8.1 shows the main features of the illustrations.

The arenas provided legitimacy for reflection: a protected spatial, social and temporal resource for discussion. In each case higher management had specifically allocated resources and defined an assignment for the groups. In each case the assignment entailed collective reflection, but this was not focussed in the specific task of the group. Its tasks were couched in terms of exchanging and evaluating experiences, defining and planning further developments, addressing and solving problems (similar to the embedded forms of collective reflection described by Cressey in Chapter 5 in this volume). They avoided the abstract, unsettling and even provocative term 'reflection' that can sometimes hinder reflection by making people either self-conscious or negatively inclined to the task. (See Boud, Chapter 13 in this volume for more on this point.)

Experience from these cases showed that the presence of experienced resource persons to support the structuring of the discussions was advantageous, especially in the early stages of the process. In the first case, the Coach group had been meeting for nearly a year before they identified the issue of 'salary revision' as a

Table 8.1 Comparison of the examples of arenas for collective reflection and sense making

	Illustration I	*Illustration II*	*Illustration III*
Organizational Development/ Transformation	*Cross-unit Professional group (State pharmacy chain)*	*Organizational Development challenges (Rail Transport Authority)*	*Strategic Development group (State pharmacy chain)*
Ambiguity	Inexperience of self-management and self-organization: work situation diffuse and unclear	High expected ambiguity due to multiple work cultures – but high level of agreement	Interpretative ambiguity: management not clear that they were unclear
Structural mechanism (Arena)	District coach group 'coaches without a coach'	Start conference	'Vertical slice' forum
Learning context	Professional role forum, highly unstructured: trial and error practice Addressed new roles and organization Process began to evolve when concrete issues formulated	Democratic dialogue (All levels and professions) Highly structured method Addressed current challenges Energy generated Clear ideas formulated	Discussion of current developments Realization of strategic plans Semi-structured by researchers Strategic idea not consciously perceived or impacting events
Model's utility	Development process in an emerging work practice Can be well described by the model but has not functioned as a tool in the process	Conference provided illustrations of the model's central concepts – ended with formulations. Study limited to initial events – no process evaluation possible	Conscious attempts were made to test the model with certain facilitation by the researchers Direct emergence of mutual understanding

practical issue that would help them formulate their roles. This group had been working on their own with occasional visits from their district manager. The groups in the other two examples had direct support from a facilitator, a professional communication and change consultant. The start conference is a recognized methodology based on Gustavsen's 'democratic dialogue' as an emancipatory process and structure. The prescriptive design of structures and processes to facilitate and promote learning is often referred to as the design of learning mechanisms and is taken up by Stebbins *et al.* (Chapters 7 and 9 in this volume).

Communication serves a general function, since it both creates a bridge between different individual's perceptions and their efforts of making sense of the organizational context, and is the active mechanism that determines the arena. In the sense of the participants making their own perceptions and ideas accessible to one another, they also subject their own and others' ideas and perceptions to a favourable critical validation.

The discussions in the arenas in our three examples illustrate Weick's concept of 'sense making as the verbal inter-subjective process of interpreting actions and events':

> ... individual thoughts, feelings and intentions are merged, synthesized into discussions during which the self gets transformed from 'I' into 'we'. This is not simply an interaction in which norms are shared, which would be a connection through social structure rather than interaction. Instead a – level of social reality – forms which consist of an inter-subject, or joined subject or merged subject.
>
> (Weick 1995: 71)

This shared-meaning construction proceeded in steps that enabled different groups to arrive at a shared understanding, so as to deal with the different examples of ambiguity that the three contexts involve. We interpret Weick's words about going from 'I' to 'we' as being about creating a sufficient mutual understanding, without intimidating any particular individual's understanding or experience. This should not be confused with ideas of fairness or democracy in terms of everyone having their say in matters. It was rather a matter of including what was perceived as being mutually understood. Actually what is described here is something as unremarkable and ordinary as thinking about what and how a task is understood, and how it can be carried out in its existing context – to contextualize.

Such processes, however, become increasingly complex as the number of those involved increases. If an entire group, and eventually as in our empirical examples an entire workplace, were to create a broader understanding of the organization and its activities then the seemingly simple becomes complex, remarkable and exciting, both for the practitioner and the researcher. Reflection in collective contexts can create learning processes, partly with respect to the development of the individual's cognitive structures, and partly in terms of the perfection of the ability to effectively and beneficially relate one's thinking and perceptions to those of others, and creating something mutually beneficial out of it.

The distinctive aspect of this chapter is to focus the communicative process involved in productive collective reflection. It presents a model including several key elements of the communication process that we maintain are critical if collective sense making, learning and shared understanding are to be realized. The examples presented are few and are only illustrations. They suffice to indicate the relevance and usefulness of the concepts. The contexts of the examples and the glimpses from the processes involved indicate that planned facilitation and structure may be expected to improve the development of collective learning in these types of situations. However, the extent and character of design in situations concerning reflection and learning is a sensitive issue. A fine line separates positive support from negative steering and where exactly that line goes is a matter for further study.

References

Antonovsky, A. (1987) *Unraveling the Mystery of Health: How People Manage Stress and Stay Well*, San Francisco, CA: Jossey-Bass.

Bjerlöv, M. (2002) 'Deutero-Learning and Sustainable Change', in P. Docherty, J. Forslin and A.B. Shani (eds) *From Intensive Work Systems to Sustainable Work Systems*, London: Routledge, 190–200.

Gustavsen, B. (2001) 'Theory and Practice: The Mediating Discourse', in P. Reason and H. Bradbury (eds) *Handbook of Action Research: Participative Inquiry and Practice*, London: Sage Publications, 17–26.

March, J.G. (1994) *A Primer on Decision Making*, New York: Free Press.

Piaget, J. (1962) *Comments on Vygotsky's Critical Remarks Concerning. The Language and Thought of the Child and Judgement and Reasoning in the Child*, Cambridge, MA: The MIT Press.

Shotter, J. and Gustavsen, B. (1999) *The Role of 'Dialogue Conferences' in the Development of 'Learning Regions': Doing 'From Within' our Lives Together what we Cannot do Apart*, Stockholm: Centre for Advanced Studies in Leadership, Stockholm School of Economics.

Weick, K. (1995) *Sensemaking in Organizations*, Thousand Oaks, CA: Sage Publications.

9   Reflection during a crisis turnaround

Management use of learning mechanisms

Michael Stebbins, A.B. 'Rami' Shani and Peter Docherty

Introduction

Crises involve acute problems perceived by management as seriously threatening the organization's sustainability or survival. They require quick and radical action, often aiming at a far-reaching transformation of the organization affecting many or all aspects of the business. This chapter addresses learning in crises using a case study from a company attempting a business turnaround, i.e. a radical improvement in its market position and business performance. Achieving the transformation will be described in four phases:

1   the pre-study phase defining the main design goals and principles;
2   the redesign phase, developing in detail the new organization, its technology and human resources;
3   the implementation phase; and
4   the evaluation of the functioning of the organization – has it 'turned around'?

The topic of learning and reflection during a business turnaround program is relatively new and uncharted. Kochan and Useem (1992) present a number of studies addressing this issue. They identify two main themes in such situations. The first is an emphasis on change that challenges and reconfigures the tacit knowledge and assumptions about how organizational boundaries, technologies, strategies and human resources should be arranged. The second concerns the emphasis on 'learning organizations'– how individuals, groups and organizations are committed to and capable of continuous learning through information exchange, experimentation, dialogue, negotiation and consensus building. Dunphy and Stace (1990) analysed transition processes in Australian companies and noted marked differences in the effectiveness of participative strategies in different phases of the transformation processes. Participative strategies are more feasible in the later phases. Many studies have shown that the efficiency and effectiveness of such change processes are dependent on the 'breadth' and 'length' in the definition of the change project. Too narrow or unbalanced definitions of the project, e.g. a marked focus on technical issues, or the omission of organizational or learning issues, delay or prevent realizing key performance targets. Similarly allotting too little time to the project may also delay reaching performance targets (Scott Morton 1992; Keen 1988).

Many researchers have addressed the conscious design of conditions to promote and support learning in organizations in such contexts, e.g. Shani and Docherty (2003). This chapter focuses on the different conditions for learning prevailing for different actors and the learning mechanisms used in different phases of a turnaround process.

The turnaround case: the health care plan organization (HPO)

Our case study is a very condensed version of a five-year longitudinal study. It illustrates both the creative realization of learning opportunities and missed opportunities. The case is of an American health plan organization (HPO) that functions within a larger network composed of diverse hospital, clinic, and other service providers. The HPO provides coordination and integration by designing health plan benefit packages, marketing the packages to employers, insurance agencies, and individual customers, contracting with hospitals, clinics, and other providers, and by handling reimbursement. Given competitive conditions in the California marketplace, improvement of both the HPO and its larger network was regarded by its board as critical. The board recruited a new president to plan and execute the turnaround process that was given the name 'the Change Initiative' (CI).

We begin with a brief review of what we know about structural learning mechanisms. The HPO case is then introduced, followed by a discussion of the implications for productive reflection and learning during change programs.

Collective reflection during change programs

The character and extent of reflection and learning during change programs varies considerably. For example, we can ask whether the change process leads to set changes, whether the process allows unplanned change which is codified, or whether there is some combination of the two processes. Are the designs blueprints to be implemented without change, recipes that may be adapted, or something else? It would seem to be clear that the nature of reflection and learning is tied to the particular change process, the company context and unique conditions within the organizational setting.

Learning mechanisms

Learning mechanisms have been designed and formulated to promote and facilitate learning in the organization and its larger network. Learning mechanisms are formalized strategies, policies, guidelines, management and reward systems, methods, tools and routines, allocations of resources, and even the design of the physical facility and work spaces. Since learning involves ongoing questioning and analysis of existing practices, it can be regarded as a disturbance of the status quo.

Depending upon an organization's environment, management might have limited interest in learning or might view learning as the principal means of competition (De Geus 1992; Garvin, 2000).

For the purposes of this chapter, we identify three broad categories of learning mechanisms: cognitive, structural, and procedural (see Table 9.1). *Cognitive mechanisms* provide language, concepts, models, symbols, theories, and values for thinking, reasoning, and understanding learning issues. These mechanisms may be manifested in company value statements, strategy documents, management-union partnership agreements, and adoption of systems such as the balanced scorecard.

In contrast, *structural mechanisms* concern organizational, technical, and physical infrastructures. These include formal discussion forums, learning-specific structures such as parallel learning structures, bench-learning structures, quality circles, and other similar formally-structured forums. *Technology-oriented structural mechanisms* include learning centres, e-learning programs, and diverse groupware capabilities. Formal articulation of communication channels, feedback channels, available data bases, and data-sharing systems are broadly considered structural mechanisms. Also, the co-location of employees during a change program and layout of the work space would be included, as they can facilitate formal and informal contacts and communications.

Procedural mechanisms concern the rules, routines, methods and tools that might promote and support learning. Procedural mechanisms include provision for specific types of learning, such as action learning and built-in critiques and debriefing. They also include test and assessment tools and methods, operating procedures, and other mechanisms to promote individual and collective learning. Table 9.1 provides a sample matrix of mechanisms used in the HPO case.

The utilization of learning mechanisms at HPO

Parallel learning structures operate parallel to the formal structure (Bushe and Shani 1991). People in the main organization are given temporary assignments, usually by participating in development projects. In the case presented in this chapter, a parallel learning mechanism composed of representatives from different levels of management was used in the early stages of the transformation process to assess and structure key values in the organization, to formulate goals for the overall change program and to identify specific targets for internal redesign and reengineering. Participation in the learning structure was temporary and would end after goal setting.

An integrated learning mechanism is a mechanism created to plan, initiate and coordinate formal and informal learning activities in an organization on a temporary or permanent basis. In the context of the case here it was the Change Initiative organization that had responsibility for the two transformation themes identified by Kochan and Useem (1992). Specifically, the themes cover the change process and associated learning processes for the duration of the change program. Structurally, an integrated learning mechanism can resemble any other department of the company in terms of roles, hierarchy, role relationships and work routines.

Table 9.1 Learning mechanisms during stages of the HPO Change Initiative program

Change program	Learning mechanisms		
Program stage	*Cognitive*	*Structural*	*Procedural*
Pre-study: selection of design principles and methods	Mission and value statements	Parallel learning mechanism Group sensing	Gap analysis
Redesign process: conduct of detailed design	Crisis turnaround strategic plan	Integrated learning mechanism I Co-ordination and support system	Action learning
Implementation: iterative adaptation and improvement	Sequential use of an iterative, experimental procedure with self-managing teams	Integrated learning mechanism II Huddle meetings as link in coordination and support	Systems to monitor outcomes with new development iterations

Since the mission of the new unit is to orchestrate change, the psychological climate in the unit and ways of working are often quite different from other departments in the formal organization (Stebbins *et al.* 1998). That is, the members have accepted the cognitive rationale for change and they have also adopted procedures that promote free exchange of information, candid feedback, and cooperation.

The change initiative to turn around the health plan organization

Background

The case spans six years and was part of an overall turn-around program for a company that at the beginning had great difficulty competing within the California health care services market. The turnaround program was simply known within HPO as the 'Change Initiative' and will be referred to as CI throughout the case description. The CI was a multi-pronged effort to address the company's market image, internal operations, structure, organizational culture, and management support system issues within a rather traditional and conservative organization. The Board of Directors felt that HPO was functioning at the bottom of the health care industry and that the company needed a major shake-up. It wanted the newly appointed president to orchestrate a turnaround effort within a company having flat membership and revenues, outdated business systems, high administrative cost ratios, and a traditional command and control work climate. He decided that business process reengineering of the core processes at HPO was the most important part of CI (Stebbins *et al.* 1998). Downsizing would enable radical rationalization by replacing 11 local service centres by three centralized service call-centres. Thus the transformation and learning tasks were enormous. A shift in direction, injection of a sense of crisis, and re-engineering of core processes were viewed as necessary to reposition the organization in the marketplace. The changes proposed were considered revolutionary within HPO.

The pre-study: stating the corporate values, mission and design principles

The new president began the change initiative program with a pre-study phase. 'Up and coming' managers who might be able to take a fresh look at the organization and its operations were given the opportunity of participating in this phase which was also a test of their suitability to be the right people to manage future stages of the CI program. Five teams composed of middle and lower managers were established to study the situation and to suggest changes. They focused on market assessment, process reengineering, human resources, communications, and management/organization structure. In addition, all team members had a collateral responsibility to help the president develop new values, a mission statement and to consider culture change. The president hoped to show that participation in redesign of HPO's core business processes was both needed and welcome.

The pre-study organization was a *parallel learning mechanism*. Besides focussing on their particular assignments, the different teams also met collectively to evaluate the organizational culture and to identify high leverage core processes for the major reengineering effort that would follow. These teams also conducted 'group sensing' meetings at all organizational levels. Sensing sessions (without managers present) were designed to identify sources of information used by employees, levels of trust, degree of candid communications and the like. Using sensing techniques such as the nominal group method, the groups collected a great amount of data on employee perceptions of the workplace. The entire pre-study group used the data to identify themes to formulate the corporate value base. On receiving the pre-study report, top management drafted new statements of the company's value base and mission. The new values stressed high performance, risk-taking, and accountability. An example of a value shift was the president's emphasis on the recognition of current high performance rather than extended loyalty to the company, admirable though that was. He underlined this by immediately initiating a new performance-based recognition system. A second example concerns his prioritizing of productivity, 'rationalization before relationships', emphasized by explicitly prioritizing the up-dating of internal systems such as electronic claims processing. The reported outcomes of the pre-study phase (Table 9.2) were selection of specific core processes to be redesigned, creation of the new values and mission statements, and managers' commitment to the next phase of the change program. The pre-study group, the parallel learning organization, was disbanded after presenting its report.

The redesign process: the detailed design of the organization, routines and IT-support

The redesign process called for more intensive involvement of HPO employees in the turnaround process. It also required utilizing qualified technical consultants and staff from outside firms: Electronic Data Services (EDS) and Deloitte and Touche (D&T). To drive and coordinate the overall effort, an integrated structural learning mechanism was created (Figure 9.1). A sales director who led one of the pre-study teams was appointed Change Manager and she had overall responsibility for the design and implementation of the change initiative (CI) from that point forward.

The Change Manager worked closely with the president to shape the redesign activities. They decided to create a large and complex structural learning mechanism for this phase of CI, namely a change initiative steering committee composed of leaders of various CI teams, headed by the Change Manager. The president felt that a combination of outside consultants and new operations executives could provide the necessary team leadership for the redesign and implementation phases. Figure 9.1 indicates the integrated learning mechanism's complexity. Notice that the re-engineering teams (operations initiative teams in the centre of the figure) relied heavily on over 10 transition support teams (facilities, training, telecommunications, etc.). For the most part, re-engineering and support teams were fully dedicated groups composed of outside consultants and internal HPO personnel on assignment from their regular duties. The point of creating such a large structure was clear: the company proposed to close 11 service offices in major cities, and transfer the work to three centralized facilities at completely new geographic locations. In each case, entirely new facilities had to be designed and constructed, and the centres would feature new physical layout, new technology, new transaction processing systems, and new work teams. Early assessments indicated that at least half of the employees in the work teams would be newly recruited.

Typically, the project teams in the redesign phase worked off-line in a separate environment creating new systems and 'model offices'. Design work involved a combination of expert consultant knowledge about technology and trends outside the company blended with internal knowledge about how the organization really worked (provided by the HPO internal staff). That is, islands for data gathering, reflection and learning were created so that project team members could create new systems. This was a 'clean slate' approach that mostly ignored existing systems and procedures. Work by the claims processing team provides an example. The team hoped to generate radical change by shifting to a Windows-based platform that would provide operators instant access to all databases they might need to process a member's claim. Consultants and HPO operators learned from each other as the engineers began to specify hardware and software requirements, subject to critique by the end users. The claims processing team had ready access to new technology successfully used in other settings and the advantage of a fast transition to simulation and testing by all members of the team.

The plan to replace 11 local community service centres with three centralized

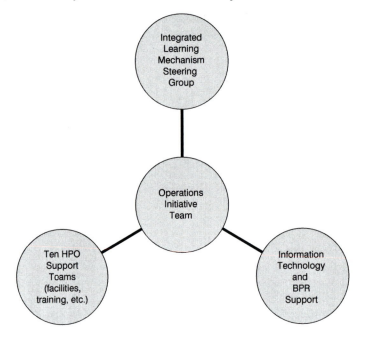

Figure 9.1 The integrated structural learning mechanism in HPO's Change Initiative program

service centres functioning as call centres was the major challenge of the design phase. The existing system featured close relationships and periodic face-to-face contacts with customers. This would change in dramatic ways with use of call centres, so the Change Manager and support teams were pressed to work closely with centre site teams during the transition. For example, in the implementation phase, training in claims processing occurred in action learning fashion (Raelin 2000). Initially, claims processing team members learned via simulations from the engineers and HPO staff who had created the new systems. After the formal training and hand-overs, team members learned with their peers by working on and then reflecting on encounters with real customers (Raelin 2000).

The implementation phase: creating three new service call centres

As noted above, the progression of the program to the implementation stage was characterized by a steady widening down through the organization of personnel participation in the work of the CI. This entailed not only an opportunity for influence, but also for learning. Implementation at the large service centres was sequential: the IT-based routines designed by the transition teams were tested, adapted and developed iteratively between the transition team and the end users in the first operative service call centre. During and after the first try at implementation, the centre staff identified enhancement features for the software as well as software bugs to be addressed by EDS and D&T consultants. Experienced employees could immediately see how new transaction processing systems were either better or worse than prior systems. In ongoing training sessions, there was time to vent frustrations and to communicate how they would like to see the system changed. The operations and support teams within the integrated learning mechanism then had to decide which changes were possible in the short run and which changes depended upon significant system rebuilds. Then the modified routines were passed on to the second service centre where the end users became involved in a similar iterative development and learning process. This potentially allowed the teams to learn from successes and mistakes at the first facility and to make adjustments at the next. Since system design work continued, trainers and managers at the first service centre could not automatically extend their knowledge to succeeding centres. Enhancements continued in real time as software 'fixes' and hardware modifications altered the initial model office concepts. For example, employee training in new processes/technology had to be continuously retooled to reflect learning at the last facility and process enhancements occurring in real time. This method of experimental iterations between the transition teams in the Change Initiative organization and the new operational teams at the various service call centres was a very important *procedural learning mechanism*.

Despite the dominant focus on technology, there were other issues and goals to be addressed. One of the overall program goals was to reduce the levels of management within HPO and to foster more self-management within the teams. While this phenomenon is well understood in the management and change literature, it is inevitably a surprise when introduced in a new setting (Pasmore 1988). Since HPO was rather conservative and hierarchical, many managers were unprepared for new roles of coaching and supporting self-management (Table 9.1). Moreover, it is doubtful that the redesign consultants were in a position to bring self-management to HPO through the 'model office' approach. Nor was the Steering Committee knowledgeable of or adept at creating self-management within work teams. Problems persisted, and some of the post-CI follow-up work addressed training for managers and employees on these issues.

As work progressed to centre start-ups, the Change Manager called for weekly 'huddle meetings', hosted on a rotating basis by one of the three new service centres. Huddle meetings became the main vehicle for getting needed resources to the centres, and assuring co-ordination between core and support teams. The huddle meetings featured conference calls across all CI teams. In the conference calls, service centre managers outlined their main needs and all other teams had three to five minutes to raise cross-team issues. For example, the facilities team leader would list specific telecommunications tasks that had to be completed before HPO employees could be moved to work stations at a new centre, and service centre team members at the site could report on unique aspects of the site that had to be dealt with during installation. The huddle meetings were overwhelmingly devoted to information sharing and problem solving around service centre progress. The three- to five-minute limits served both to encourage teams to meet ahead of huddle sessions to reflect on progress and identify what they needed in the way of organizational support, and afterward to work further on key issues with relevant information, advice and support.

The transition from 'model office' to 'real operations' and from one service delivery model to another requires special attention to change processes, managerial skills and communications. Opening new centres was a pressured time for all parties, particularly in enrolment and claims processing services that were previously handled by the now disbanded small community-based centres. The leaders of the integrated learning mechanism provided scheduled meetings and changeover deadlines that helped created a sense of urgency and commitment. The huddle meetings in particular provided early warning of unanticipated problems, on learning needs and breakdowns and on relevant exchanges of experience.

However, not everything went smoothly. The Change Manager's plan was to move new processes to centre managers as soon as possible to facilitate learning and system testing and to foster the creativity and commitment of employees who had to live with redesigned work. Members of the steering committee attempted to facilitate this transition, but it was not easy and the change management team observed that the project groups and consultants had a hard time giving up control to permanent managers and teams in the service centres. The president decided to force the issue and he terminated support from reengineering consultants and officially closed the CI program after two years.

The evaluation phase: immediate and intermediate outcomes

In reflecting on the overall CI program, the president and senior management at HPO felt that the immediate outcomes confirmed the appropriateness of the learning mechanisms chosen at each phase. They felt in principle that the choice of learning mechanisms depends on the situation at hand and each phase of the Change Initiative offered different conditions for informal learning and collective reflection. Management's assessment of the learning achieved during the turnaround process entailed improved managerial competencies to plan and conduct change programs and a heightened readiness on the part of many team leaders to take on managerial tasks in the organization. However the company still felt the need to utilize outside consulting firms in information technology and management in future reengineering projects.

Executives at HPO were keenly aware of major outcome indicators prior to, during, and after the change program. The Change Manager hoped to achieve balanced results as measured by improved productivity, customer satisfaction, and employee learning. Ongoing monitoring of these indicators showed mixed results. The program was enormously successful in terms of productivity and financial impacts. Over a two-year period, employment at HPO fell by 1,000 employees, or 25% of the workforce. The company achieved a 50% reduction in floor space, a 77% reduction in time to enrol new groups, and a 60% increase in data entry productivity. Administrative costs as a percentage of revenue declined from 23.1% in the second year to 17.5% four years later. At the end of the program, HPO claimed to be able to do the same work with 25% fewer employees. In annual reports, management attributed the cost savings to new technology and changed core processes.

On the down side, HPO lost hundreds of experienced supervisors and operations workers who did not want to transfer to the new service centres. Moreover, customer service indicators fell 25% during and after the transition to the service centres and they did not return to prior levels until six months after the project. Although the Change Manager spoke highly of the company's training activities and commitment to learning throughout the program, the reality was that customers had been better treated under the old community service model. Thus, her goals for balanced outcomes were not achieved both during and directly after the change program.

Discussion

The character of the transformation process

Kochan and Useem (1992) refer to transformation as a coin with two sides: the change process and the learning process. The company board framed the transformation process in terms of a turn-around, a crisis that called for a major shake-up and the new president had a clear track record of accomplishing such change processes. His focus was relatively short term, more on change than learning and more on rationalization and quick results than customer and personnel relationships. Thus learning was directed to getting personnel into the required mindset for the change initiative and for promoting development activities that would give quick results. Thus there was limited discussion building into the new organization characteristics that would promote continuous systemic change once the formal program ended. Learning mechanisms were created and dismantled when the immediate ends were met. Moreover, consultants had been used to conduct tasks that the organization could not, so that the company has limited capability to carry out similar tasks in the future.

The priorities attached to different issues and aspects of the change process were made clear at the outset in the value statements and choice of methods and consultants. The early decision on centralized call-centre service units entailed heavy downsizing with the elimination of 11 centres and the personnel at risk were not troubled to participate. The concentrated focus of the change process, reengineering of processes and the development of IT-support for the new processes led to real reflection and learning for full time participants in CI. However, other important issues and aspects of the change process, such as individual and team competencies and customer relations took a back seat. The sequential as distinct from parallel or integrated tackling of such issues is not uncommon. Neither are its consequences. Other studies point to performance delays between two and four years due to the informal and incremental learning and adaptation processes that must be worked through to realize the potential of the technical systems (Keen 1988; Scott Morton 1992; Docherty and Stymne 1995). While paying formal attention to all relevant issues and stakeholders legitimate needs and ambitions will take more resources than a few prioritized ones, the overall costs incurred to realize the potential performance levels may well be lower in the holistic, integrated approach.

Participation, collective reflection and the use of learning mechanisms

Considering participation, transformation processes are, with exception, initiated from the top down. Dunphy and Stace (1990) note that the processes are more efficient and effective when the CEO formulates the change strategy authoritatively. The transformation process then proceeds with a series of decisions cascading down the organization, steadily bringing more and more people into the change process. At HPO, the CEO's basic principle was not to involve people until it was absolutely necessary; firstly managers in the pre-study project. That gave the participating managers a shared understanding of the need for the transformation and where the main thrust should be made, around the core processes. However, the CEO and his upper management team determined the priorities in the values and mission statements that served as a cognitive learning mechanism for those involved in CI. It may be noted, however, that other companies have made such value statements that include all the key stakeholders and learning processes as core processes (Shani and Docherty 2003).

As the decision and change activities cascaded down the organization management chose different learning mechanisms. The pre-study was conducted using a parallel learning mechanism that allowed collective reflection in groups of the personnel in 'sensing' exercises, followed by collective reflection in subproject group, then in a plenary pre-study group. In addition, the procedural learning mechanism, gap analysis, led to clear targets for change in the next phase of the overall change program. The redesign phase was controlled and facilitated by the Change Initiative program organization that had responsibility for both the change and the learning activities. In the redesign work contact with operative personnel or system end users was relatively limited. HPO relied on a few experienced operators during system development and did not combine structural and procedural learning mechanisms until the implementation phase. At that point, the alliance between development teams and end users featured intensive reflection and productive learning (Tables 9.1 and 9.2).

The role of structural mechanisms in fostering reflection and learning

HPO created unique learning mechanisms that nurtured the change initiative and proved to be valuable in integrating and guiding the separate initiatives that were taking place simultaneously (see Figure 9.1 and Tables 9.1 and 9.2). The learning mechanisms facilitated knowledge and concept development and enabled people to learn change management skills. The formal learning of the new systems in the implementation phase had to be altered continuously as both hardware and software

Table 9.2 Productive reflection and learning: some examples from HPO coupled to structural learning mechanisms

Learning mechanisms created by HPO	Productive reflection examples	Action and results	Retrospective comments
Parallel learning mechanism to conduct scanning and sensing	Review and revise value and mission statements. Identify and debate promising areas for redesign	Revised and affirmed basic values and mission statement. Selected specific core processes to be redesigned. Unfreeze HPO through diverse activities that signal commitment to change	Parallel learning mechanism inadquate due to lack of representation from key stakeholders (employees, health care providers, and employer customers). Crisis perception inducing activities were effective in gaining commitment to change programs
Integrated learning mechanism (ILM) to conduct, redesign and test/redesign, and to handle transition to permanent organization	Discover and test the ILM's purpose and structure. Careful selection of consultants and internal actors to staff the ILM. Create ILM structure of steering group, core project teams and support teams. Initiate multiple modes for communication and problem solving among IM teams and HPO organization	Establish HPO as firmly in control of change program. Create multiple projects, managed to goals and time lines. Sensing and early warning of problems that must be addressed by redesign teams. Resolve problems tied to start-up of new in large service centres	Key players from the local community service centres to be later downsized were left out. Inadequate communications with employer customers and network health care providers on changes in process. New work teams were inadequate due to staffing problems, lack of employee knowledge and experience. Decline in service indicators might have been avoided

were improved along the way. The action learning process for permanent work teams at the centres, together with collective reflection in the programme management group and coupled to the huddle groups, allowed periodic critique and reconsideration of change program goals, concepts and actions. In some ways then, the integrated mechanism fostered communities of practice (Drath and Palus 1994). In completing the Change Initiative task, those who participated in the various CI groups developed a shared history, created meaning together. In addition, members of the new teams developed shared routines and practices (Wenger 1998).

Employee stakeholders at the core of the new service centres became more and more directly involved in the implementation phase of the change program. However, those employed in community units to be closed were not included. If a greater effort had been made to involve local employees additional skilled and experienced personnel might have transferred to the new centres. In retrospect, managers who were involved in the change process felt that many of the serious issues connected with staffing the new centres and with customer service difficulties might have been alleviated if there had been an involvement of local employees in the change program (Table 9.2).

Other stakeholders were left out of deliberations. Clinic and hospital partners also experienced changes in service due to creation of new enrolment and claims review processes conducted by the regional centres. This may account for at least some of the drop in customer satisfaction during and shortly after the change program. To a great extent, health care providers and the consuming public were ignored. Irrespective of the extent of customer involvement in the change program, it is clear that stronger communications with stakeholder were warranted. The involvement and communications with such stakeholders was largely confined to the rollout of new products that occurred very late in the change program.

The implications for reflection and learning during turnaround

Comparing the HPO case with the Prime Optics case in Chapter 7 in this volume, the HPO leaders clearly had a different strategy for design and implementation of the change program. The president of HPO had direct control of the pre-study team (parallel learning mechanism) and determined the new value and mission statements as well as the projects selected for re-engineering. In contrast, in the Prime Optics case, the divisional manager was involved at the kick-off and goal-setting stage, but did not appoint a leader or create a working integrated learning mechanism for the overall change program. In the HPO case, the Change Manager was the full-time leader of the learning mechanism and she reported directly to the president. She was responsible for co-ordination and support for the transition teams to facilitate the exchange of experiences and the adoption of an experimental learning perspective in the redesign and implementation phases. The transition team participants had the opportunity to test the program rationale and plans for the projects, and (later) to collectively review and revise plans for facilities, core transaction processing systems, staffing and training.

The case illustrates some difficulties in transferring 'laboratory' or model office systems design to 'real-world' operating organizations. The original 'blueprint for change', the new IT-based routines, were reconceived as 'recipes' to be modified according to experiences at the new centres. While engineers and other change agents were clearly able to help with start-up and training issues for work teams, the transition organization had difficulties with the breadth and depth of the changes to the systems required by the users. The development teams had strong ownership of the new systems and experienced difficulties relinquishing control to operations groups. These are classical IT-development issues that can be addressed by more holistic socio-technical design approaches, greater user involvement and a longer planning horizon (Docherty *et al.* 1977; Scott Morton 1992).

This case shows that there are fairly good opportunities to organize arenas and methods to promote and facilitate collective reflection and learning during change programs. In the case at hand, the competitive threat was real, and the CEO and his managers were able successfully to resolve many economic and human issues through judicious use of cognitive, structural, and procedural learning mechanisms at different stages of the change program. Both the successes and failures documented in this case provide insights for consultants and executives who hope to promote productive reflection and learning during crisis turnaround programs. The case also suggests that future experimentation with learning mechanisms will depend on such factors as the nature of the industry, the character and severity of the company crisis, the history and culture of the organization and the values and competence of top management.

References

Bushe, G.R. and Shani, A.B. (Rami) (1991) *Parallel Learning Structures: Increasing Innovations in Bureaucracies*, Reading, MA: Addison Wesley.

De Geus, A. (1992) *The Living Company*, Boston, MA: Harvard Business School Press.

Docherty, P. and Stymne, B. (1995) *Mediators of IT-Effectiveness*, Stockholm: Instutite for Management of Innovation and Technology, Stockholm School of Economics, Working Paper 1995: 72.

Docherty, P., Herber, S., Magnusson, Å. and Stymne, B. (1977) *How to Succeed with Systems Development: An Analysis of Five Cases*, Stockholm: Economic Research Institute.

Drath, W. and Palus, C. (1994) *Making Common Sense: Leadership as Meaning-Making in a Community of Practice*, Greensboro, NC: Center for Creative Leadership.

Dunphy, D. and Stace, D. (1990) *Under New Management: Australian Organizations in Transition*, Sydney: MacGraw Hill.

Garvin, D.A. (2000) *Learning in Action*, Boston, MA: Harvard Business School Press.

Keen, P.G.W. (1988) *Competing in Time: Using Telecommunications to Competitive Advantage*, 2nd edn, Cambridge, MA: Ballinger.

Kochan, T.A. and Useem, M. (1992) 'Creating the Learning Organization', in T.A. Kochan and M. Useem (eds) *Transforming Organizations*, New York: Oxford University Press, 391–406.

Pasmore, W.A. (1988) *Designing Effective Organizations: The Sociotechnical Systems Perspective*, New York: Wiley.

Raelin, J. A. (2000) *Work-Based Learning: The New Frontier of Management Development*, PH OD Series, Prentice Hall.

Scott Morton, M.S. (1992) 'The Effects of Information Technology on Organizations and Management', in T.A. Kochan and M. Useem (eds) *Transforming Organizations*, New York: Oxford University Press, 261–79.

Shani, A.B. (Rami) and Docherty, P. (2003) *Learning by Design: Building Sustainable Organizations*, Oxford: Blackwell Publishers.

Stebbins, M. and Shani, A.B. (Rami), Moon, W. and Bowles, D. (1998) 'Business Process Reengineering at Blue Shield of California: The Integration of Multiple Change Initiatives', *Journal of Organizational Change Management*, 11, 3: 216–32.

Wenger, E. (1998) *Communities of Practice: Learning, Meaning and Identity*, Cambridge: Cambridge University Press.

10 Interactive critical reflection as intercultural competence

Victor J. Friedman and Ariane Berthoin Antal

As a result of rapid globalization culture has become a central issue in terms of the nature of work and organization. This chapter looks at productive reflections in work contexts involving individuals from different national cultures engaged in complex tasks. Emphasizing the role of reflection is important because mainstream approaches to cross-cultural management stress culture-specific knowledge and adapting individual and organizational behaviour to expectations based on general models of cultural difference.

In this chapter we shall argue that cultural knowledge and a focus on adaptation can actually inhibit learning. Furthermore, we shall argue that an interactive process of critical reflection lies at the core of 'intercultural competence'. This process, which we call 'negotiating reality', entails: (1) an active awareness of oneself as a complex cultural being and the effect of one's own culture on thinking and action; (2) an ability to engage with others to explore tacit assumptions that underlie behaviour and goal; and (3) openly testing with others different ways of thinking and doing thing (Berthoin Antal and Friedman 2003; Friedman and Berthoin Antal, forthcoming).

The challenge of intercultural competence: beyond adaptation

Practical culture guides often offer specific advice about cultural differences and culturally appropriate behaviour to help managers adapt to a wide range of business and social situations in various countries (e.g. Chaney and Martin 2000; Harris and Moran 1991). A strategy of cultural adaptation is based on the assumption that if people know enough about different cultures, they can intentionally shift into a different cultural frame of reference and modify their behaviour accordingly. While it makes sense to prepare oneself for a new culture with background information, adaptation is inadequate for dealing with the dynamic interactions between culturally complex beings in culturally complex contexts (Osland and Bird 2000). The adaptation approach treats the application of insight as relatively unproblematic. It skirts the issue of how people can break out of their own cultural frameworks and expand the range of interpretations and behaviours they can draw on.

The adaptation approach to cross-cultural competence has taken much of its inspiration from research on the influence of national cultures on values, assumptions, perceptions, and the behaviour of people in organizations (e.g. Adler 2002; Early and Erez 1997; Hofstede 1991; Trompenaars and Hampden-Turner 1997). In particular, this research has drawn on models for classifying national cultures by their differences. These models provide a powerful explanatory framework for making sense of intercultural problems in management and a guide as to how potential cultural conflicts can be anticipated, avoided or handled more effectively.

There are, however, significant conceptual and practical drawbacks to treating national culture as a distinct, overarching system for guiding behaviours. Such an approach tends to classify individuals and groups in terms of a single culture, failing to account for the fact that individuals are complex cultural and psychological beings (Hong *et al.* 2000; Sebenius 2002). It also posits a causal link between cultural values and behaviour that is too simple and deterministic. In fact, it may be dangerous, and even insulting, to adopt a particular behavioural orientation under the assumption that it is appropriate with a 'typically Japanese' or 'typically Spanish' counterpart (Berthoin Antal and Friedman 2004). Furthermore, adaptation amounts to a form of manipulation when people believe they are sufficiently expert in cultural codes to control others and get them to acquiesce to their own way of doing things.

One way of dealing with the issue of cultural complexity is to view culture as a kind of repertoire drawn from a variety sources that provides a limited set of resources 'which people may use in varying configurations to solve different kinds of problems ' (Swidler 1986: 273). Rather than seeing behaviour as determined by a particular culture, this approach sees people as possessing a repertoire generated by the various cultures that have influenced them. A person's cultural repertoire not only offers a range of responses to its members, but it also *constrains* the range of responses available to an individual.

The claim that people draw on cultural repertoires does not imply that constructing a strategy of action is a conscious process. To the contrary, individuals tend not to consider how their cultural backgrounds shape their repertoires until they experience misunderstandings or their behaviour does not generate the response they would have expected within their usual cultural community (Adler 2002). *Cultural competence* is the ability to generate appropriate strategies of action with little conscious thought. *Intercultural competence*, on the other hand, demands a more critically reflective process, entailing the ability to explore one's repertoire and actively construct an appropriate strategy for a given situation.

Negotiating reality: critical reflection as intercultural competence

Research comparing more successful international managers with their less successful peers confirmed the importance of treating each interaction as unique and solving problems through observation, listening, experimentation, risk taking, and active involvement with others (Ratiu 1983). We have coined the term 'negotiating reality' to name this kind of competence. The practice of negotiating reality draws on theory and methods from 'action science' (Argyris *et al.* 1985; Friedman 2000) and the engagement of 'identity conflict' (Rothman 1997; Rothman and Friedman 2001). It operationalizes cultural repertoires as tacit, mental 'theories of action' that guide everyday behaviour (Argyris and Schon 1974; Friedman 2000). Thus, negotiating reality involves openly and interactively reflecting on the components of theories of action: perceptions of the situation, underlying assumptions, the goals people are trying to achieve and the strategies they employ to achieve them. Bringing cultural repertoires within the realm of awareness and choice provides opportunities for joint 'single-loop' and 'double-loop' learning (Argyris and Schon 1974).

Negotiating reality does *not* imply cultural neutrality and clearly reflects the authors' own cultural repertoires (national, religious, ethnic, intellectual, scientific, professional). We maintain that *no* point of cultural neutrality exists but that: (1) all people are of equal importance and worthy of equal respect; (2) as cultural beings, people differ because they possess different repertoires of ways of seeing and doing things; and (3) the repertoire of no individual or group merits *a priori* superiority or right to dominance. Thus the best we can do is to be open about our repertoires, testing them with others and being open to change.

In the following section we present a case study that illustrates the challenge of intercultural competence and the need for a negotiating reality. It was written by Rajiv[1] in the context of a seminar we taught on 'Cross-cultural Management Competencies' at the Leipzig Graduate School of Management (HHL). For the purposes of this chapter, the introductory and concluding sections of the case have been summarized, while attempting to stay as close as possible to Rajiv's words and meanings. The text in the dialogue has been selected from a number of vignettes that Rajiv reconstructed from memory.

Rajiv's case: leading a multi-cultural team

Bill, Ryoko, and Rajiv – three of managers in a German multi-national corporation – were brought together as a team to develop a plan for the entry into a new business. Bill was an American with an undergraduate degree in Business Administration. Ryoko was Japanese and had a Masters Degree in Human Resources. Rajiv was Indian and an engineer. All three had joined the company as management trainees two years before and this project was an opportunity to give their careers a boost. They reported to Mr Hecht a German manager, who asked Rajiv to coordinate the activities of the group and set a very accelerated time frame. Rajiv was doubtful about the feasibility of this time frame, but felt he had to agree.

Having assumed responsibility for leading the team, Rajiv was worried about co-ordinating the team activities and meetings. This group of people had never worked together before and were as diverse as could be. He considered the options before him. He could try 'cultural dominance', which meant doing things in the way of his home culture and trying to convince the others to adjust to his style. However, he felt that the cultural differences were too wide and that it would be unhealthy to force his way on the others. He could try 'cultural avoidance', which meant acting as if there were no conflicts or differences, but he rejected this precisely because he felt that healthy conflict could give rise to new solutions. He also considered 'cultural accommodation', in which he could try to imitate the other cultures. However, he wondered how could he do so with both an American and Japanese on the same team?

None of these options appealed to him, so Rajiv decided that his strategy would be to try to follow what he called 'Madhyapantha' (the Middle Path), or 'cultural compromise', and to 'convince the others to do the same'. He believed that this strategy would enable them to develop new solutions to problems while respecting each of the underlying cultures extent and creating synergy.

The dialogue in Table 10.1 illustrates one of Rajiv's attempts to put his strategy into practice. It took place at the very first meeting of the group.

In reflecting back on what he learned from the case, Rajiv wrote that 'to the Westerner, future is short term and something controllable from the present'. He explained Bill's desire to take small steps and reviewing them before moving on as the result of a culturally grounded belief that 'the steps of the present would continually define the results of the future'. Rajiv interpreted Bill's statement about 'crossing the bridge when it comes' as meaning that 'it would make more sense to get going in short steps and when the future showed some problem, it could be solved with inputs from the present'. He perceived Ryoko, on the other hand, as 'a typical Oriental person' who 'had a more longer-term vision of time' and used this attribution to explain why she 'talked about getting the bigger picture before starting off with the project and meeting with less frequency'. Rajiv added that 'the Westerner looked at life situations as many small problems each of which he would like to solve at a time … (but) a person from the East has a more adapting (sic) nature and would absorb difficulties … unless confronted with a really tough one'. Therefore, he concluded that 'it was … natural (for Ryoko) to expect that she would not face so many problems so frequently and thus wanted to meet after two weeks'.

Rajiv also observed that Bill made an upfront promise to meet a certain deadline that was difficult to achieve and Bill eventually failed to meet it. He wrote that 'an American would, perhaps, … make a promise to meet customer needs and would somehow manage to explain it to the customer' if he failed to deliver, but that 'the Japanese would not promise to meet a deadline unless she was absolutely sure she would actually meet it'. He also noted that 'Bill, an American was eager to get to the point right from the word go. He wanted to start the project right away' whereas 'Ryoko, a Japanese, wanted to build some kind of a relationship before going in to the project details'. Rajiv also explained the differences between his colleagues behaviour in group discussions as reflect the contrast between a 'specific, low context style' (Bill) and a 'diffuse, high context style' (Ryoko).

Table 10.1 Rajiv's strategy in action

I must set the direction of the meeting at the outset. This will help me establish my leadership in the group. He didn't even let me finish! I think that was rude. I will not let him dominate. I will lay down my agenda for the day.	**Rajiv**: Good Morning Bill and Ryoko, we will today decide on the entire course of action for our project and for that …
	Bill: Yeah, that would be great, let's start off. I will look into sales, right?
	Rajiv: Right. We will follow the brief outline that Mr Hecht has given us. We will cover all the issues mentioned …
Oh, God! He interrupted me again! This girl is so polite. She's listening to me. In fact she a bit too quiet. As a leader I must ask her to speak up.	**Bill**: And more than that too, I suppose!
	Rajiv: Ryoko, don't you want to say something?
Ah! She wants an overview of the project. A long-term perspective is what she is looking for.	**Ryoko**: Yes, I understand that we are supposed to do our individual bits but what are we trying to achieve at the end of it all? What would we have in our hands after one month, say?
Bill has a completely different outlook. He doesn't want to see much ahead. How am I going to handle these two contrasting styles of viewing things?	**Bill**: We would cross that bridge when it comes, Ryoko. Let's first look at the deliverables for the few days.
Isn't she dilly-dallying things a bit? Or is she trying to say something, which she is not being able to express?	**Ryoko**: Yes, but before we start away with the work can we talk to each other and have a discussion of what each of us actually feels about this project. What overall and long term ideas do we have?
He seems to be in a hurry. He must be very smart at his work. But we need a balance. After all we must follow the Madhyapantha. I must intervene, as I am the leader. We must strike a balance. We must get the bigger picture as Ryoko suggested and also start the work on time.	**Bill**: I think that would be a waste of time. I would rather start my fieldwork in the next half an hour.
	Rajiv: I think what we can do is, we can discuss the inter-relationships of our individual parts of the project and then disperse to our work. We can then meet and review the bigger picture and see how the things are falling in place.
	Bill: That's OK with me.
Now the next issue is of the frequency of the meetings. I hope they will not disagree. Well, that's too often. I wonder whether I myself will be able to do my job that fast. Perhaps this guy is really fast with his work. I must oppose this.	**Rajiv**: But how frequently do we meet?
	Bill: I suggest once every two days. That way we can constantly monitor whether we are going in the right direction in solving the smaller problems.

Ah! That helps my cause. But once in two weeks is like ages. A lot of things can change in that time. Something in between perhaps? I must keep both of them happy. Only then can we do some meaningful work. I must give them the feeling that both their opinions are being valued in the group.

Good, at least he agrees.

I'm definitely going to face some severe scheduling problems. These two people seem to be working at very different paces. Look at the contrast. One speaks of half an hour while the other talks of two full days!
Bill is getting a bit excited. I must calm him down before things go out of control. I hope Ryoko would not mind ... Oh no, she did mind I think! She is red all over her face. I must intervene. Bill is bossing around. I must take control. I must manage both of them. The Madhyapantha again! Why does Ryoko want two days? Does she want to know about the personnel manager before asking him questions? Perhaps I can help her do that and that would solve our problem.

I must set the forward path as we end the meeting today. The date of the next meeting is what I want to decide on.

Good Lord! What's this guy talking about? He must be real fast. Let's see what Ryoko has to say.

She wants more time. I wouldn't say anything on this, because I would rather take some more time and complete the job. But how do we keep pace with Bill? I wonder whether he can *really* do the work in two days.

Ryoko: I think that would be a bit too frequent. I don't think we would face so many problems that we need to meet so frequently. Perhaps once in two weeks would be enough.

Rajiv: I think we can settle for twice a week. In case we face some more problems, we can always contact each other and decide on a time and place to meet depending on the severity of the problem.
Bill: Fine. In the meantime, Ryoko, can you meet the personnel manager and get some important information from him in the next half an hour?

Ryoko: I think I will take some more time. Perhaps a couple of days would be better.

Bill: You need a couple of days to get some information? That's crazy! I think you can do it in one hour.

Ryoko: That would be difficult.

Bill: What difficulty are you referring to? I will fix the appointment for you. You just have to meet him personally. It's just that you are handling the HR issues and I am not. Otherwise I and Rajiv would have gone.

Rajiv: Ryoko, would it help if the two of us meet the personnel manager over dinner tonight and then you can go ahead getting the information we need?

Ryoko: That would be fine, I suppose.

Rajiv: So what deadline do we fix for the first module of our work?

Bill: I'll be ready by 6 p.m. day after tomorrow.

Rajiv: And you, Ryoko?
Ryoko: Not before next week. But then I am sure I can do it by next week.
Rajiv: Right, so we meet day after, and see what Bill has to say. We'll also see how much Ryoko has progressed. Of course, I will start of my work as well and get back to you.

In commenting on his own performance, Rajiv wrote that 'I thought that I had performed pretty well because I could solve most of the disputes by a process of following the concept of cultural compromise and thereby achieving cultural synergy,' suggesting that was 'able to make the other two members of the group appreciate the cultural characteristics of each other'. On the other hand he felt that he had 'failed to a large extent in coming out of my shell of possessiveness of my leadership position'. He admitted that 'even as Bill was discussing his problems, I was busy thinking about the fact that he could not meet the deadline he had promised and that he could not prove himself to be superior to me and thus could not pose threat to my leadership position'. Furthermore, Rajiv admitted that he failed to express his own doubts about the time frame because 'he was more concerned about agreeing to what the boss said rather than being honest and telling him that the target might not be achieved'. The team, in fact, failed to meet this deadline and subsequently Mr Hecht told Rajiv that it would have been better if he had shared his concerns about meeting the deadline.

Comparing Rajiv's espoused theory with his theory-in-use

Rajiv's case dealt with the problem of managing a multi-cultural project team. In particular, it raises issues relating to control and to the temporal aspect of the task, which are among the fundamental dimensions of human experience that culture shapes (Kluckhohn and Strodtbeck 1961). Our analysis focuses on Rajiv's strategy for dealing with this complex problem. The dialogue enables us to compare Rajiv's 'espoused theory' (i.e. what he intended to do) with the 'theory-in-use' implicit in his actual behaviour (Argyris and Schon 1974).

On the espoused level, Rajiv emphasized learning and openness to other points of view. His espoused theory, as inferred from what he wrote before and after the dialogue, contained the following features:

- He was aware of entering a complex and potentially problematic cultural situation and he consciously planned a strategy for dealing with it effectively.
- He exhibited a relatively high level of cultural awareness and theoretical sophistication. Although he did not cite academic sources, Rajiv's terminology (e.g. dominance, avoidance, accommodation, compromise) strongly resembled concepts of conflict management (e.g. Thomas 1976). His analysis after the dialogue made use of theoretical terms such as 'high-low context cultures' and quite detailed knowledge about 'typical' thinking and behaviour in American and Japanese culture.
- He saw himself as also part of the 'problem' and was wary of imposing his perspective on the others. He chose 'cultural compromise': (*Madhyapantha*) as his preferred strategy because he believed it would be respectful of other cultures, and would create 'synergy'. He rejected 'avoidance' because he felt that 'healthy conflict' could lead to 'new solutions'.

• He showed the ability to be self-critical and see himself in perspective. In reflecting on the dialogue, Rajiv admitted feeling threatened by Bill, which led him to attend to his own fears about leadership rather than to problems that needed to be dealt with. In addition he recognized having made in error in not being more forthright about the time frame with his superior.

At the theory-in-use level, however, Rajiv's strategy closely resembled the adaptation approach. On the basis of knowledge of 'typical' cultural behaviour, he attempted to determine unilateral a set of norms for group functioning that would be acceptable to the representatives of each culture on the team. In so doing, his learning goals seemed to slip away:

• Rajiv followed a clear behavioral pattern: He raised an issue in the form of a question, allowed both sides to state their points of view, and then made a decision that he believed would 'keep both of them happy'. This pattern repeated itself three times in the dialogue.
• Rajiv focused on maintaining control over the process and he acted as if he were responsible for generating the compromise ('I must set the direction of the meeting at the outset. This will help me establish my leadership in the group'; 'I must take control. I must manage both of them'; 'How am I going to handle these two contrasting styles of viewing things?'.)
• Whenever a disagreement arose, Rajiv quickly looked for a compromise that would end the potential conflict ('I hope they will not disagree', 'I must calm him down before things get out of control', 'I must keep both of them happy').
• He made interpretations about Ryoko's and Bill's behaviour, but he kept these to himself and took action. For example, when Ryoko said she wanted two days, he asked himself whether she wanted time to meet the personnel manager personally. However, he never asked Ryoko to make her reasoning explicit. Instead, operating on his untested assumption about her thoughts and feelings, he proposed having dinner with the manager. Ryoko's response – 'That would be fine, *I suppose*' (our italics) – left her real feelings ambiguous.

Despite Rajiv's good intentions and conceptual sophistication, he was unable to engage in a process of critical reflection when he encountered conflict and misunderstanding. Rather it might be said that he *uncompromisingly* implemented cultural compromise. Although he did not wish to impose his own cultural perspective on the others, the dialogue shows that he imposed *Madhyapantha*, using his own cultural repertoire to unilaterally interpret the situation and define the solution. Moreover, Rajiv was unaware of these contradictions in his reasoning and behavior, which is likely to have been driven by what action science calls 'Model I' governing values: control, protection of self and others, and rationality (Argyris and Schon 1974; Friedman 2000).

The practice of negotiating reality

The goal of a negotiating reality strategy is to maximize learning while not sacrificing long-term effectiveness. Such a strategy would attempt to enact 'Model II' values: valid information, free and informed choice, and internal commitment (Argyris and Schon 1974; Friedman 2000). It is beyond the scope of this chapter to go into a full description of such a strategy (see Berthoin Antal and Friedman 2003; Friedman and Berthoin Antal, forthcoming), but it is possible to summarize its key components:

1 *Make perceptions of the situation explicit. Test them openly.* One way of putting this strategy into action would be for Rajiv to share his view of the problematic situation (i.e. cultural differences) as well his proposed strategy for dealing with it (i.e. the Middle Path) – and to invite feedback from the others. In doing so, he would encourage open reflection about the framing of the situation and what to do about it. Such a discussion may lead to the discovery of new perspectives and new ways of acting.

2 *Share and test attributions about the reasoning and behavior of other.* Rajiv's perception of the problem is based on his assumptions about Bill and Ryoko based on their cultural backgrounds. Rather than simply acting on these assumptions, Rajiv could make them explicit and ask the others whether he has understood correctly. This strategy increases mutual understanding and joint control over how the task is defined and carried out.

3 *Make views explicit, but combine 'advocacy' with 'inquiry'.* Advocacy means clearly expressing and standing up for what one thinks and desires. Inquiry means exploring and questioning both one's own reasoning and the reasoning of others. In addition to being explicit about his preference for the Middle Path, Rajiv could clearly state the reasons why he believes this strategy makes sense. At the same time he could ask others whether his arguments make sense and to point out where he might be mistaken. Negotiating reality does not mean compromise for the sake of agreement. To the contrary, it encourages people to passionately argue for what they believe is right, but to be equally passionate about trying to discover where the might be mistaken.

4 *Inquiring more deeply into the perceptions and assumptions behind a conflict.* This strategy would have been useful when Rajiv felt that the conflict was beginning to get out of hand. Rather than automatically seeking a compromise for each perceived conflict, Rajiv might inquire into the roots of the conflict, bringing to light different views of reality, values, assumptions, and needs. This strategy not only encourages mutual understanding, but helps people become more reflective about what they want and why they want it. When someone digs deeply into a particular position or expresses strong emotions, it often reflects a threat to strong 'identity needs' that need to be acknowledged and addressed (Rothman 1997). Although negotiating reality stresses exploring the reasoning behind behavior, it does not mean avoiding emotions. To the contrary, it encourages people to be explicit about why they feel so passionately about something.

There are numerous other ways that Rajiv might have put these strategies for negotiating reality into practice. The essence of negotiating reality, however, is shifting from intra-psychic, private reflection to joint, open reflection. This approach does not necessarily ensure consensus, but it can counteract processes of escalation and mutual misunderstanding. It brings differences out into the open as objects of inquiry, making conflict an opportunity for learning. In this way, negotiating reality brings more behavior into the realm of conscious choice and increases the likelihood that people will be able to produce the kinds of outcomes they intend.

As Rajiv's case illustrates, this shift requires more than good intentions. It entails 'unlearning' (Hedberg 1981) deeply embedded behavioural patterns and learning new ways of thinking and acting under conditions of uncertainty and even threat (Friedman 2000; Friedman and Lipshitz 1992). While the difficulty of learning to negotiate reality should not be underestimated, we believe that this kind of inter-cultural competence does not require exceptional talent and can be learned (Berthoin Antal and Friedman 2003). It is also important to understand the role of the organizational context in promoting, or inhibiting, negotiating reality. For example, structure and power relations may influence the openness of individuals to engage in critical self-reflection (see Boud, Chapter 14; and Schenkel, Chapter 6 in this volume).

Conclusion

This chapter has argued that the culturally complex and dynamic context of work and organization requires an approach to intercultural competence based on interactive critical reflection. This approach, or negotiating reality, enables people actively and collaboratively to engage differences. It enables organizational actors to take into account the complexity of culture without being overwhelmed by it. It facilitates the continual testing, enrichment, and improvement of individual and organizational cultural repertoires in a constantly changing world. Negotiating reality contributes not only to learning but also to the ability of people to exercise free and informed choice in the process of constructing their behavioral world. In this way, it may contribute to creating the kinds of communities of practice that Nyhan (Chapter 11 in this volume) has described as a network of relationships of giving and receiving in which the good of each cannot be pursued without also pursuing the good of all those who participate in those relationships.

Note

1 All of the names are pseudonyms.

References

Adler, N.J. (2002) *International Dimensions of Organisational Behaviour*, 4th edn, Cincinnati: South-Western.
Argyris, C., Putnam, R. and Smith, D. (1985) *Action Science: Concepts, Methods, and Skills for Research and Intervention*, San Francisco, CA: Jossey-Bass.

Argyris, C. and Schon, D.A. (1974) *Theories in Practice: Increasing Professional Effectiveness*, San Francisco, CA: Jossey-Bass.

Berthoin Antal, A. and Friedman, V. (2003) 'Learning to Negotiate Reality', Discussion Paper SP III 2003-109, Berlin: Wissenschaftszentrum Berlin für Sozialforschung.

Berthoin Antal, A. and Friedman, V. (2004) 'Overcoming Dangerous Learning. The Role of Critical Reflection in Cross-cultural Interactions', Discussion Paper SP III 2004-106, Berlin: Wissenschaftszentrum Berlin für Sozialforschung.

Chaney, L.H. and Martin, J.S. (2000) *Intercultural Business Communication*, 2nd edn, Upper Saddle River, NJ: Prentice Hall.

Early, C.P. and Erez, M. (1997) *The Transplanted Executive. Why you Need to Understand how Workers in other Countries see the World Differently*, New York: Oxford University Press.

Friedman, V.J. (2000) 'Action science: creating communities of inquiry in communities of practice', in H. Bradbury and P. Reason (eds) *The Handbook of Action Research*, Thousand Oaks, CA: Sage, 159–70.

Friedman, V.J. and Berthoin Antal, A. (forthcoming) 'Negotiating Reality: An Action Science Approach to Intercultural Competence', *Management Learning*.

Friedman, V.J. and Lipshitz, R. (1992) 'Shifting Cognitive Gears: Overcoming Obstacles on the Road to Model 2', *Journal of Applied Behavioural Science*, 28, 1: 118–37.

Harris, P. and Moran, R.T. (1991) *Managing Cultural Differences*, 3rd edn, Houston, TX: Gulf Publishing.

Hedberg, B. (1981) 'How Organisations Learn and Unlearn', in P.C. Nystrom and W.H. Starbuck (eds) *Handbook of Organisational Design*, Vol 1, New York: Oxford University Press: 3–27.

Hofstede, G. (1991) *Cultures and Organisations: Software of the Mind*, Maidenhead: McGraw-Hill.

Hong, Y., Morris, M.W., Chiu, C. and Bennet-Martinez, V. (2000) 'Multicultural Minds: A Dynamic Constructivist Approach to Culture and Cognition', *American Psychologist*, 55, 7: 709–20.

Kluckhohn, F.R. and Strodtbeck, F.L. (1961) *Variations in Value Orientations*, Evanston IL: Row, Petersen & Co.

Osland, J.S. and Bird, A. (2000) 'Beyond Sophisticated Stereotyping: Cross-cultural Sensemaking in Context', *Academy of Management Executive*, 14, 1: 1–12.

Ratiu, I. (1983) 'Thinking Internationally: A Comparison of how International Executives Learn', *International Studies of Management and Organisation*, 13: 1–2, 139–50.

Rothman, J. (1997) *Resolving Identity-based Conflict: In Nations, Organisations, and Communities*, San Francisco, CA: Jossey-Bass.

Rothman, J. and Friedman, V.J. (2001) 'Conflict, Identity, and Organisational Learning', in M. Dierkes, A. Berthoin Antal, J. Child and I. Nonaka (eds) *Handbook of Organisational learning and knowledge*, Oxford: Oxford University Press: 582–97.

Sebenius, J. (2002) 'The Hidden Challenge of Cross-border Negotiations', *Harvard Business Review*, 80, 3: 77–85.

Swidler, A. (1986) 'Culture in Action: Symbols and Strategies', *American Sociological Review*, 51, 2: 273–86.

Thomas, K. (1976) 'Conflict and Conflict Management', in M. Dunette (ed.) *Handbook of Industrial and Organizational Psychology*, Chicago: Rand McNally, 889–935.

Trompenaars, F. and Hampden-Turner, C. (1997) *Riding the Waves of Culture*, 2nd edn, London: Nicholas Brealey Publishing.

Part IV

Challenges and complexities

11 Collective reflection for excellence in work organizations

An ethical 'community of practice' perspective on reflection

Barry Nyhan

Introduction

In this chapter, collective reflection is understood as the means through which the members of an organization or a work-based community of practice reflect and learn together about how to attain organizational excellence in all its dimensions – human, social and economic. The chapter argues that the capacity for 'ethical reflection', understood as deliberation and decision making about how to contribute to the excellence of a community of practice, is intrinsic to collective reflection. Thus, an 'excellent' community of practice is also an 'ethical community of practice'. The latter is constructed and sustained by its members' capacity for ethical reflection about achieving the shared goals/goods of the community.

The starting-point for this chapter lies in the author's work with other colleagues about how modern work organizations can achieve organizational excellence through addressing a complex array of learning goals – those of *management* for greater efficiency and productivity – and those of *employees* to find meaning and satisfaction in their work and develop their potential. An organization that meets the above criteria in addressing the bottom-up humanistic and developmental interests of employees as well as top-down management interests can be said to aspire to become a learning organization (Nyhan *et al.* 2003a). Peter Senge's definition of a learning organization is one 'where people continually expand their capacity to create the results they truly desire and where people are continually learning how to learn together' (Senge 1990, p. 3)

However, despite the impressive literature presenting 'compelling portraits' of learning organizations, there appears to be a wide gap 'between vision and actuality' (Snell 2001). The reason for this according to Snell is the lack of an ethical foundation to learning organization thinking and practice. He points out that it is '*morality* rather than technique or method that provides the foundations of a learning organization. Failure to achieve the characteristics of learning organizations thus reflects a lack of ethical practices, principles and virtues' (Snell 2001).

The critique of Snell raises the question – what is the nature of the 'ethical practices, principles and virtues' that could transform 'learning organization vision' into 'learning organization actuality'? In his answer to this question Snell puts forward 10 propositions derived from different ethical theories rather than answer it in a focused way.[1]

At the same time that the author of this chapter was addressing this question, the members of the SALTSA group project on 'reflection and learning at work' were asking how best collective reflection can take place in organizations. They saw collective reflection as a prerequisite for generative as distinct from instrumental learning. This requires, amongst other things, sharing, truthfulness, trust and confidentiality etc. – all ethical issues. This led me to make a link between the two questions, about the relationship between collective reflection on the one hand, and on the other, the ethical practices, principles and virtues required to create and sustain learning organizations promoting excellence (see Figure 11.1).

In this chapter, it is argued that to answer the first of these questions one must also answer the second one. Thus, the enactment of ethical practices in organizational contexts presupposes a capacity for collective reflection (deliberation and judgement) about the attainment of excellence. Likewise collective reflection for excellence entails ethical reflection.

This chapter, therefore, attempts to answer these two questions in an integrated way through in the main drawing on the 'community of practice' ethical theory of Alasdair MacIntyre (1999, 1990, 1985, 1981) but also other modern writers (many of them like MacIntyre) drawing on the thinking of Aristotle (see, for example, Dunne 1993 and Carr 1995). Although MacIntyre uses the term 'practice' as distinct from 'community of practice' (see Lave and Wenger 1991) he sees a 'practice' as a community construction through which people learn together and collaborate to achieve a common goal (good) that meets the criteria of human excellence. This means that in order to achieve excellence at work (as in all other human social systems) the members of an organization must be capable of continually reflecting together about how to construct (continuously maintain and reconstruct) an ethical community of practice. Ethical practices characterized by 'reflective doing' are an intrinsic dimension of excellent practices. This means that excellent practices cannot be realized without people deliberating and finding meaning together, in other words reflecting together and working together in collaborative community settings.

It is acknowledged that in the context of today's pluralist society the introduction of the notion of ethics raises all sorts of contentious issues which can not be easily

Figure 11.1 Learning organization, ethical practices and reflection

resolved. The author recognizes that there is a risk in entering into these waters in a book that is about learning and reflection. However, in joining those authors who have pointed out the need to explore ethics in the field of organizational learning (see Contu and Willmott 2000 as well as Snell 2001), in the field of HRD (Elliot and Turnbull 2003) and Gardner *et al.* (2001) and Martin (2000) who have written books specifically about the relationship between ethics and the meaning of work in modern society, it is hoped that this chapter will contribute towards an understanding of how people can learn together to create, what is termed 'an ethical community of practice' at work.

Following this introductory section, the chapter goes on in section two to present briefly some of the critiques of modern organizational theory and practice that point out an exaggerated concern for controlling people to achieve short-term economic benefits without regard for building sustainable work systems based on human, social as well as economic values. Expanding on this, section three of this chapter argues that the failure of much modern management and organizational theory is due to an excessive focus on 'means' and 'technique' to the exclusion of a discussion on 'purpose' and 'meaning' in work. It is argued that unless the members of an organization can find agreement about the meaning and purpose of the work of their organization, then that organization is not a self-sustaining and developing community of practice. A concern with purpose and meaning is the central ethical issue that needs to be addressed in fostering excellence in work organizations.

The next section goes on to explore the meaning of excellence in a community of practice perspective. A prerequisite for the attainment of excellence is the social construction of an ethical community created and sustained by the *internal* habits and virtues of 'giving' and 'receiving' – that is the *lived* practice of the members of a particular community. The goals/goods sought after by this community are not purely instrumental external goals such as money or prestige but are the internal goals/goods of excellence that define and are distinctive of a particular community or social system.

Section five goes on to examine what is meant by a capacity for ethical reflection in line with a community of practice ethics-based framework. This is contrasted with a code-based framework. The manner in which one learns this capacity is also discussed. The chapter ends with a concluding comment.

Critiques of contemporary organizational theories

As well as Snell, there are many authors, in particular in the field of adult and community education but also vocational education and training who are critical of learning organization thinking (Brown and Keep 2003; Fischer 2003). They see it as being rooted in a prescriptive business-school management concept promoting organizational effectiveness in an exclusive economic sense. They criticize the use of sophisticated cultural and psychological theories by modern management theorists to maximize benefits for the company without paying a great deal of attention to ensuring personal learning benefits for employees/workers or society at large.

In the same vein, these critics talk about being let down by the non-fulfilment of the optimistic forecasts in the 1980s concerning the emergence of more human-centred workplaces in the post-Tayloristic era that would improve the quality of working life for all (see Piore and Sabel 1984). They point out that the reality for many workers, today, is a reincarnation of Taylorism in the form of neo-Taylorism or perhaps disguised in the form of 'lean-production' or 'flexible working'. There is also a sense of disillusionment about the potential of information communication technologies (ICT) not being exploited to create more autonomy and freedom at work, as predicted by many commentators. In fact, it is argued that in many situations the opposite is the case with ICT being used as an instrument for the introduction of new types of technocratic control and surveillance.

Radical critics of modern organizational theories, such as the learning organization, see them as nothing more than an effort by management to delude people into becoming 'organizational men and women'. For example, see Chapter 14 by Elmhold and Brinkmann in this volume which expounds on Michel Foucault's critiques of modern work. Sennett sees modern organizations as corroding people's character (Sennett 1998). Victor and Stephens (1994) talk about the 'dark side of the new organizational forms'. Dobson (1997: 128) quoted in Snell (2001) states that 'market values' and the instrumental 'rational pursuit of material goods' have 'corrupted business'. He goes on to state: 'What I see is individualism, acquisitiveness, and the elevation of the values of competitive economic activity to the status of a natural law' (Dobson 1997: 131).

Ethics is about purpose and meaning and not so much means and techniques

Snell's explanation for the failure of the implementation of learning organizations is that the focus of learning does not go beyond *instrumental* techniques or *utilitarian* methods. The focus is on the *means* of working and not the *purpose* or *meaning* of working. In their book entitled *Good Work* (Gardner *et al.* 2001) the authors set out to examine 'the relationship between excellence and ethics'. They ask why is it that experts primarily teach techniques to young professionals, while ignoring the values that have sustained the quests of so many creative geniuses?

Gardner *et al.* (2001) propose that work has three defining purposes or values. In the first place they talk about *mission* – 'each realm of work has a central mission, which reflects a basic societal need and which the practitioner should feel committed to realizing' (ibid.: 10). Second, they refer to *standards* – 'each profession prescribes standards of performance. Professionals should be able to employ, as a standards test, the question: which workers in a profession best realize their calling and why? A list of admired workers, along with their virtues, should reveal the standards embodied in the profession' (ibid.: 10). Third, they refer to *identity*, which refers to 'a person's deeply felt convictions about who she is, and what matters most to her existence as a worker, a citizen and a human being. A central element of identity is moral – people must determine for themselves what lines they will not cross and why they will not cross it. Rich lives include continuing internal conversations about who we are, what we want to achieve, where we are successful and where we are falling short' (ibid.: 11).

In an earlier work by E.F. Schumacher (1980), coincidentally having the same name *Good Work*, the author argues that 'good work' enables us to fulfil the following three purposes:

- 'First, to provide necessary and useful goods and services;
- second, to enable every one of us to use and thereby perfect our gifts like good stewards; and
- third, to do so in service to, and in cooperation with, others, so as to liberate ourselves from our inborn egocentricity'.

This threefold function makes work so central to human life that it is truly impossible to conceive of life at the human level without work. 'Without work, all life goes rotten', said Albert Camus, 'but when work is soulless, life stifles and dies'. Work is ultimately not a fulfilling experience unless one learns how to continuously achieve these purposes.

Of course in introducing the topic of ethical values into a discussion about learning at work one can be dismissed as being idealistic or naive. After all learning to be efficient and productive are rather practical and pragmatic matters that do not have much to do with ethics. Real ethical issues only arise from time to time and then because of the different views that people have about morality it is almost impossible to come up with any kind of consensus. Ethical discussions are therefore to be avoided if at all possible.

Likewise for some of the above, but also other reasons, many researchers in the field of learning theory are reluctant to delve into questions about ethics except in an implicit manner. The enlightenment distinction between *fact* and *value* holds good. Whereas we can analyse empirical *facts*, *values* are about 'subjective feelings' that cannot be got hold of. Furthermore, in the postmodernist environment[2] ethical relativism holds sway. Ethical issues regarding integrity, truthfulness and courage are not dealt with explicitly to any great extent by modern learning theorists such as Engeström (1987) and Lave and Wenger (1991) even in discussing the building of community that obviously requires truthfulness, sharing and trust.

However, some researchers, in particular those from a philosophical background, argue that we must think philosophically if we are to answer the fundamental questions about human learning and development[3] and this entails making the link between ethics and the attainment of excellence in work organizations. In a populist but serious book with the rather strange title of *If Aristotle ran General Motors* (Morris 1997), the author, who is a professional philosopher, argues that the aim of ethics according to Aristotle is to make us 'good men' – not morally good men as the word 'morally' would be interpreted today, but rather successful fulfilled human beings. The Greek term *Ta Ethica* is derived from the word *Ethos* which means the nature or disposition or customs of a community (see *The New Oxford*

Dictionary of English). Ethics, therefore according to Morris consists in enquiring into how human beings are to behave based on the character of human beings, and how human beings should live in order to fulfil their potential.

Thus, work organizations as Camus stated are meant to be communities in which human beings achieve their fulfilment. This requires that work is carried out in a way that fits in with the ethical values underpinning human excellence. While workplace designers and managers may be under short-term pressures to build instrumental systems, in the long run they avoid facing up to the human dimension of work. The Swiss writer Max Fischer said of the European guest-worker programme of the 1960s – 'we wanted workers, but we got people'. Charles Handy reminds us that 'in the pursuit of economic growth and efficiency, we can be tempted to forget that it is we, individual men and women, who should be the measure of all things. It is easy to lose oneself in efficiency, to treat that efficiency as an end in itself and not as a means to other ends' (Handy 1994: 1).

Achieving excellence in a community of practice – 'giving and receiving'

The neo-Aristotelian philosopher MacIntyre[4] explores the concept of 'practice' as the community context within which people create the conditions for the attainment of human goods. Although MacIntyre does not use the term 'community of practice', drawing on the Aristotelian concept of practice, he sees it as being essentially community centred – those sharing in a practice work together towards the attainment of a common good.[5] This perspective radically challenges the values underlying liberal individualism that is the hallmark of modernity. For MacIntyre, human beings can only learn about and achieve their fulfilment (excellence) through sharing in the life of a community (of practice) through 'receiving' and 'giving' in that community. A human being is by nature a social and political being and cannot be conceived of as a pure individual. Furthermore, a community is sustained by the internal habits and virtues (lived practices) of its members that have been learnt experientially in and through sharing in the practice of that community.

For MacIntyre a practice, such as a work organization,[6] comprises a set of social relations in which and through which people collaborate to achieve a certain dimension of human excellence that is distinctive of their practice, e.g. an engineering company is striving for excellence in all dimensions of an engineering company – producing quality products, having a good working environment, providing opportunities for activities that challenge people to develop collectively and individually, maintaining the profitability of the company, etc. Central to this notion of practice is that the goods (goal or purpose) to be aspired to are goods that are internal to the practice and not purely external goods such as money or power. A practice does not follow an instrumental logic focusing on something outside or external to it. Rather, the good of the practice is pursued for its own sake. A practice according to this perspective can be described as – *the collaborative actions and reflections (or reflective actions) of an established group in realizing the goals of human excellence (or human 'goods') that are distinctive of and have an internal value for that group* (see MacIntyre 1981 and also Nyhan 2003b). Beck *et al.* (1994) in writing about 'reflexive communities', and drawing on the work of MacIntyre, refer to these internal goods as 'substantive goods' that relate, for example, to 'workmanship' and 'the good of the firm'. These goods have to do with the 'ethical life' of those sharing a practice.

Central to the work of MacIntyre is the notion of a community working co-operatively for a shared goal – a common good. A practice such as a work organization is 'a network of relationships of giving and receiving' in which the good of each cannot be pursued without also pursuing the good of all those who participate in those relationships. 'We cannot have a practically adequate understanding of our own good, of our own flourishing, apart from and independently of the flourishing of the whole set of social relationships in which we have found our place' (MacIntyre 1999: 107–8). He goes on to state that:

> Market relationships can only be sustained by being embedded in certain types of non-market relationships, relationships of uncalculated giving and receiving, if they are to contribute to overall flourishing, rather than, as they so often do, undermine and corrupt communal ties. Norms of giving and receiving are then to a large degree presupposed by both our affective ties and by our market relationships. Detach them from this background presupposition in social practice and each becomes a source of vice: on the one hand a romantic and sentimental overvaluation of feeling as such, and on the other a reduction of human activity to economic activity.
>
> (MacIntyre 1999: 117–18)

In his book, entitled *Meaning Work – Rethinking Professional Ethics*, Martin (2000) rejects what he calls the doctrine of 'separate spheres', which places 'ethics and economics' in two different compartments of one's life –'the private' and 'the public'. Applying the doctrine of the 'separate spheres' to the world of work, means that while ethics should govern one's private life, one's work life (public life) is to be guided primarily by economic self-interest values. The latter is the classical libertarian viewpoint.[7]

The meaning of ethical reflection in a community/ organizational setting

For MacIntyre, communities of practice go about achieving their common goals through a process of 'practical reasoning with others' which can be seen as collective reflection. Reflection is the highest form of human reasoning or learning. Indeed, it is the distinctive capacity that makes human beings human. Reflection 'is a feature of the peculiar way we belong to the world' (Eagleton 2003: 60). The word reflection connoting 'serious thought or consideration' and having its origin in the Latin word *reflectere* means 'to bend back' – to be reflexive (see *New Oxford Dictionary of English*).

Reflecting in a community setting entails having a capacity for mature deliberation, decision making, judgement and evaluation about one's actions – present, past and future – and how they relate to, impact on and are affected by the actions of others. (All reflection by those participating in the community therefore is social even if it is done alone, in the sense that one is always in some way dependent on others just as they are dependent on you.) This form of human reasoning which has ethical and intellectual dimensions is given the name of *phrónêsis* by Aristotle. Eikeland (2001) describes *phrónêsis* as follows:

> *Phrónêsis* is specifically an ability to deliberate about and choose means for achieving ethically and politically good objectives. (It presupposes knowledge of ethical and political 'virtue'. This also means that deliberation in order to reach more instrumental or selfish objectives is not included.) *Phrónêsis* demands, in addition to this, that you know the ethically right thing to do in the situation, deliberately choose to do it, and are able to justify it and convince others about the right means for achieving it. It is not just *de*scriptive, but *pre*scriptive as well.
>
> The main question and challenge is how does one *become* a person of good judgement. I think it needs little reflection to realize that 'good judgement', that is 'spontaneously' and skilfully both 'seeing correctly through' the situation you are in the middle of, and knowing 'the right good thing to do', and being able to persuade or convince your companions of the same view or letting yourself be persuaded of something even better, and being able to put the decision and action through as well, is one of the most difficult things to do.'
>
> (Eikeland 2001: 148–9)

Learning the capacity for reflection in an ethical community of practice

According to MacIntyre, in line with the Aristotelian perspective, one learns the capacity for *phrónêsis* or ethical reflection through participating in the life of a community of practice. Similar to the manner in which a 'beginner learner' acquires skill in the community of practice of Lave and Wenger (1991) and the manner in which the 'novice' of Dreyfus and Dreyfus (1986) becomes an 'expert' through participating in the tradition of a professional practice, so developing the capacity for ethical reflection is learnt firstly through sharing (as a 'novice') in the richness of a living community and gradually over time gaining experience – becoming an 'expert'. (An 'expert' in the etymological meaning of the Greek word '*empeirognomon*' literally means someone who has the capacity to give advice based on experience.)

Developing the capacity of reflection is not a pure cognitive or rationalistic process through which one discovers the validity of moral principles or learns rules or codes of behaviour, as Kohlberg (1981) following Kant, puts forward. Rather, it is acquired through an amalgam of cognitive, affective and behavioural processes – that is, a holistic and prolonged 'living' of a practice. One learns the capacity for *phrónêsis* through actively participating in – sharing in and contributing to – the excellence of the practice of one's community. In other words, one learns to reflect through joining in the reflections of others, participating in the social exchanges of one's community, while at the same time 'acting' as a community builder in contributing to the achievement of the common goals (goods) of one's community. In this way one acquires the virtue of *phrónêsis* which is a capacity for good decision making and acting.

This concept of ethics based on a community *internally* self-constructing its ethical community of practice is very different from the approach to ethics which entails drawing up a 'code of ethics' based on *external* norms of 'best practice', the former entails a three-sided collective process (see Table 11.1). The contrast is between a system of ethics based on personal conviction about the values of one's community and one based on laws and rules. Aristotle is quoted as saying – 'if all laws were to be abolished, it would not make much difference to our way of life'. Martin (2000) argues for a similar perspective, in many respects, when he asserts that it is necessary to build a work-based ethical system on 'personal moral commitments' as distinct from one based on 'duties' and 'codes of conduct', which he traces back to the rationalistic (duty-based) moral theory of Kant. He comments that the latter approach is the one adopted by most companies who wish to establish ethical ways of behaving. He refers to this as the 'consensus paradigm' of business ethics.

Concluding comment

One of the central points made throughout the chapters in this volume is that 'making sense of one's work' is a critical issue for people in modern work organizations. This is about finding meaning in one's work. One of the 'malaises of modernity' is a widespread decline in meaning' (Taylor 1992). The possibilities of meaningful work appear to be disappearing for many people, as forces, seemingly outside of their control, dominate their lives. In fact many people – managers and workers – are struggling to find meaning as conflicting demands drag them this way and that.

Fostering a capacity for reflection and providing spaces for reflection at work is put forward in this book as one of the ways to find meaning. But, the concept of reflection itself can be interpreted in many ways. The chapter of Elmhold and Brinkmannn in this volume points out that the modern humanistic discourse on reflection at work can merely be a camouflage for a dangerous form of control in which people are 'self-controlling' themselves in line with the old bureaucratic external control models.

This chapter argues that if reflection is to contribute to resolving the problem of meaning then it must include an ethical dimension. The capacity for collective ethical reflection is a prerequisite for genuine collaborative work in which everybody can find meaning and realize their goals.

If organizations are to achieve excellence in all its dimensions – social *and* economic *and* personal – they must become ethical communities of practice. This is much more that an ethics based on adopting 'external codes of practice' but rather building ethical communities founded on internal convictions about the values of excellence and the practice of the virtues associated with these values. Organizations must build ethical practices from within.

Table 11.1 'Community of practice' versus 'code based' ethics

Community of practice based ethics	Code/rules based ethics
Learnt through participating in and sharing reflections on the life of a community	Learnt through rational reasoning/ theoretical reflection
Socially constructed but also built on the inherited tradition of a community's practice	Externally derived from universalist principles
Integration of cognitive and affective actions	Based on cognitive processes
Rooted in identity and character formation	Based on reasoning power and understanding
Virtue based	Principle, code and rule based
Critical engagement in the narrative of a community	Critical analysis of universalist rules
Embedded in a context	Application of universalist rules
Objective/universalist and subjective/ context based rationality	Objective/universalist rationality

Notes

1 The 10 propositions are as follows:
   1. Critical trust and transparent decision-making.
   2. Communal business cultures accountable to Aristotelian and Kantian ethics.
   3. Avoidance of mercenary and exploitative discourses of appropriation.
   4. Commitment to improving collectively a record of meeting stakeholders' moral claims.
   5. Humanity and transparency in the face of stakeholders' criticism.
   6. Leadership that is virtue-seeking and humble in admitting shortcomings.
   7. Freedom of speech and other civil liberties.
   8. Tradition constituted and tradition constitutive inquiry.
   9. Compassion for employees.
   10. Help to those who are in need. (Snell 2001: 323–36)
2 Eagleton (2003: 13) describes postmodernism as the 'contemporary movement of thought which rejects totalities, universal values, grand historical narratives, solid foundations to human existence and the possibility of objective knowledge. Postmodernism is sceptical of truth, unity and progress, opposes what it sees as elitism in culture, tends towards cultural relativism, and celebrates pluralism, discontinuity and heterogeneity'.
3 In making the link between philosophical analysis and education and learning, the philosopher John Dewey (1996) well known for his work on the concept of reflection, argues that education is the laboratory in which philosophical theories are tested. In fact, a philosophical theory can be seen as forming the basis for a theory of education.

4 Alasdair MacIntyre is best known for his book *After Virtue* (1981) which is a critique of the 'modernist project'. However, he adopts a different stance to the postmodernists in arguing for the classical philosophical tradition initiated by Aristotle and continued within different communities through history including today. MacIntyre makes a radical critique of modernistic technocratic empirical rationality and its lack of a foundation for ethical thinking. He argues that human beings must regain faith in their natural capacities to reflect about what it means to be human. However, this is more than knowledge, as people must build social practices or communities that foster the virtues required to enable people to fulfil their potential as human beings. (For a critical review of the work of MacIntyre see Horton and Mendus 1996.)

5 Carr (1995) contends that current understandings of the concept of 'practice' are flawed and that it is only when we give historical depth to philosophical analysis (beginning with Aristotle) that we will arrive at an adequate understanding of the meaning of practice.

6 Whereas MacIntyre does not go into any great depth in his writing on work organizations as communities of practice and indeed in some places, using his strict definitions of a 'social practice', excludes them from consideration in not meeting his criteria, his work has been taken up by many authors in their analysis of modern work organizations (for example, see Martin 2000; Beck *et al.* 1994. See also, Solomon (1992) who develops the notion of a corporation as a community.).

7 Martin expounds on the libertarian view as follows – 'This libertarian outlook has dominated economic thinking since its first powerful articulation by Adam Smith in the *Wealth of Nations*, published in 1776. In his famous words, "It is not from the benevolence of the butcher, the brewer, or the baker, that we expect our dinner, but from their regard to their own interest" (Smith, 1976). By 'benevolence', Smith means desires and emotions aimed at promoting the happiness of others, for their sake rather than solely for ulterior self-interested ends. Smith's sweeping generalization is that merchants seek personal gain *and not* the good of others, certainly not the good of the wider public. To be sure, in order to acquire personal gain, merchants must please customers, and in the long run that means producing quality goods at competitive prices. In this way, self-seeking individuals benefit the wider community without intending, trying, or even wanting to do so. Each merchant is "led by an invisible hand to promote an end which was not part of his intention," certainly not part of an altruistic intention: "I have never known much good done by those who affected to trade for the public [*sic*] good. It is an affectation, indeed, not very common among merchants, and very few words need be employed in dissuading them from it." (Smith 1976).' (Martin 2000: 12).

References

Beck, U., Giddens, A. and Lash, S. (1994) *Reflexive Modernisation: Politics, Traditions and Aesthetics in the Modern Social Order*, Cambridge: Polity Press.

Brown, A. and Keep, E. (2003) 'Competing perspectives on workplace learning and the learning organisation', in B. Nyhan *et al.* (eds) *Facing up to the Learning Organisation Challenge. Selected European Writings*, Vol. II, Luxembourg: Office for Official Publications of the European Communities.

Carr, W. (1995) *For Education – Towards Critical Educational Inquiry*, Buckingham: Open University Press.

Contu, A. and Willmott, H. (2000) 'Knowing in practice: a "delicate flower" in the organisational learning field', *Organization*, 7, 2: 269–76.

Dewey, J. (1966) *Democracy and Education. An Introduction to the Philosophy of Education*, New York: Free Press.

Dobson, J. (1997) 'MacIntyre's position on business: a response to Wicks', *Business Ethics Quarterly*, 7, 4: 125–32.

Dreyfus, S.E. and Dreyfus, H.L. (1986) *Mind over Machine*, Oxford: Basil Blackwell.

Dunne, J. (1993) *Back to the Rough Ground: 'Proneseis' and 'Techne' in Modern Philosophy and Aristotle*, Notre Dame, IN: University of Notre Dame Press.

Eagleton, T. (2003) *After theory*, London: Allen Books.

Eikeland, O. (2001) 'Action research as the hidden curriculum of the western tradition', in P. Reason and H. Bradbury (eds) *Handbook of Action Research: Participative Inquiry and Practice*, London, Thousand Oaks, New Delhi: Sage: 145–55.

Elliot, C. and Turnbull, S. (2003) 'Reconciling autonomy and community: the paradoxical role of HRD', *Human Resource Development International*, 6: 4.

Engeström, Y. (1987) *Learning by Expanding: An Activity-theoretical Approach to Developmental Research*, Helsinki: Orienta-Konsultit Oy.

Fischer, M. (2003) 'Challenges and open questions raised by the concept of the learning organisation', in B. Nyhan *et al.* (eds) *Facing up to the Learning Organisation Challenge. Selected European Writings*, Vol. II. Luxembourg: Office for Official Publications of the European Communities, 33–49.

Gardner, H., Csikszentmihalyi, M. and Damon, W. (2001) *Good Work: When Excellence and Ethics Meet*, New York: Basic Books.

Handy, C. (1994) *The Empty Raincoat – Making Sense of the Future*, London: Hutchinson.

Horton, J. and Mendus, S. (eds) (1996) *After MacIntyre – Critical Perspectives on the Work of Alisdair MacIntyre*, Cambridge: Polity Press.

Kohlberg, L. (1981) *The Philosophy of Moral Development: Essays on Moral Development* (volume I), San Fransico: Harper and Row.

Lave, J. and Wenger, E. (1991) *Situated Learning: Legitimate Peripheral Participation*, Cambridge: Cambridge University Press.

MacIntyre, A. (1999) *Dependent Rational Animals: Why Human Beings Need the Virtues*, Chicago: Open Court.

MacIntyre, A. (1990) *Three Rival Versions of Moral Enquiry: Encyclopaedia, Genealogy, Tradition*, London: Duckworth.

MacIntyre, A. (1985) 'Moral arguments and social context: a response to Rorty', in R. Hollinger (ed.) *Hermeneutics and Praxis*, Notre Dame, IN: University of Notre Dame Press.

MacIntyre, A. (1981) *After Virtue: A Study in Moral Theory*, London: Duckworth.

Martin, M.W. (2000) *Meaningful work. Rethinking Professional Ethics*, New York and Oxford: Oxford University Press.

Morris, T. (1997) *If Aristotle ran General Motors*, New York: Holt and Company.

Nyhan, B., Cressey, P., Tomassini, M., Kelleher, M. and Poell, R. (2003a) *Facing up to the Learning Organisation Challenge. Key Issues from European Perspective*, Vol. I, Luxembourg: Office for Official Publications of the European Communities.

Nyhan, B., Kelleher, M., Cressey, P. and Poell, R. (eds) (2003b) *Facing up to the Learning Organisation Challenge. Selected European Writings*, Vol. II, Luxembourg: Office for Official Publications of the European Communities.

Piore, M.J. and Sabel, C.F. (1984) *The Second Industrial Divide: Possibilities for Prosperity*, New York: Basic Books.

Schumacher, E.F. (1980) *Good Work*, London: Sphere Books (ABACUS).

Senge, P. (1990) *The Fifth Discipline. The Art and Practice of the Learning Organization*, New York: Doubleday.

Sennett, P. (1998) *The Corrosion of Character – the Personal Consequences of Working the new Capitalism*, New York: W.W. Norton and Company.

Smith, A. (1976) *An Enquiry into the Nature and Causes of the Wealth of Nations*, R.H. Campbell and A.S. Skinner (eds) New York: Oxford University Press.

Snell, R.S. (2001) 'Moral foundation of the learning organisation', *Human Relations*, 54, 3: 319–42.

Solomon, C. (1992) *Ethics and Excellence*, New York: Oxford University Press.

Taylor, C. (1992) *The Ethics of Authenticity*, Cambridge, MA: Harvard University Press.

Victor, B. and Stephens, C. (1994) 'The dark side of the new organisational forms: an editorial essay', *Organization Science*, 5, 4: 479–82.

12 Reflecting on workplace change

A trade union perspective

Monica Breidensjö and Tony Huzzard

Introduction: from competence development to collective reflection

Many of the newer organizational models impacting on working life have been informed by the managerial doctrine of leanness that seeks to eliminate any waste in labour processes that does not add value to customers (Womack *et al.* 1990). This doctrine stands in contrast to other views that stress the need for reflection, learning and innovation from within the workforce as key aspects of longer-term dynamic performance and sustainability. It would appear that the doctrine of leanness has clear tensions with reflective practices in that little scope is offered for the necessary time and space associated with organizational learning and development. The application of lean approaches in Sweden in particular has provided few opportunities at the workplace for employees to reflect. In many instances the consequences of the quest for leanness have been new regimes of 'management by stress' (Parker and Slaughter 1988) rather than the optimistic visions associated with the rhetoric of 'learning organizations' (Senge 1990).

This chapter explores the tensions between leanness and learning from the perspective of the trade unions. How are unions and union representatives seeing emergent trends at the workplace and the tensions between competing ideologies for managing work? What is the union experience of reflective activity on work processes at Swedish workplaces? How are union strategies evolving in response to what appears to be a growing gap between the rhetoric of learning and the reality of leanness and downsizing? What can we contribute as actionable knowledge from the Swedish experience?

We argue that unions have considerable potential for supplying new 'learning spaces' (Fulop and Rifkin 1997) at workplaces where they organize employees and thereby can provide new sources of added value to firms and public sector organizations as resources for reflection. There is a growing recognition in the organizational learning literature that learning and thereby reflection in organizational contexts is best understood as processes of social interaction rather than an aggregation of individual cognitive processes (Vince 2002). Our emphasis here is thus on reflection at the collective level. In our view, developing a specific union role in learning spaces wherein collective reflection can open up new opportunities for learning can also enable unions to draw on new bases of legitimacy and influence in labour processes. In short, we see no shortage of reflective activities in unions; on the other hand these need to be more systematically harnessed as means of creating learning spaces at workplaces. In effect, the unions need to reflect on their reflection.

We precede our discussion by focusing on the challenges to unions of lean production and the possibilities for unions in a 'knowledge economy' from the empirical context of an apparent increase in lean production in Sweden. The chapter then continues with a conceptual discussion in which first we establish some of the key theoretical issues and tensions associated with reflection and second, we clarify our definition of the concept and present a model of collective reflection and its centrality in processes of organizational learning. We also make a distinction between event-driven and non-event-driven reflection and illustrate this through empirical examples. Following a discussion on the implications of lean production on union strategy, we conclude the chapter with some reflections of our own.

Leanness versus learning: a new challenge for the unions?[1]

Whilst we should be wary about claims to widespread transformation in working life (Thompson and McHugh 2002), change is undoubtedly afoot in terms of new management doctrines. How have the unions reacted to these changes? Is there a new strategy emerging or are the unions still asking themselves what path will strengthen unions and their members in this new situation? The central task of struggle for a fair distribution of surpluses remains, but the question is whether that alone will be satisfactory for union members in a working life trajectory of continuous change. At the same time there is an ongoing discussion within many unions on how to create opportunities for members to develop their professional competencies in different ways. The discussion concerns both education at different levels and professional and social development at the workplace through new models of work organization. The main focus has been on the right to education throughout one's working life so as to enhance one's employability (Garsten and Jacobsson 2004). There are increasing demands for new skills in labour processes, and thus for employability, in order to survive in insecure labour markets. Such a view has prompted unions to advance competence development up their respective agendas. It could even be argued that the right of all to education and skills development is a new expression of 'solidarity' (Huzzard 2004).

As already argued, the 'lean organization' has hampered the development of new learning possibilities at work. The trade union way to tackle this has mostly been by concluding agreements with the aim of supporting their members in these precarious situations, either financially or through education to help make it easier to obtain a new job. Trade union support has been highly focused on giving backing to members in the transition period between jobs. It has been more difficult, however, to create long-term solutions to prevent this insecurity.

Some unions have tried, by producing printed material, to promote an ongoing discussion on the need for current competence development at the workplace that is beneficial both from the employees' and the employers' point of view. Other unions have focused on solely supporting the individual members' competence development. It is thus evident that most efforts to promote competence development have their focus on education *at the individual level*. Of course formal education is needed for many purposes. But this is easy compared to trying to create learning organizations. For educational efforts there are structures and resources, with aims often set by society. But for most workplaces the learning organization remains a utopian dream. Focusing on competence development by education may be necessary, but it is an insufficient means for solving the problem of the growing precariousness of working life. Moreover, there is the difficulty that in the established education system we can always pose the question 'Who is allowed to learn?'. We should also perhaps pose the question 'Who is not allowed to learn?' – it is a system that both enables and excludes.

It is also argued that organizations designed to learn with time to reflect on and develop their work practices can enhance competitive advantage (Shani and Docherty 2003). If this is true, then it would suggest that learning organizations may contribute positively to economic growth. Unions have a strong interest in this. The current situation at most workplaces, however, is that inadequate care is taken of existing knowledge. In particular, firms committed to downsizing run the risk of jettisoning key components of organizational memory (McKinley et al. 1995). It is also clear from Swedish research that there is over-qualification as well as under-qualification of employees suggesting that many workers cannot fully use their competence at work (Svensson 2004); accordingly, the 'knowledge economy' is a partly underutilized one. We thus need to develop the economic lexicon to recognize not only undercapacity in the physical economy of production, but also undercapacity *in the intellectual economy*.

To sum up, the unions are in a situation where they might consider broadening their central task of negotiating wages to also form a strategy for promoting learning organizations and adding value through supporting reflective activities at the workplace, or even conducting such activities directly themselves. Several factors appear to favour such an approach:

- It could help members obtain up-to-date professional knowledge and gain social competence;
- It could be a fruitful way to make work more creative and developmental for all union members; and
- It could contribute strongly to firm development and thus economic growth.

But in a context of increasing leanness what might such practices of reflection consist of? Before answering this it will be necessary both to define the term reflection and to provide it with greater conceptual clarity, a task we undertake in the next section.

Conceptualizing reflection

In our view, reflection can be usefully conceptualized as a means of *contrasting and confronting experience with expectations through dialogue*. By experience we mean the experience of what employees have done in their work and how they have acted in a given context. Typical questions asked here are: what did I/we do? What was the outcome? What contextual factors of time, space, external relationships, resources etc. were of significance? By the same token, employees will usually have some expectation of the outcomes of their actions. This is guided by existing knowledge that is partially derived from past learning outcomes. The perceived outcomes of one's actions (experience) are then contrasted with the expectations of such actions. Thereby a process of reflection starts. This process, in turn, can entail interrogation on matters such as: Was it (the action) a success or a failure? What do we do now? What do we do differently in the future? What are the significant contextual factors? And, crucially, what were the assumptions underlying what we did?

Acknowledging the role of reflection in learning processes is of course not new. Theorists of experiential learning such as Dewey (1910/1933) saw the reflection at the core of such learning as being intimately associated with action, in particular that of problem solving. Dewey made the distinction between everyday action (whereby the role of reflection was questionable), and action prompted by external triggers such as unforeseen obstacles, uncertainty and difficulty. These latter examples of disruption set off processes of reflection. In our view, this distinction is useful and can be understood as that between routine and non-routine action. In contrast to Dewey, however, we would advance the possibility that reflection might also occur on routine actions on a regular basis and 'reflection routines' might become an essential activity of a learning workplace union.

The emphasis on reflection in Dewey's work is clearly on the individual learner. The same can be said of another prominent exponent of reflection at work, Donald Schön, notably in his text 'The Reflective Practitioner – How Professionals Think in Action' (Schön 1983). In contrast to these authors, however, our emphasis here is on reflection at the collective rather than individual level. Following Vince (2002), we see reflection as an organizing process rather than an activity of the 'reflective practitioner'. Reflection is thus not just a potential means for individual development and perhaps even emancipation, but also part of an ongoing organizing process within a social collectivity or 'community of practice' (Lave and Wenger 1991). As such, it is part of a dynamic that has its own assumptions, institutionalizing tendencies and rules of belonging. Yet these very same features of organizing, which help to enhance security and reduce uncertainty, also have a constraining role (Vince 2002). Reflection is thus characterized by an inherent tension between coherence and constraint, a tension best managed by the act of collective questioning the assumptions on which such coherence and constraint is built.

Nevertheless, whilst reflection is a collective process, it is informed by individual level competencies. These are not just a matter of expert knowledge on the issues associated with the labour process at hand, but also concern social competence for individuals and thereby feed-forward processes from previous learning outcomes. Such outcomes also feed forward to influence expectations. These in turn can be seen as learning outcomes that, as mentioned, are a basic resource for reflection. A diagrammatic representation that synthesizes our conceptualization of reflection is depicted in Figure 12.1.

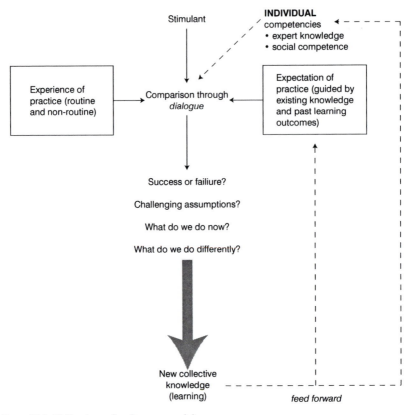

Figure 12.1 Collective reflection – a model

Reflection in practice

Scandinavian unions, together with their counterparts from works councils in Germany, are in many respects pioneers in the active participation in discussions at workplaces on work organization and technological development. For example, Sandberg *et al.* have reported on how a number of Swedish blue-collar unions have exploited the co-determination arrangements to advance union agendas on what they called 'development issues' (Sandberg *et al.* 1992). Clearly, such approaches require active participation, in co-operation with local management in development projects that can be seen as learning processes. In many respects union visions of 'good work' that guided union approaches in such projects represented a radical break from the work practices of Taylorism requiring a thorough questioning of traditional assumptions in the labour process. Such learning required the ability to surface such assumptions, stand back from them and engage in critical interrogation. In other words, the practice of reflection was a central prerequisite for such learning to occur. Similar practices of union learning and reflection were also evident in the AMBIV development projects at Volvo Umeverken and Assa Abloy reported in Huzzard (2000).

Clearly, then, the research to date provides no shortage of evidence that unions have considerable experience of reflective activity at the workplace on developmental issues. Yet although unions appear to be tapping into the discourse of learning (Huzzard 2000), the crucial distinction between learning through exploitation and learning through exploration is not generally made (March 1991). This is important as the doctrine of leanness does not at all deny the desirability of learning, rather it puts a one-sided emphasis on exploitation in that it stresses the codification and diffusion of the work practices that best reach the ideals of waste elimination. In this sense it is a technology for the standardization of routines across an organization and thereby sits uneasily alongside the practices of reflection that are more closely related to the notion of learning through exploration. The challenge now is for unions to develop approaches to learning that explicitly counter the logic of leanness whereby all practices, including reflection, are eliminated that do not immediately and clearly add to the bottom line.

If unions are to have an intervening role in countering the logic of lean production and promoting alternative approaches to organizational learning, when might such interventions occur? What is the nature of the stimulant identified in the model (Figure 12.1)? First, such a stimulant can be something that occurs externally to a union and to which it is forced to respond such as workplace rationalization, closures or changes to political actors and regimes resulting from elections. Second, it can be something that occurs from within its own regular activities – what we might call its own reflective practice or routine reflection.

We can thus talk about both event-driven reflection and non-event-driven reflection – a distinction that can be usefully illustrated with reference to two empirical examples of union reflective practice. The Swedish Association of Health Professionals (SAHP) has been engaged with major upheavals in the provision of health care in the Stockholm area, in particular the closure of units at a smaller hospital and their transfer to another hospital nearby – Söder Hospital. How did the union act? There was considerable ambition from the local union to listen to the members and to let everyone talk about their reactions and have a say about the union actions in response. There were general meetings at which all members took part. The union obtained support from an employee–consultant who helped process the various items of information connected with the closure and to broaden out the discussions. The smaller hospital had no financial problems but the politicians had decided that the decision was the best way to save money. Information about the closure was published by the media before being formally presented to employee representatives. This affected the union membership negatively. During the subsequent process, the experience and upheaval of closure caused a considerable degree of ill-health, especially among the union leadership.

The unions obtained organized support in the form of reflective conversations with a psychiatrist, both individually and in groups with the local union committees. The aim was that the unions should be able to take care of and support rank-and-file members as well as members who had leading positions in the organization. Reflective conversations also took place with the director of the hospital. The meetings were held every second week over the period of a year. During the process, the psychiatrist and the director of the hospital represented the employer in what became reflexive dialogue. The key attitudes underlying the approach were 'How do we best solve this problem?' and 'an opportunity for development must be to hand'.

This is an example of reflection during an actual change process. The union representative from SAHP felt that the union was also granted the time and took the opportunity to hold an open and reflexive dialogue with its members. The local union took a position with regard to what came out from the dialogue. The union leaders felt that both they individually and the union as a collective had learnt a great deal from this process: in her words 'they got stronger'. The way of acting from the union side changed from relying on traditional methods into a more supportive, coaching role that supported reflection at the workplace within a context of downsizing and leanness.

In contrast, non-event-driven reflection can be illustrated with reference to some tested techniques for reflective practice in unions that are not connected to any external trigger, such as an actual change process. Sif, a white-collar union with members across various industrial sectors, has recognized for some time the importance of enhancing its innovation processes in membership service delivery through carefully listening to its members. Its efforts in this regard have been seen as an explicit component in boosting group creativity and organizational learning internally (Björkman 2005). In effect, Sif has acknowledged that the traditional channel of union decision-making, namely its representative structure, has shortcomings in that it does not easily accommodate dialogue, reflection and learning.

A key technique for enhancing services has become what the union calls 'design dialogue groups'. The design dialogue groups share many features of focus groups. However, whereas most focus groups tend to be led by consultants or market research firms who have some expertise in the area, for example that of providing skilled moderators, Sif has opted to develop such competencies internally through 'internal service developers'. The main emphasis of the dialogue development groups has been that of reflection on internal union matters. But such reflection has, in some respects, turned the attention of the groups outside Sif towards what is happening externally and what types of membership support is required at today's and tomorrow's workplaces. For example, groups have included dialogues on issues connected with pay negotiations as well as more specific audits of the work environment, a key issue in the context of lean production.

Discussion: Reflection and learning spaces

It is generally accepted that organizational learning does not just consist of an aggregation of individual learners – learning also occurs collectively at group, organizational and inter-organizational levels. Such collective learning necessarily occurs through processes of interaction. Yet such processes can diverge widely in their format. Developmental learning involves a great deal more than simply the diffusion of explicit knowledge, for example that of benchmarking of 'best practice' within standardized routines: this is lower level learning. Higher levels of learning generally require the ability of actors to surface their individual and collectively held assumptions or 'theories of action' (Argyris and Schön 1978), step outside them and interrogate them critically. As noted earlier in the chapter, such activities are central features of reflection. Yet almost by definition such activities cannot be conducted through collective bargaining or joint consultation where participants are engaged in positional thinking and advancing particular interests in what are invariably zero-sum situations.

As stated, the focus of learning under lean production is that of exploiting and diffusing existing knowledge of waste elimination rather than the generation of new knowledge for development through collective reflection. A wealth of literature has demonstrated that the most suitable form of interaction underpinning learning for development is that of genuine dialogue (see e.g. Gustavsen 1992). Such dialogue, it is argued, can only occur where three conditions are fulfilled: equality and the absence of coercive influences; listening with empathy; and bringing assumptions into the open (Yankelovich 1999). True dialogue, understood in this way, cannot occur in traditional industrial relations arenas. Accordingly, new arenas for allowing genuine learning and reflection at workplaces are surely needed in organizations seeking the high road to sustainability and competitiveness.

The absence of reflective practices at workplaces, particularly low-road workplaces characterized by the doctrine of leanness, is naturally a problem for employees. At the same time, it opens up new possibilities for unions in taking the initiative for establishing high-road practices – ideally with management involvement. Of particular use in this context is Fulop and Rifkin's concept of 'learning spaces' (Fulop and Rifkin 1997). In their view, learning spaces only occur 'when people in the organization communicate in certain reflective and "authentic" ways about information, experiences and feelings …' (ibid.: 46). Such situations require a release of control by management and 'a relaxation of privileging forces' (ibid.: 58). Fears about self-disclosure are removed and 'people have freedom to think and explore and to question such things as managerial control. Managers are meant to reflect on and engage in practices that are not controlling or "managing"' (op. cit.). Learning spaces are also characterized by a suspension of truth or knowledge claims and require management, union representatives and employees to engage in reflective practice and be party to a discourse of learning.

Learning spaces, designed and moderated through union expertise where dialogue and reflection are central, can thus be platforms for putting critical questions to firms in ways that can have developmental potential. The aim for unions here is not to defend or advance the sectional interests of employees. Such activity will continue as core union work, but will be undertaken elsewhere. Learning spaces might conceivably involve joint reflection on decisions to outsource, the trajectory of technology, job redesign, customer and supplier relations and various risk analyses. On the other hand, it may well be the case that some outcomes of such reflection may need to be bargained over and thereby transferred to other arenas.

The Söder Hospital illustration shows how reflection occurred at the moment when union actors were forced to confront the experience of closure with their expectations of ongoing job security. The individual competencies of union leaders on handling change situations and redundancy were being fed into the collective dialogue (see Figure 12.1). In contrast to Söder Hospital, the Sif dialogue groups show how 'reflection routines' in learning spaces might be undertaken on a more regular basis without reference to any specific critical event. The dialogue groups afforded the possibility for confronting expectations with experience in a less strained setting. Both cases, although different in the sense that the reflective practices had different origins, suggest that there are possibilities here for a new role for unions at workplaces. Such roles may be both operational in the sense of being grounded from day-to-day issues which might be rather mundane in nature as well as strategic in the sense that new competencies and ideas for alternative, innovative trajectories for workplaces could be fed into decision-making processes in both firms and public sector organizations.

Implications for unions and union strategy

Swedish unions have discussed the role and significance of competence development for many years, formed programmes and put forward demands to employers to grant employees with the right to development at work. Many projects have focused on competence development, mainly as an option for members interested in developing their professional competence through taking part in formal education, courses etc. But attempts have also been made to form learning processes at workplaces to foster collective learning through dialogue and reflection. The question now is whether, firstly, the unions can proactively take on responsibility for capturing these experiences and channelling them into developmental work, and secondly, move on from individual competence development to forming collective strategies for learning processes at work. Quite clearly, in an environment of perceived change, a whole series of developmental responsibilities have opened up for unions: supporting members, supporting unemployed members, recruiting under-represented employees, co-operating with management in personnel and organizational development, and developing the union itself in response to such challenges.

Swedish unions have, throughout the last century, built a strong position around their core activity of wage negotiations. Locally and centrally there is good knowledge of laws, agreements and how to negotiate. There is also, in general, an overall union strategy, often debated by members at conferences etc. There are well-known and well-established structures for negotiations, both at central and local level. The legitimacy of unions is built on their strongly established role as wage negotiators. This is not the case, however, when it comes to reflection and learning at work although there is a strong awareness that these are fields that demand long-term initiatives from the unions. In order to strengthen individual job security and employability, the promotion of developmental opportunities for members is becoming a key issue for the unions (Huzzard 2004).

If unions choose to take on the task of fostering learning as an integrated part of a work situation, this will call for changes in the priorities of the unions as well as in working methods and union structures. If a union takes the developmental prospects for the individual member as a key component of union strategy, it will imply a change in priorities. This can also be described as a broadening of competence as the notion of solidarity is broadened out from economic solidarity to also include the right for everyone to develop and learn at work (Huzzard 2004). This, in turn, will call for the unions to acquire more knowledge about learning processes and the interrelation between learning and the organization of work. It will be necessary to build a long-term strategy in the field. In forming a strategy on the right to learning at work, the challenge is to find ways to secure the right for every member to acquire the necessary prerequisites for learning at work. Above all, it will be necessary to show the members in practice that they all have an important role in such a strategy.

The challenge for unions is not just that of understanding the significance of learning at the workplace and their role in this. It is also about appreciating the distinction between learning as a means of standardizing the elimination of waste and learning as a means of fostering development. The latter, clearly, sees reflection as having a productive role rather than simply being seen as an expendable cost. Such an understanding, however, requires more than mere insight – it has significant implications for union praxis. More time will have to be used to engage in dialogue and discussion with members at the workplace about the developmental aspects of work and both their own and the union role in this. Many members are not used to stating their opinion in discussions. But all must be involved and this may require special efforts and new methods from unions in terms of membership support. Unions that have worked with learning at the workplace have described their new role as changing into being a coach for the members rather than being an expert – the 'representative with all the answers' (Huzzard 2000). This might also lead to new forms of influence at work.

Trade union pedagogical methods including training might have to change. There have to be links between local learning processes and courses that can support them. Shop stewards will have to take care of both individual and collective needs. They will also have to face discussions and obstacles derived for instance from the fact that many wage systems are not compatible with the co-operative ideas of learning organizations. The career system may also be a hindrance.

If the developments described here lead to a new locus of legitimacy amongst competent union representatives at the workplace this must result in an internal discussion about union structures, strategic planning and priorities. If the idea of the learning organization is to endure, it has to be supported at all levels of the organization. It is also important to discuss the distribution of work in terms of learning facilities between local and central levels. At the central level it might be an important task for unions to ensure that the training and education structures of society support workplace development.

Conclusion: reflecting on reflection

Whilst lean production clearly articulates the desirability of learning in organizations as a means of improving competitiveness and performance (Womack *et al.* 1990), this generally assumes a bias towards the exploitation of existing knowledge rather than the exploration of new knowledge through the practice of collective reflection. Learning under lean production focuses on standardization that is largely functional and subject to corporate control (Berggren 1995). In this chapter we have argued that unions can have an important role in weaning both private and public sector organizations away from such a bias in learning and focusing instead on learning for development through collective reflection.

Famously, Antonowsky (1987) has argued that instead of analysing working life through diagnosing its various ills, we should instead seek to identify the key components of organizational wellness. It is in this spirit that we explore in this chapter a potential new role for unions as competent suppliers and guarantors of reflective practices at workplaces, as an alternative to the doctrine of leanness. There is considerable evidence that Sweden's intellectual economy is underutilized at both individual and collective levels; union facilitated processes of dialogue-based reflection could be a fruitful means for bringing underutilized capacities out of the shadows and deploying them to add value.

A learning organization draws its strength from including all workers and (all) knowledge that is created daily by workers. The point is that the ongoing generation of new knowledge cannot be achieved solely by sending workers onto courses. Many different means of learning must be tried. One of the most important of these is to create new forms of work that allow and encourage reflection with the aim of systematically taking care of the knowledge that accumulates on the job. This could be a way to create a sustainable work system (Docherty *et al.* 2002). Unions, moreover, could make this a strategic way of empowering their members.

Even if there have been many projects aimed at developing aspects of work organization, change is a very slow process. Traditional forms of work organization building on the notion that knowledge comes from the top still have wide cognitive purchase. And knowledge is power – this is a threat to those who think they will lose power and who cannot see the advantages for their organization. In order to make individual knowledge common knowledge (Dixon 2000), certain new prerequisites are needed. A learning organization presupposes not only a new organization but also new attitudes and competencies at the workplace as well as a new conception of leadership.

The message for unions seems to be that in a context of lean production they need to reflect on their existing reflective practices. There is no shortage of reflective activity in unions: they are more innovative organizations than is often portrayed in the mass media. The challenge, however, is to harness some of their more internally focused tools for reflection for external purposes by setting up learning spaces in developmentally oriented high road firms and public sector organizations.

Note

1   There is some disagreement in the literature about what, precisely, characterises a 'learning organization'. We side here with those who critique versions of the concept that are managerial, unitarist and based on dialogue that is ultimately univocal. Our preference is for a pluralist view that recognises diversity, takes seriously the problematic reality of unequal power relations and sees dialogue as multivocal, and having the aim of increasing understanding and respect for difference rather than aiding the pursuit of managerially defined outcomes.

References

Antonovsky, A. (1987) *Unravelling the Mystery of Health. How People Manage Stress and Stay Well*, San Francisco: Jossey-Bass.

Argyris, C. and Schön, D. (1978) *Organisational Learning: A Theory of Action Perspective*, Reading MA: Addison Wesley.

Berggren, C. (1995) 'The Fate of the Branch Plants – Performance Versus Power', in Å. Sandberg (ed.) *Enriching Production*, Aldershot: Avebury.

Björkman, H. (2005) 'Learning from Members: Tools for Strategic Positioning and Service Innovation in Trade Unions', PhD thesis, Stockholm School of Economics.

Dewey, J. (1910/1933) *How We Think*, New York: Heath.

Dixon, N. (2000) *Common Knowledge: How Companies Thrive by Sharing what they Know*, Boston, MA: Harvard Business School Press.

Docherty, P., Forslin, J. and Shani, A.B. (Rami) (eds) (2002) *Creating Sustainable Work Systems: Emerging Perspectives and Practice*, London: Routledge.

Fulop, L. and Rifkin, W. (1997) 'Representing Fear in Learning in Organizations', *Management Learning*, 28, 1: 45–63.

Garsten, C. and Jacobsson, K. (eds) (2004) *Learning to be Employable: New Agendas on Work, Responsibility and Learning in a Globalizing World*, Basingstoke: Palgrave.

Gustavsen, B. (1992) *Dialogue and Development*, Assen/Maastricht: Van Gorcum.

Huzzard, T. (2000) *Labouring to Learn: Union Renewal in Swedish Manufacturing*, Umeå: Boréa.

Huzzard, T. (2004) 'Constructing the Competent Individual: Trade Union Roles, Responses and Rhetoric', in C. Garsten and K. Jacobsson (eds) *Learning to be Employable: New Agendas on Work, Responsibility and Learning in a Globalizing World*, Basingstoke: Palgrave.

Lave, J. and Wenger, E. (1991) *Situated Learning: Legitimate Peripheral Participation*, Cambridge: Cambridge University Press.

March, J.G. (1991) 'Exploration and Exploitation in Organizational Learning', *Organizational Science*, 2, 1: 71–87.

McKinley, W., Sanchez, C.M. and Schick, A.G. (1995) 'Organizational Downsizing: Constraining, Cloning, Learning', *Academy of Management Executive*, 9, 3: 32–44.

Parker, M. and Slaughter, J. (1988) *Choosing Sides: Unions and the Team Concept*, Boston, MA: South End Press.

Sandberg, Å., Broms, G., Grip, A., Sundström, L., Steen, J. and Ullmark, P. (1992) *Technological Change and Co-determination in Sweden*, Philadelphia, PA: Temple University Press.

Schön, D. (1983) *The Reflective Practitioner. How Professionals Think in Action*, New York: Basic Books.

Senge, P. (1990) *The Fifth Discipline. The Art and Practice of the Learning Organization*, New York: Doubleday.

Shani, A.B. (Rami) and Docherty, P. (2003) *Learning by Design: Building Sustainable Organizations*, Oxford: Blackwell Publishers.

Svensson, L. (2004) 'Lifelong Learning: A Clash Between a Production and a Learning Logic', in C. Garsten and K. Jacobsson (eds) *Learning to be Employable: New Agendas on Work, Responsibility and Learning in a Globalizing World*, Basingstoke: Palgrave.

Thompson, P. and McHugh, D. (2002) *Work Organizations: A Critical Introduction*, 3rd edn, Basingstoke: Palgrave.

Vince, R. (2002) 'Organizing Reflection', *Management Learning*, 33, 1: 63–78.

Womack, J.P., Jones, D.T. and Roos, D. (1990) *The Machine that Changed the World*, New York: Harper Perennial.

Yankelovich, D. (1999) *The Magic of Dialogue: Transforming Conflict into Co-operation*, London: Nicholas Brearley.

13 Creating the space for reflection at work

David Boud

In contributing to a book about reflection at work in the first decade of the twenty-first century it is impossible to ignore an earlier phase of activity about the role of reflection in learning. While much of this did not focus directly on the workplace, it provided much of the language we use today to talk about reflection. During the 1980s and 1990s there was an explosion of activity in the area of professional education around the themes of reflection and reflective practice. These were clustered around notions of reflective teaching (Cruikshank *et al.* 1981), reflective practice (Schön 1983, 1987) and reflection and learning (Boud *et al.* 1985). Each of these ideas had a slightly different focus – on the practice of teaching, professional practice and experiential learning. However, they each shared an emphasis on learning from experience and the ways in which conscious reflection can influence learning (Moon 1999).

While there has been development of these ideas over the past 20 years, what is striking is the extent to which they have informed the curriculum in many professional areas even when the application of these ideas differed from the expectations of their original proponents. Indeed, it would now be unusual to find university courses in any of the professions that did not in some way acknowledge the importance of reflection or reflective practice in professional formation. Similarly, in the wider area of adult education and experiential learning ideas of reflection are commonplace.

What then of the world of work? Except where there has been direct influence from the above through continuing professional education, reflection is not a concept normally used in working life. Reflection is spoken about in its conventional everyday sense, not as a marker for a conceptualized practice. The challenge in writing a chapter on reflection at work therefore lies in deciding whether to ground it in the extensive ideas that have developed in the world of education or to look at the practice of work and locate it there. What I have chosen to do is to consider these two separate domains together.

The chapter starts by summarizing some ideas about reflection in education that have been discussed in earlier chapters. It then focuses on a study of informal learning in workplaces I have been involved in. Illustrations of work practice are drawn from these studies to ground discussion of reflection in the world of work. These are then used as a lens through which to examine ideas of reflection taken from the world of education. The question addressed is how does workplace practice challenge or extend these earlier ideas. The chapter concludes by identifying some features of an agenda for further exploration of reflection at work. It suggests that creating a space for reflection is not a simple matter of structuring new kinds of activities in workplaces. To understand what might be possible, it is necessary to examine ways in which learning occurs or is seen to occur at work, how workplace identity is constructed and how the demands of work both limit and generate possibilities for reflection. It points to the dilemma of over-formalizing reflection in workplaces: it provokes resistance and can inhibit learning, but opportunities for reflection can occur if the needs and desires of participants are taken into account.

Ideas about reflection and learning

Despite the diversity of the literature on reflection and reflective practice in education, there are themes common to most frameworks. This commonality probably arises from shared roots in Deweyian philosophy. The first theme is that of reflection as a means of examining experience. A simple example is in the Kolb-Lewin learning cycle where it is one stage of a four step process of concrete experience, reflective observation, abstract conceptualizing and active experimentation (Kolb 1984). While Kolb says little about the nature of the reflective observation stage and seems to take reflection as self-evident, he locates it as having a key role in learning from experience.

The second theme in the reflection literature is a focus on re-examining experience to notice tensions and contradictions. Experience is not taken for granted. Situations in which individuals are content with what they are doing may be less fruitful for reflection than those in which they are aware of matters unresolved. Examining such experience is regarded as an important place for exploration, as a way of prompting understanding and of throwing up dilemmas to be examined. Indeed, the literature on reflection is characterized by a focus on situations in which learners 'explore "a state of perplexity, hesitation, doubt" (Dewey 1933), "inner discomforts" (Brookfield 1987), "disorienting dilemmas" (Mezirow 1990). Uncertainties, discrepancies and dissatisfactions are said to precipitate reflection and are central to any notion of reflection' (Boud and Walker 1998).

Third, while it may occur unprompted, reflection is taken in the literature to be a conscious, volitional process. It involves an act of working with experience in order to learn something from it. Although it may be seen as an active process, this does not imply that it is necessarily susceptible to simple intervention or instrumental approaches. The literature is replete with authors urging practitioners not to make crude interventions under the guise of promoting reflection, and subsequent bemoaning of ways in which this has been inappropriately enacted. The volition and desire of the learner is a strong theme, but the mobilization of learners is frequently frustrated by the context in which reflection is encouraged (Boud and Walker 1998). One feature of the context of formal education that is frequently identified as inhibiting learning (Sumsion and Fleet 1996; Stewart and Richardson

2000) is that of student assessment. Contradictions between the acknowledgement of personal uncertainty and lack of knowledge required in reflection with the need for assessment products which position students as confident knowers subject to the judgement of others, have been seen to inhibit reflection.

Most important of all in the educational literature, reflection is frequently regarded as an act of the individual which, while it might be facilitated by taking place in a group setting or on a one-to-one basis, is essentially about individual learners extracting meaning from their own experience. Even when it takes place with others, it does so in order that the individual can benefit from the diverse perspectives of others, as in debriefing group activities. This can allow the individual to realize that others do not necessarily share their own point of view and thus prompt further reflection on their own experience.

Alongside the commonalities in discussions of reflection, there are many variations in the ways in which it is conceptualized. Different authors vary in the emphasis they give to reflection-in-action, reflection-on-action and reflection in anticipation of action. Some indeed question the value of talking about reflection-in-action (Eraut 1995). There is also variation in the extent to which reflection is embedded in a theory of learning or a theory of facilitating learning. Finally, some authors ignore the role of feelings and emotions in reflection and implicitly regard it as a cognitive process, while others give these a central role.

Views from the workplace[1]

Unlike formal courses that may use a reflection strategy as part of some deliberate intervention to promote learning, reflective ideas are not commonplace in workplaces even those in which learning vocabulary is used, such as educational institutions or enterprises with explicit organizational learning strategies. Reflection, in a conventional sense, is more likely to be seen as accompanying a break from routine or something perhaps needed to puzzle through a difficult problem. There is relatively little research on everyday learning as viewed by workers. As part of a recent research study on the theme of 'uncovering learning at work' four work groups were studied in detail. The employer was a large public organization involved in vocational education and training and two of the four work groups were of teachers. Observations were made, interviews conducted and meetings held with them over a two-year period. The overall goal was to examine informal learning in the workplace and to consider the implications of this for the ways in which learning can be enhanced at work. The following vignettes highlighting particular incidents are taken from this study. The incidents were selected because reference to them recurred throughout the study and they represent issues that were the focus of extended discussion with participants. They are used here to provide a base of experience through which to view some theoretical ideas about reflection.

The journey home

Just before the formal start to a meeting between one of the work groups and the research team, two very experienced vocational teachers related a discussion they had as they drove home the previous evening. It was about their difficulties in working with a new group of students from backgrounds quite unlike any they had previously encountered. Their hour-long drive had been occupied with trying to understand how to cope with the new situation they faced. They were at a loss about what to do, as their normal strategies did not seem to work with the new students. Their discussion spilled over into the research meeting, as it was obviously something that greatly exercised them. They were not expecting the 'educational experts' present to offer a solution. Rather, they were presenting their dilemma as a challenge they faced at work. Later, during the formal part of the meeting, the pair was adamant when asked that they were not learning from each other, they were simply having a conversation!

This incident is typical of many situations in workplaces. A problem arises for which an obvious solution cannot be found. However, the problem is such that it cannot be passed on to someone else as it relates directly to the expertise of those experiencing it and no one else can reasonably be expected to deal with it.

The particular setting was only mentioned incidentally in discussion. It is characterized as significant for a number of reasons. It takes place on a long journey of about an hour that provides time without intrusion of other activities. It is a setting that prompts conversation about what is on one's mind about events shared by the other person. The act of driving and being a passenger provide a neutral informal focus away from a deliberate conversation which one or other of the parties has chosen to initiate. In this case, being friends as well as colleagues doing the same kind of work, conditions for interaction and reciprocal communication as peers were present without being contrived. The question arises of whether so much time would have been allocated to reflection in any other setting. Our observations of the workplace suggest this would have been almost impossible as workplaces are not conducive physically to extended discussions and it would have broken the norms of the workplace to take such a period of time out from 'productive' activities. However, in the study we noticed how participants referred to the 'spaces' they used for conversation. These often involved taking refreshments, such as in a lunch room, and they acted as hybrid spaces that were neither working nor social, but constituted a varying combination of the two (Solomon *et al.* forthcoming).

The journey acted as a kind of debriefing after work. The intensification of reflection during a car journey produces an occasion for reflection. In a car, social norms make it permissible to both talk and not talk. They also create a space that is clearly marked out as informal as it is normally unacceptable to deliberately schedule 'serious business' when one of the parties is partially distracted by the need to concentrate on driving. Nevertheless, the driver, during routine parts of the trip, is available to think and converse freely.

Learning despite staff development

A second example involved a member of another workgroup of professionals involved in outreach work. As part of a discussion about workplace learning, some members of the group referred critically to an activity common in the organization – a staff development day. This is an occasion during which employees from different units meet to examine particular issues. In this organization it is typically arranged on a state-wide basis by a disciplinary grouping or staff development centre.

After others had made critical remarks about the value of such meetings when there is so much work of one's own to do one of them remarked:

> It's usually run as a meeting where they give us information, and we've got the opportunity to ask questions. But one of the biggest values of it is that during the breaks, we network furiously. And it's amazing what you can pick up in terms of new ideas or what's been tried and hasn't worked, when you've been thinking about trying the same thing. And you can modify it or adjust it because you've learnt from their experience just listening to them.

Another reported, 'If it's formalized, you just get another meeting', implying that someone else's agenda was being followed, not their own. While comments were made about the lack of opportunities in sessions to do what one wanted the staff development day was of benefit for what was not on the program. That is, it allowed those involved in similar kinds of work to network with each other, and sometimes permitted intense reflective discussion among those with common interests of a kind that did not occur in the planned sessions.

Reflective activities are often attempted to be scheduled as part of training activities, but the level of engagement and interaction is often far less than that which spontaneously occurs when the formal event creates informal spaces for learning. The incident described illustrates how an activity designed for one purpose – perceived here to be that of passing on knowledge of new developments – can be used to meet other needs, to meet and share what one wishes. The day allowed spaces for reflection to be created by participants even though they were subordinated to the main agenda and not explicitly acknowledge as part of the event.

I can't allow myself to be a learner here

In interviews and discussions with participants there were numerous examples where the tension between being identified as a learner when being a worker was mentioned (Boud and Solomon 2003). One person with a management position summarized it as follows:

> Well I do [learn] but I wouldn't present myself as a learner because that would suggest that you didn't know what you were doing.

Another, who was a part-time teacher, described it as follows:

> ... when I've got students around me, I don't seem like I'm learning ... I'm the one with the knowledge that's being passed over. I've got the experience. But when I'm in the presence of [colleagues] ... I'm on the other side of the

situation where I'm the learner. But when the students have got me and I'm in control ... I don't think of it as 'I am the learner'.

A member of another work group employed part-time used the metaphor of a learner-driver:

> I think sometimes when we say the word learning, you think of someone driving a car, 'L' plates ... You kind of think they haven't been in the job for too long ...

Not surprisingly, identification of oneself as a learner makes it problematic to simultaneously portray oneself as a competent worker.

In these cases identity as an effective worker overshadowed other competing identities, for example, as someone who does not know, or as a person who has much to learn. The researchers did not believe that these work groups untypically constrained learning because members reported many examples of ways that learning was facilitated by the conditions in which they worked. The normal processes of everyday work and the need for acceptance as a colleague who could contribute to the tasks positioned workers into being 'non-learners'. The effect is greater at some times than at others. For example, in the example of the part-time teacher the demands of coping with a group of students were so great that thinking of oneself as a learner, or indeed considering reflecting in their presence, was almost inconceivable.

If we know so much about reflection, why aren't we doing it?

The final example involved members of the research team and occurred in their workplace – the university. As adult educators and indeed as academic advocates of the practice (Boud 2001) we discussed the possibility of keeping a personal learning journal as part of the project and each agreed to keep one. A few months later when reviewing the situation we discovered that none of us had done so. We had engaged in a number of practices that involved standing aside from our immediate tasks, such as examining our own meetings, but we did not adopt the formalism of an explicit reflective activity such as a learning journal (Solomon *et al.* 2001).

Nevertheless, we did turn our working experiences in the research project into an object of reflection. The naming of our work practices as learning experiences signalled the beginning of a shift. It led to a brief consideration of what devices could be used to facilitate this learning. But the initial choice of keeping a learning journal as such a device was not taken up. The reason for this is that this, in itself, did not provide enough impetus to sustain the activity. It was an additional task that was an end in itself. It was not a performance directly linked to our more pressing project needs, such as finalizing the complex contractual details and negotiating our entry into work sites. Nor was it a performance that was connected to the accountabilities related to our organizational responsibilities as researchers and educators. No doubt as a reflexive practice the learning journal could have facilitated our individual learning. Yet the learning journal, as a text without an audience or an obvious and immediate link to the research or our organizational goals, was an activity that could be easily overlooked in our already overloaded working lives.

However, professional matters intervened. As researchers, one of our required work performances is participation in international academic and professional communities and as the focus of the research was relevant, the research team agreed to use the chance to present two papers as an opportunity to explore the research practices involved in collaborative projects. The papers gave the team a shared objective – a common instrumental focus that would work towards both individual and organizational goals. We gave ourselves a project within the project – to reflect on our collaborative process, not for its own sake, but to theorize it for conference papers, thus providing a focus and motivation for investigating our work practices as learning ones. The writing of conference papers became an integral part of our work schedules. This meant that the taking up of reflexive devices that focused on our learning was no longer seen as superfluous. Indeed we allocated time during our project planning meetings to 'work' on our learning with a focus on the writing of the papers.

Writing conference papers, as a legitimate professional 'performance', provided not only an opportunity to formally consider ourselves as workplace learners, but also located these performances within an acceptable discourse (Solomon *et al.* 2001).

We were unable to reflect using a strategy with which we were familiar (that is, keeping a learning journal) because of the demands of work. We therefore deployed other constraints as positive influences to pursue similar ends. That is, we used the pressures of performativity to enable reflection to occur that was more legitimate. The team noticed that the strategy they ended up using was in effect instrumental, rather being consciously instrumental from the start, and also that it was not one imposed by others. These are both features that distinguish reflection in this context from that typically promoted in courses.

Issues arising from the vignettes

There are many observations about workplace learning that can be made from these examples. However, if the examples are examined from the point of view of reflection at work it is possible to identify some key issues. The most important of these is that the nature of work, and the ways in which it is perceived by those engaging in it, influence opportunities for and conceptions of reflection. However, this is an influence, not a determination. Within this we can also see some important threads. These are the need for an appropriate occasion for reflection to occur and the location of reflection as part of workgroup practice. Other issues include resistance that occurs when formalities of work intrude into spaces for reflection, and the paradox of reflection both needing to be legitimized as part of work while simultaneously being rejected if it is a formal expectation.

Finding an occasion of reflection

In our transcripts we did not identify examples of work group members choosing to set up an explicit time for reflection or similar activities. The domain of work was characterized by a task orientation in which priorities of the organization provided the legitimation for planned activities and other activities occurred below the level of explicit scrutiny. To choose to reflect can seem self-indulgent or an excessive formalization of what is perceived to be an essential act. Excuses need to be made for it and opportunities taken as part of other everyday activities – the drive home, over tea or coffee. It works as part of something else, not as an activity in its own right.

There are limits to the individualized view of reflection commonly represented in the literature. Reflection may be an individual or group activity, not necessarily framed only by individual concerns. While it is possible to read an individual perspective into many of the accounts, a stronger characterization comes from the shared perspective of work. Reflection occurred with a peer (in the car journey), with other workers (on the staff development day) or as part of a common workplace project (in writing conference papers). The context of work was important throughout and framed the nature of the activities in which people engaged and the opportunities taken.

Perceiving oneself as 'off-the-job' can be important for reflection. That is, disengagement 'off-line' whether that be at the place of work or separate from it. It appears to be important that the immediate demands of production be absent in the moment, that is, there is no task-related agenda requiring attention. However, being 'on-the-job' can create different kinds of opportunities as the example of writing conference papers illustrates. The occasion of reflection was reconceptualized as an engagement in a different but legitimate part of the job that provided more immediate satisfaction.

Our study points to the paradoxical nature of occasions of reflection. Both performativity – in the case of needing the impetus of writing papers – and the absence of performativity – away from the immediate demands of work – can prompt reflection. Formalizing it as an expected activity can inhibit it, but the absence of formalization does not necessarily foster it. There is a risk in formalizing the informal. Formal elements of tasks can inhibit informal interaction in otherwise task-driven workers as can be seen in the example of the reaction to the staff development day. Staff cannot be expected to be any less task-driven at an event organized by the institution in which they work than in their everyday job.

This illustrates the dilemma for those who wish to intervene. We need to recognize that both formality and informality are needed for reflection, and that we cannot readily prise these features apart. As in the study of informality and formality in learning by Colley *et al.* (2003), we need to accept that any consideration of reflection needs to acknowledge both and be conscious of how they interact.

All formal activities have informal elements that may support or undermine them. Similarly, some elements of formality may be needed to make informal activities work well.

Reflection and informal practices

A feature in the data from the workgroups was the presence of two worlds of work. One was the normal public world of the organization in which work tasks were undertaken, institutional policies followed and expected outcomes realized. This was the world that was formally documented and recognized as legitimate by managers and workers. Various formal workplace learning practices – training courses, staff development events – were acknowledged and undertaken. Alongside this was the informal world experienced on a day-to-day basis by all those who worked in the organization. This was represented in everyday 'chat' (conversations between peers) and informal practices (having tea, meeting colleagues, travelling to work). This was not simply a social world apart from work, but was an intrinsic part of it. The two worlds coexisted. They interpenetrated each other and created spaces that were neither clearly in one or the other. Chat sometimes was about leisure activities, but most of that we could discern was about work. Much reflection took place through chat. Social activities and work overlapped. Conversations moved between the social and the work related from moment to moment (Solomon *et al.* forthcoming).

Such chat between colleagues is an important transitional space and site for reflection. It is a kind of collective processing of what is occurring at work. It is a way of making sense of one's experiences through describing one's own experiences to others and gaining perspective on one's own through their stories. It is exactly what is referred to in the literature on reflection as 'returning to experience' (Boud *et al.* 1985). That is, a recapturing of one's experience of events through description. It is interesting to note, however, that the model of learning from experience from which this term is taken has two subsequent elements that constitute the reflection process: attending to feelings and re-evaluation of experience. Both could be seen in our data, but attending to feelings was not a strong feature, perhaps because this requires a more intimate setting away from the presence of researchers and is seen as less legitimate to report in interviews.

Throughout our study we observed numerous ways in which participants resisted moves to formalize the informal. This ranged from denial that they were learning anything from each other (in the car trip), to exploiting the formal staff development day for their own ends, to avoiding the label of learner and rejecting our own prescriptions from the world of formal education. Occasions of reflection were overwhelmingly informal, but they could be seen as taking place close to the intersections of what Habermas refers to as the life world and the system sphere of work and learning. Nonetheless, there was strong resistance to seeing reflection as part of the system world.

Part of the original design of the research project was a stage in which some of the practices identified through the study would be developed as formal interventions to 'improve' learning at work. This idea was abandoned at an early point once it became clear that the richness of learning we identified could be compromised by attempting to move it into the system world of the organization. Welton (1995) has argued for the importance of adult educators protecting the life world from such intrusions. Our study gave evidence of the reasons for this.

Where does this leave the notion of reflection in the context of work?

A naïve view would suggest that finding space for reflection at work is simply a matter of scheduling time away from the immediate pressures of production in an environment conducive to review of one's experience. While there may be occasions on which this is possible, our analysis troubles this view. We have seen here that reflection occurs frequently through chat, in the midst of work activities, with others. The challenge of finding an occasion for reflection is closely linked with the dynamics of work. It involves the point of intersection between the system world of the organization and the life world of the members of the organization. It requires recognition of the spaces in between these two worlds in which new possibilities can be considered. And it requires finding identities for workers that fit the complexities of the environment in which they operate.

Creating capacity for reflection at work involves the legitimizing of the third space between conventional polarities. That is, between the life world and the system world, the formal and the informal, the structured and the emergent. There are some parallels here between promoting reflection and what the organizational learning practitioners talk of as knowledge creation. Nonaka and his colleagues (Nonaka *et al.* 2001) used the Japanese term *ba* as a context in which knowledge is shared, created and utilized and suggest that the generation and regeneration of *ba* in workplaces is key to creating organizational knowledge. The elaboration of *ba* may be fruitful for considerations of reflection in work.

Knowledge from the literature on reflection can be used, but it must be read with the experience of work and organizations in mind. The present project reinforces concerns from education that reflection should not be introduced as a formal learning intervention. The idea that human resource development practitioners run programs to inject reflection activities into workplaces is problematic. It is not unlike the practice of getting students to fill in a reflection checklist after a clinical placement. While not necessarily worthless, it betrays a limited and limiting view of the phenomenon of reflection at work.

It is not a simple matter of someone organizing time and space for reflection to occur. The formal strategy of having reflection times in workplaces is as contrived and as artificial as it is to schedule time for physical activity in offices. There may be a few organizations in which this would fit with the culture, but these would be rare. Time for reflection may be at least as worthwhile as time for exercise, but to create occasions in which a designated group interrupts whatever they are doing to engage in it sets it apart from normal work, when it is part of it. A more fruitful direction may be to identify what gets in the way of reflection within any given setting and find ways of removing the constraints. Reflection can be structured, but it needs to be done in ways sensitive to how people talk about learning at work and to the performance expectations of normal workflow.

Reflection at work can still be seen as a volitional act, but circumstances frame it. The exigencies of work and daily life create spaces (the long drive home together, the coffee break in the workshop) that would not be deliberately structured for reflection. What is needed is the taking up of reflection as a part of workplace discourse to legitimize it and to enable work to be organized to permit it to flourish.

The vignettes discussed in this chapter also draw us strongly to the importance of how learning and reflection are discursively constructed. In some circumstances we cannot think of ourselves as engaging in such activities, while other people observing us might find these entirely appropriate ways of identifying what it is that we do. Like learning, reflection is frequently not part of the language we use to describe what we are doing even when we might subsequently reinterpret our activities as reflective ones. Again, like learning, there will be occasions on which it would be fruitful to identify our activities as reflection – so we can draw upon the repertoire of resources the literature on reflection offers – and other occasions when to do so would be overly contrived.

Finally, the idea of creating space for reflection at work should not be taken literally. Sometimes it involves a physical space (a place to make tea and chat); sometimes it involves time out of work activities. It may mean finding spaces within work processes that enable disengagement and re-engagement for brief periods. Most important of all, creating space for reflection is a metaphor for renewal and development. By having it as part of the agenda for working life we are reminded that for ourselves and for our organization there are important things beyond the present task.

Note

1 Workplace is used here to refer to any setting in which work takes place, whether paid or unpaid, intellectual or manual, public or private. Similarly, 'worker' is used as a term to describe anyone who engages in work, of whatever kind, at whatever evel of responsibility.

References

Boud, D. (2001) 'Using journal writing to enhance reflective practice', in L.M. English, and M.A. Gillen (eds) *Promoting Journal Writing in Adult Education*, New Directions in Adult and Continuing Education No. 90, San Francisco: Jossey-Bass, 9–18.

Boud, D., Keogh, R. and Walker, D. (1985) 'Promoting reflection in learning: a model', in D. Boud, R. Keogh and D. Walker (eds) *Reflection: Turning Experience into Learning*, London: Kogan Page, 18–40.

Boud, D. and Solomon, N. (2003) 'I don't think I am a learner': acts of naming learners at work', *Journal of Workplace Learning*, 15: 7–8.

Boud, D. and Walker, D. (1998) 'Promoting reflection in professional courses: the challenge of context', *Studies in Higher Education*, 23, 2: 191–206.

Brookfield, S.D. (1987) *Developing Critical Thinkers: Challenging Adults to Explore Alternative Ways of Thinking and Acting*, San Francisco: Jossey-Bass.

Brookfield, S.D. (1995) *Becoming a Critically Reflective Teacher*, San Francisco: Jossey-Bass.

Colley, H., Hodkinson, P. and Malcolm, J. (2003) *Informality and Formality in Learning*, London: Learning and Skills Research Centre.

Cruikshank, D., Kennedy, J., Williams, E., Holton, J. and Fay, D. (1981) 'Evaluation of reflective teaching outcomes', *Journal of Educational Research*, 75, 1: 26–32.

Dewey, J. (1933) *How We Think: A Restatement of the Relation of Reflective Thinking to the Educative Process*, Lexington, MA: D.C. Heath.

Eraut, M. (1995) 'Schön shock: a case for re-framing reflection-in-action', *Teachers and Teaching*, 1, 1: 9–22.

Kolb, D.A. (1984) *Experiential Learning: Experience as a Source of Learning and Development*, Englewood Cliffs, NJ: Prentice-Hall.

Mezirow, J. (1990) *Fostering Critical Reflection in Adulthood: A Guide to Transformative and Emancipatory Learning*, San Francisco: Jossey-Bass.

Moon, J.A. (1999) *Reflection in Learning and Professional Development Theory and Practice*, London: Kogan Page.

Nonaka, I., Toyama, R. and Byosière, P. (2001) 'A theory of organizational knowledge creation: understanding the dynamic process of creating knowledge', in M. Dierkes, A. Berthoin Antal, T. Child and I. Nonaka (eds) *Handbook of Organizational Learning and Knowledge*, Oxford: Oxford University Press: 491–517.

Schön, D.A. (1983) *The Reflective Practitioner*, London: Temple Smith.

Schön, D.A. (1987) *Educating the Reflective Practitioner: Towards a new Design for Teaching and Learning in the Professions*, San Francisco: Jossey-Bass.

Solomon, N., Boud, D., Leontios, M. and Staron, M. (2001) 'Researchers are learners too: collaboration in research on workplace learning', *Journal of Workplace Learning*, 13, 7: 274–81.

Solomon, N., Boud, D. and Rooney, D. (forthcoming) 'The in-between: exposing everyday learning at work', *International Journal of Lifelong Education*.

Stewart, S. and Richardson, B. (2000) 'Reflection and its place in the curriculum on an undergraduate course: should it be assessed?', *Assessment and Evaluation in Higher Education*, 25, 4: 369–80.

Sumsion, J. and Fleet, A. (1996) 'Reflection: can we assess it? Should we assess it?', *Assessment and Evaluation in Higher Education*, 21, 2: 121–30.

Welton, M. (ed.) (1995) *In Defense of the Lifeworld: Critical Perspectives on Adult Learning*, Albany, NY: State University of New York Press.

14 Discursive practices at work

Constituting the reflective learner

Claus Elmholdt and Svend Brinkmann

Much of the literature on workplace learning sees reflection as an ability belonging to human subjects as individual learners, in principle detachable from social practices. We believe that this notion of the reflective learner has certain serious shortcomings, and that a more adequate analysis needs to understand the reflective learner as part of, and created by, discursive practices, that is how people act, interact, and speak in everyday social realities. In this chapter, then, our focus is on the question of how reflective learners are constituted in discursive practices at work. How do discursive practices work to constitute reflective learners? This chapter throws light on the question of productive reflection and learning at work, attempting to transcend an individualistic view of self-reflection by presenting reflection at work as a collective, contextualised and pragmatic activity. This chapter raises the question: what do discursive practices of reflection produce? We argue that the answer to this is reflective subjects.

We will trace the notion of reflective learning historically, and show how it has become embedded within contemporary practices and discourses on workplace learning making reflective learning an imperative for most employees. Today, employees should be adaptable, flexible, willing and able to reflect and to learn. Contemporary learning discourse applies to those who work and learn in contemporary organizations. Following Hacking (1995), we refer to this as the looping-effect of human kinds. Inspired by Michel Foucault, we wish to indicate that theoretical discourses have practical effects.

In short, the chapter aims at questioning rather than celebrating ideas of productive reflection and learning at work. We identify two preconceptions in much of the literature on individual and organizational learning and suggest two alternative conceptions. The first is the reflective subject as an ontological foundation for learning as distinct from the reflective subject as constituted in reflective practices. The second is the idea of reflective learning as 'good for all', on the one hand, and reflective learning as situated in power relations, on the other. The focus of the chapter is primarily critical, but we conclude with a more constructive outline of possible scenarios for the reflective learner of the future.

The notion of reflection at work

We presume that people have always learned at work but that the specific character of workplace learning has altered remarkably in relation to changing societal and organizational structures. In particular, the role of reflection has changed significantly from the workshops of mediaeval times, through the bureaucratic organizations of industrial society, towards the post-bureaucratic organizations of the knowledge society. The self-reflective life-long learner is a relatively new idea informed by contemporary discourses on workplace learning. These discourses have successfully brought together arguments pointing to the need for employees to be capable of adapting to changing societal conditions, on the one hand, with humanistic arguments that stress self-development and self-actualization, on the other.

The craftsmen of mediaeval Western societies banded together in guilds. They valued tradition-bound professional knowledge, and insisted on apprenticeship as an appropriate educational form to hand down expertise from one generation to the next. Guilds and apprenticeships ensured social recognition, security, and stability (Black 1984). The principal learning mechanisms of apprenticeship have been identified as observational and model learning, guided participation and rehearsal of skills (Elmholdt 2004). Learning was related to a gradual taking over of tasks that were meaningful in the local community of practice.

In order to understand the role of reflection within traditional apprenticeship education, it is useful to distinguish between two types of reflection. First, reflection directed inwards at the self and separated from immediate action. In what follows, we refer to this as self-reflection. Second, reflection directed outwards at the ongoing situation in which somebody is acting. The former kind of reflection, which is often referred to as reflexivity or meta-reflection, played a minor role in traditional apprenticeship, but has come to play a major role in shaping the late-modern subject and employee (Rose 1999). The latter kind of reflection, identified by Schön (1987) as reflection-in-action, can be seen as integral in situations of ongoing action, and aims at solving a concrete problem at hand. Reflection-in-action 'serves to reshape what we are doing while we are doing it' (Schön 1987: 26). With reflection-in-action, Schön manages to merge thinking and acting conceptually, thus developing a notion that seems able to comprehend the kind of reflection inherent in traditional apprenticeship.

With the industrial revolution of the eighteenth and nineteenth centuries, the manufacturing of goods moved from craft production towards industrial production in huge factories organised by the hierarchical division of labour. The goal of the industrial worker's learning was to know as little as necessary in order to fulfil simple tasks efficiently at the assembly line (Jarvis *et al.* 2003: 131). With scientific management Taylor introduced time and motion studies in order to optimise the performance of tasks and simplify the jobs to such an extent that workers could be trained to perform a specialised sequence of motions in a single optimal way. Workers were expected to know only what they needed in order to complete the simple tasks they were given, while a few highly skilled workers could be used as managers. There are some similarities between traditional apprenticeships and training for industrial work. In both cases the body of knowledge was largely given, and the level of mastery was transparent and attainable. One dissimilarity is seen in the fact that the craftsman's level of mastery was skilled manufacturing of highly *complex* trade products, whereas the industrial worker's level of mastery was performance of *simple* repetitive tasks.

With the emergence of what is called the post-industrial society, the innovation economy, or the knowledge society (Stehr 1994), the role of reflection in workplace learning has changed towards a focus on self-reflection. Physical exertion, manual dexterity, and endurance of industrial work have gradually been displaced by knowledge work requiring attentiveness and an ability to reflectively analyse problems and make decisions (Stehr 1994). A fundamental characteristic of the new innovation economy is a market-driven demand for flexibility and change. This has involved a changed valorization of self-reflection in workplace learning. The potential for flexibility and change in self-reflective learning, which was viewed as unnecessary or even harmful in medieval guilds and industrial production plants, has become centrally important in the post-bureaucratic organizations of the knowledge society.

Reflection in contemporary perspectives on workplace learning

The dominance of self-reflection in contemporary learning discourse is strikingly illustrated by the post-modern re-emergence of the notion of apprenticeship (Kvale 2003) in the form of a life-long apprenticeship without hope of ever attaining mastery, as argued by Rikowski (1999). What has to be mastered constantly changes, and so the processes of learning and reflection become more important than the content of what has to be learned. Recent post-modern versions of apprenticeship focus on identity aspects of learning. Learning is seen as participation involving changing to become a different person (Lave and Wenger 1991). This underlines the shift to a more (self)-reflective form of apprenticeship in which the body of knowledge is never given and the level of mastery therefore never attainable. Apprenticeship learning in its new guise is mobile, flexible, and adaptable. It may therefore not be accidental that it is now finding a distinct revival in theories on workplace learning since it well suits the needs of a contemporary knowledge society (Edwards 2003). However, it also emphasises the collective unity of working and learning in local communities of practice, which might serve as small islands of resistance against overarching individualistic learning discourses of flexibility and change demanded by the market (Kvale 2003).

Today, self-reflective learning is largely assumed to be a good thing, sometimes contrasted with non-reflective learning, which is, explicitly or implicitly, understood as less valuable, if not outright oppressive and harmful. Several conceptual pairs differentiate self-reflective from non-reflective forms of learning, for example, non-reflective/reflective learning (Jarvis *et al.* 2003), and single-loop/double-loop learning (Argyris and Schön 1974).

Non-reflective learning is 'the process of accepting what is being presented and memorizing or repeating it' (Jarvis *et al.* 2003: 70). Reflective learning on the other hand involves thinking *critically* about the situation (ibid.: 70). Reflective learning is identified with a potential for change, as it questions key variables instead of just accepting and repeating a given body of knowledge, like non-reflective learning does. Reflective learning is understood as the outcome of a process of critical thinking, detached from immediate action and directed inwards at the self, using one's own identity as a measure for creating meaning. Taking a humanistic approach to adult education, Jarvis and others promote self-development and self-actualization through critical thinking. However, the liberating potential of reflective learning might turn out to be dubious when inscribed in contemporary discourses on workplace learning, if reflective learning merely comes to function as an instrument for adaptation to society's increasing demands for flexibility (Contu and Willmott 2003).

Perhaps the most influential pair of organizational learning concepts is the notion of single-loop and double-loop learning. In the repetitive single-loop '... we learn to maintain the field of constancy by learning to design actions that satisfy existing governing variables', whereas in the critical, creative, and innovative double-loop 'we learn to change the field of constancy itself' (Argyris and Schön 1974: 19). Single-loop learning, related to reflection-*in*-action, is deemed 'appropriate for routine and repetitive issues – it helps get the job done'. Double-loop learning, related to reflection-*on*-action, 'is more relevant for the complex non-programmable issues – it assures that there will be another day in the future of the organization' (Argyris 1992: 9). Such formulations make it clear that the kind of self-reflection found in double-loop learning is in high demand because of its potential to secure the organization's survival and competitive advantage.

Another recent development in organizational learning theory is the concept of the learning organization (Senge 1990; Marquardt 1996), which explicitly conflates humanistic ideals of individual liberation through self-development and self-actualization, with the liberal markets' increasing demands for flexibility and change. This is clearly illustrated by Senge's euphoric definition of the learning organization as a place:

> where people continually expand their capacity to create the results they truly desire, where new and expansive patterns of thinking are nurtured, where collective aspiration is set free, and where people are continually learning how to learn together.
>
> (Senge 1990: 3)

Reflective learning is held to be an innate, authentic capacity and desire of the individual worker. So, the self-reflective learner is seen as a pre-given ontological foundation for the learning organization. The individual's capacity to learn is treated as a natural resource that needs to be set free and nurtured by the right management in order to accomplish the twin goals of individual self-development and increasing organizational competitiveness. A shared interest in learning between the individual and the organization is tacitly taken for granted.

In this section, we have sought to demonstrate how contemporary perspectives on workplace learning largely take the self-reflective subject for granted as an ontological foundation for learning, and assume that self-reflective learning is automatically a good thing. Three reasons for giving importance to self-reflective learning were identified in the literature. First, self-reflective learning is potentially a liberating mechanism for accomplishing the humanistic ideals of self-development and self-actualization. Second, self-reflective learning is a strategic answer to consumer society's increasing demand for flexibility and change. Third, and most remarkably, is the trend towards a conflation of humanistic and liberal motives, found for instance in the literature on the learning organization and in the extensive discourse on lifelong learning. While this was originally initiated to emancipate the worker, today it has turned into a possibly threatening demand (Alheit and Dausien 2002). Contu and Wilmott also note the confluence of liberal and humanistic motives in the literature on workplace learning. They argue that despite the emancipatory focus of self-reflective learning, certain governing variables, such as those leading the individual to serve rather than to subvert the organization, remain unexamined (Contu *et al.* 2003: 936).

The reflective subject in discursive practice theory

In much of Western history, the individual subject was the unquestioned starting-point for social, political and psychological analyses, including the analysis of learning processes. What is sometimes referred to as 'the philosophy of the subject', notably articulated in the seventeenth century by René Descartes, was taken for granted in Western culture and in the human sciences. The subject was positioned as an ontologically primary and primitive category, able to understand and master the outer world through individual reflective processes. Genuinely valuable learning was thus often conceptualised as the kind of individual self-reflection that transforms pure experience into genuine knowledge. We do not, it was often presupposed, really learn in our everyday mode of functioning. Learning occurs only in those rare situations, particularly in schools, where we critically and self-reflectively are able to transform messy experience into pure knowledge.

Until the 1960s there were few theoretical alternatives to 'the philosophy of the subject'. However, from the middle of the twentieth century, a general decentering of the subject took place across the human and social sciences. The individual subject was no longer seen as ontologically primary, but rather as an effect of something else; socio-economic structures in some versions of Marxism; impersonal linguistic structures in some versions of structuralism; or an effect of power relations in Michel Foucault's work. It is the latter which will concern us here. Foucault's objective was '… to create a history of the different modes by which, in our culture, human beings are made subjects' (Foucault 1994: 326). We are not simply subjects as such, according to Foucault; we are *made* subjects through processes of subjugation and subjectification. If we have become self-reflective subjects today, it is because we have been made such subjects. In contemporary flexible capitalism (Sennett 1998), we are constantly encouraged to take a reflexive stance towards ourselves, which is not a natural capacity, but something historically new that we have been trained and disciplined into doing.

Foucault argues that modern subjectivity emerged from new structures, practices and techniques of subject regulation and control. Surveillance strategies in prisons, clinics, schools and factories, and confessional practices in different therapeutic settings have been particularly important in constituting modern forms of subjectivity. The modern reflexive self has been established through discursive practices of self-examination, self-observation and self-analysis. Such practices are invested in power relations, and this forms the basis for Foucault's claim that power is productive and normalizing rather than purely repressive. Power produces subjectivities, above all, self-reflective subjectivities. We are thus not ontologically self-reflective subjects in a universal way. We become these when we participate in reflective practices, i.e. practices that are informed by intellectual technologies that force us to take reflexive stances towards ourselves. As psychologist Arne Poulsen says: 'Psychological reflectivity is a historical and societal product' (Poulsen 1995: 5), a product brought into being by '[t]he advent of psychology, helping people to acquire an increasingly mediated relation to their daily activities' (ibid.: 17).

A key site for the production of self-reflective subjectivities is the workplace. This insight has been the springboard for various Foucauldian analyses of modern and post-modern organizations (see McKinlay and Starkey 1998). A Foucauldian approach relocates the focus away from pre-given subjects and from the economic basis and class interests as in Marxism, and towards the concrete social and material technologies of the workplace. According to Foucault, one is not made a subject through language and discourse alone, as some social constructionists tend to argue, but in real material practices (Foucault 1984). It is for this reason that we prefer to talk about 'discursive practices' in this chapter. This is intended to underscore the material and technological aspects of the production of subjectivities in addition to the symbolic and linguistic aspects.

Surveillance technologies work in today's organizations to constitute the subject. In post-bureaucratic organizations, surveillance often takes the shape of *self-surveillance* or *participatory* surveillance (Driver 2002) rather than managerial surveillance. The increased use of networking and teamwork enables managers to renounce their authority. However, this does not mean that power and control disappear, but that they change to participatory self-control. A therapeutic and confessional ethos is also widespread in current work discourse, for example in job advertisements, where companies routinely 'seek employees who wish to develop professionally *and personally*'. The relationship between organization and employee is no longer just represented in a formal language of rights and privileges, but has been supplemented by the soft, intimate language of personal relations. The discourse on the learning organization at times approaches religious imagery stressing such ideals as the 'transcendent values of love, wonder, humility and compassion' (Kofman and Senge quoted in Driver 2002: 38).

In contemporary organizations, the self has become a commodity to work on, and the self's reflective relationship to itself has become a therapeutic relationship with the goal of flexibility, autonomy, self-direction and learning (Edwards 2003). For example, 'We seek to provide opportunities for personal growth and professional development. To achieve this we actively encourage learning and development in all our people' (from the website of British Telecommunications). Current forms of power work through appeals to personal growth, learning and development, all of which have become techniques of management in contemporary organizations.

Post-bureaucratic organizational forms especially work to constitute hyperreflexive subjectivities. In such organizations, which often lack visible controls and authorities, individuals are continually asked to reflexively monitor themselves and their relations to others. Gradually employees become more engaged in different kinds of emotional labour at work, where they are asked to be specific *kinds* of people, rather than mere professionals with skills independent of their private personalities. This is seen not just in traditional emotion-laden fields such as nursing, but also in production sectors where modern forms of teamwork require that people have 'soft' interpersonal skills and sensitivities (Elmholdt 2004). The organizational shift from hierarchies to networks and teamwork demands increasing self-reflectivity. This is not just liberating, but also threatens to stifle personal character and makes it hard to work out a coherent structure in one's life narrative (Sennett 1998). If everything has to be reflexively negotiated, learned and re-learned as shifting situations demand in our short-term economic interests, then how do we pursue those long-term goals that seem important in our lives?

In this section we have sought to illustrate the fruitfulness of seeing the reflective subject as constituted by reflective practices in current workplaces along the lines suggested by Foucault rather than sticking to 'the philosophy of the subject', where the reflective subject is seen as the ontological foundation for learning. The latter view still has a strong hold today, however, since it matches the reigning neo-liberal ethos that conceives of learning as a project of individual self-development very well (Contu *et al.* 2003). By questioning the ontological universality of the subject as reflective learner, we become able to ask *in what ways* – good and bad – subjectivity is produced in today's workplaces and post-bureaucratic organizations.

Looping-effects

One of the ways in which reflective learners are constituted today is by the way different theoretical formulations of social practices infuse the workplaces. Everyday practice and theoretical reflection do not exist completely detached in different, unrelated sites. Rather, theories, and notably learning theories, are able to affect social practices. It is fruitful to understand ideas and theories, not as abstractions existing only in the minds and books of researchers, but as intellectual technologies, 'ways of applying thought in and to the world, making the world thinkable and practicable in certain ways' (Rose 1992: 352). Theories and ideas are closely conn-ected to ways of understanding and acting. In today's knowledge society, humans are affected in diverse ways by the theories formulated by researchers in the human and social sciences.

Philosopher of science Ian Hacking, who is explicitly inspired by Foucault, has thoroughly analysed what he calls 'the looping effect of human kinds' (Hacking 1995). Human kinds indicate 'kinds of people, their behaviour, their condition, kinds of action, kinds of temperament or tendency, kinds of emotion, and kinds of experience' (ibid.: 351–2). In contrast to natural kinds, such as chemical compounds, human kinds are affected by our theorizing about them. They are affected by how they are described and classified, and they interact with their classifications, sometimes affecting the classifications themselves. When new descriptions become available, then there are new things for humans to be and do.

Previously, the self-reflective learner was analysed as human kind; a recent historical invention created by organizations' need for a flexible and adaptable workforce. This human kind belongs in a larger learning discourse, which includes such notions as the learning organization and life-long learning. Looping effects come about when employees become construed, or willingly construe themselves, according to the ideas of life-long learning in learning organizations originally formulated by researchers and practitioners. In this way, theoretical formulations and practical life tune in to one another. If one expresses an unwillingness to learn and develop on the job today, one will be looked at with suspicion. Learning has become a *sine qua non*.

An all-pervasive learning discourse has given us a world of new opportunities. Nevertheless, it has also brought with it new dangers, as we have seen. As Sennett (1998) argues, becoming a life-long learner in a learning organization, continually asked to reflect and negotiate, might entail life-long rootlessness and insecurity concerning one's identity. What we learn from Foucault is that subjects do not intentionally decide how to understand and construe themselves from some standpoint outside existing practices and power relations. Rather, we are made subjects in concrete practices invested in power relations. So most often we quite unreflectively take over canonical and practice-embedded ways of understanding ourselves as we participate in different communities of practice.

Conclusion: scenarios for the reflective learner

We have argued that a universal conception of the individual reflective subject as a pre-given instrument for workplace learning is inadequate. We have suggested instead that the reflective subject should be understood as historically and contextually constituted by discursive practices at work, embedded in a cultural context of increasing demands for reflection, flexibility and change. Moreover, we identified the notion of the reflective subject as the ontological foundation for learning with a 'philosophy of the subject', which continues to dominate Western thought. We suggested an alternative, decentred notion of the reflective subject inspired by Foucault's analyses, and Hacking's description of the looping effect of human kinds. It is not only inadequate, but also potentially harmful, to understand self-reflective learning as a natural ability to be mobilised by the right social technologies and managerial initiatives. The danger is that if self-reflection is construed as a natural endowment to be set free, it may become impossible to ask how cultural discourses themselves contribute to constitute the reflective learner, thereby impeding the possibility for cultural critique.

In conclusion, we wish to outline some possible future scenarios for the reflective learner at work. Although we have focused on a relatively homogenous and individualistic 'learning discourse', there are other, contradictory streams in the water, as in the collective contributions to this volume. The following scenarios should therefore be seen as analytic tools that are hopefully good to think with, but it should be borne in mind that none of them tell the whole truth.

The hegemony of the reflective subject

The discourse of self-reflective learning has almost become hegemonic, threatening to corrode character and people's devotion to long-term goals (Sennett 1998). Contemporary discourses on workplace learning conflate humanistic motives of self-development and self-actualization with the consumer market's motives of increased competitiveness, thereby impeding cultural critique of the imperative to learn and reflect continuously. The reflective learning discourse may produce self-deceptive subjects. As Michaela Driver notes: 'Once someone has accepted the principle that the organizational purpose reflects their own, then criticizing this purpose in any manner becomes increasingly difficult, and the element of self-deception becomes a strong force for control and conformity' (Driver 2002: 40). In the worst case scenario it can be predicted that the individualistic discourse on reflective learning will not be superseded until companies begin to lose money when employees, stressed by the learning imperative, become too sick to work.

The reflective subject as critical subject

A more positive scenario depicts the reflective subject as a critical subject. When people learn to reflect and evaluate possibilities, they may put these acquired skills to use in criticizing debilitating conditions, including those conditions under which their self-reflective skills were cultivated and disciplined. A version of this argument was put forward by Foucault, who thought 'that new human capacities may come into existence as effects of forms of domination, only to then become bases of resistance to those same forms of domination' (Patton 1998: 71). If the reflective subject is to become a critical subject, then certain standards of evaluation concerning how reflection should be put to use, are required. One way ahead will be to focus on the ethical aspects of human reflection, thus enabling employees to reflect together about how to build an 'ethical community of practice' (see Nyhan, this volume). The reflective subject is thus not necessarily constrained by the imperative to learn and reflect, but can possibly use the reflective capacities to do good. In the same vein, one can view our critical comments in the present chapter as possible only because of a high degree of reflection and self-reflection.

The reinvention of bureaucracies

Foucault once remarked that 'the ethico-political choice we have to make every day is to determine which is the main danger' (Foucault 1984: 343). A main danger in industrial society's bureaucratic organizations was exploitation through a unique focus on non-reflective learning of repetitious routine work. The humanistic discourse pointing to the need for meaningful work, creativity, responsibility and self-reflexivity, was a legitimate liberating response to the dominance of hierarchic-bureaucratic organizational structures. Today, these structures no longer represent the main danger. Rather, the post-bureaucracies themselves, networking and team-working, with their soft, personalised forms of power, have become a main danger, as du Gay argues in his defence of bureaucracy against the new managerialism (du Gay 2000). Reinventing bureaucracies with a human face could be one way to achieve more transparent forms of power and more visible hierarchies and tasks, thus creating conditions that support people's characters and long-term goals to a higher degree.

The learning subject in communities of practice

With an exclusive focus on individual self-reflection, existing well-functioning structures in workplaces risk being disrupted. It should not be overlooked that in order for self-reflective or double-loop learning to take place in an adequate manner, it must rest on a persistent reproduction of stable forms of practice in the workplace. Non-reflective learning is also a necessary form of learning, and forgetting this can have dire consequences for organizations that uniquely promote innovative learning at the expense of reproductive learning (Elmholdt 2004). Furthermore, the unity of working and learning in local communities of practice may serve as small islands of resistance against the intense disciplining to flexibility and change demanded by the market (Kvale 2003). A focus on developing and nourishing local communities of practice can substantiate the claim that subjectivity is contextually constituted, and yet overcome the claim that certain overarching discourses (e.g. the learning discourse) determine how local practices are organised.

References

Alheit, P. and Dausien, B. (2002) 'The 'double face' of lifelong learning: two analytical perspectives on a 'silent revolution', *Studies in the Education of Adults*, 34: 3–20.

Argyris, C. (1992) *On Organisational Learning*, Oxford: Blackwell.

Argyris, C. and Schön, D.A. (1974) *Theory in Practice: Increasing Professional Effectiveness*, San Fransisco: Jossey-Bass.

Black, A. (1984) *Guilds and Civil Society in European Political Thought from the Twelfth Century to Present*, Ithaca, NY: Cornell University Press.

Contu, A., Grey, C. and Örtenblad, A. (2003) 'Against learning', *Human Relations*, 56: 931–52.

Contu, A. and Willmott, H. (2003) 'Re-embedding situatedness: the importance of power relations in learning theory', *Organisation Science*, 14, 3: 283–96.

Driver, M. (2002) 'The learning organisation: Foucauldian gloom or Utopian sunshine?', *Human Relations*, 55: 33–53.

du Gay, P. (2000) *In Praise of Bureaucracy: Weber – Organisation – Ethics*, London: Sage.

Edwards, R. (2003) 'Ordering subjects: actor-networks and intellectual technologies in lifelong learning', *Studies in the Education of Adults*, 35: 54–67.

Elmholdt, C. (2004) *Landscapes of Learning in the ICT World – Learning as an Aspect of Change in Social Practice*, Aarhus: Department of Psychology, University of Aarhus.

Foucault, M. (1984) 'On the genealogy of ethics: an overview of work in progress', in P. Rabinow (ed.) *The Foucault Reader*, London: Penguin.

Foucault, M. (1994) 'The subject and power', in J.D. Faubion (ed.) *Power: Essential Works of Michel Foucault*, vol. 3, London: Penguin.

Hacking, I. (1995) 'The looping effect of human kinds', in D. Sperber, D. Premack and A. J. Premack (eds) *Causal Cognition: A Multidisciplinary Debate*, Oxford: Clarendon Press.

Jarvis, P., Halford, J. and Griffin, C. (2003) *The Theory and Practice of Learning*, London: Kogan Page.

Kvale, S. (2003) 'En premoderne mesterlære i et postmoderne samfund?' (Premodern apprenticeship in a postmodern society), in K. Nielsen and S. Kvale (eds) *Praktikkens læringslandskab: Om at lære gennem arbejde* (A landscape of learning in practice: learning through work), Copenhagen: Akademisk Forlag.

Lave, J. and Wenger, E. (1991) *Situated Learning: Legitimate Peripheral Participation*, Cambridge: Cambridge University Press.

Marquardt, M. (1996) *Building the Learning Organisation*, New York: McGraw-Hill.

McKinlay, A. and Starkey, K. (1998) *Foucault, Management and Organisation Theory*, London: Sage.

Patton, P. (1998) 'Foucault's subject of power', in J. Moss (ed.) *The Later Foucault: Politics and Philosophy*, London: Sage

Poulsen, A. (1995) 'Modernity and the upgrading of psychological reflectivity', *Journal of Phenomenological Psychology*, 26: 1–20.

Rikowski, G. (1999) 'Nietzche, Marx and mastery: the learning unto death', in P. Ainley and H. Rainbird (eds) *Apprenticeship: Toward a new Paradigm for Learning*, London: Kogan Page.

Rose, N. (1992) 'Engineering the human soul: analyzing psychological expertise', *Science in Context*, 5: 351–69.

Rose, N. (1999) *Governing the Soul: The Shaping of the Private Self*, 2nd edn, London: Free Association Books.

Schön, D.A. (1987) *Educating the Reflective Practitioner: Towards a new Design for Teaching and Learning in the Professions*, San Francisco: Jossey-Bass.

Senge, P.M. (1990) *The Fifth Discipline: The Art and Practice of the Learning Organization*, London: Century Business.

Sennett, R. (1998) *The Corrosion of Character: The Personal Consequences of Working the new Capitalism*, New York: W.W. Norton and Company.

Stehr, N. (1994) *Knowledge Society*, London: Sage.

15 Feminist challenges to mainstream leadership through collective reflection and narrative

Silvia Gherardi and Barbara Poggio

Productive reflection is a methodology for opening spaces within organizations to re-think goals of how employees are formed. It can become a way of unlocking vital creative forces in those in work and at the same time engage organizational members in the creation of new identities, meanings and communities inside work, while bringing together changes in work practice. It envisages a new form of engagement where the psychological contract between an organization and its members is negotiated and re-negotiated.

In this chapter we situate productive reflection within a post-structuralist feminist perspective. We first deconstruct the managerial ideology that sustains the traditional intervention in the field of organizational learning. Later we illustrate the meaning of feminist methodology to show how experiential learning and collective reflection in groups can be rooted in feminist practices. We illustrate, by means of an example of a workshop on leadership, how productive reflection may be inscribed within an organizational training course for women managers. We discuss how this methodology may empower both women and men in the workplace and lead to small but significant changes in organizational culture and leadership practices.

We show how feminism as a situated practice can enhance understanding of what counts as leadership and how groups of women middle managers in bureaucratic organizations came to use an opportunity for productive reflection in their workplace. Having set the theoretical framework that inspired the design of the workshop, we illustrate its methodology and focus on narrative as the way to elicit experiential learning while elaborating it within the group. The collective reflection thus produced has the power to better understand individual experience, but at the same time put under scrutiny organizational practices and look for changes in actual behaviours or beliefs.

The concern to challenge what constitutes knowledge, whose knowledge is valued and how it is legitimated is central to post-structuralist feminist studies. A feminist politics of knowledge inside organizations aims to prompt open-ended learning processes and practices that can encourage reflection and value experiential learning. Feminist approaches to leadership initially examined and criticized ways in which social studies of women and men, and of sex and gender more broadly, have been androcentric. Its aim was to develop an explicitly feminist positioning alongside feminist transformations of scholarship in the field. This approach contains the basis for a broader critique of how 'knowledge' is constructed, in so far as it depends on the possibility of representing a reality that does not exist outside its representation in language. It is through language that researchers constitute the object of their knowing, their subjectivities as knowers, and what counts as knowledge as distinct from what is 'not knowledge', that is, the 'other' in the discourse, the silenced term. The precarious position of any claim to knowledge opens spaces for a distinctive feminist 'politics of knowledge' which points to the local operation of power and the crucial role of discourse in sustaining hegemonic power. Gender in fact has to do not only with bodies, and power, but also with the politics of knowledge, and therefore with organizations as containers of different bodies and sexualities, as arenas of power/knowledge, and with organization theory as a system of knowledge representation (Gherardi 2003).

Organizational learning as a managerial technique

Organizational learning is theoretically constructed as a managerial technique that acts as a discourse of disciplining which contains specific biases. There is a normative bias, a bias towards systematic and purposeful learning and a bias towards improvement. These biases are comprised of a specific structuring of power/knowledge that sustains and perpetuates them as a discourse of power, even though other discourse positions are possible. Feminist reconception of knowing and active reflecting is one of these other positions. Foucault's concept of discipline has been usefully applied in postmodern analyses of power/knowledge relations (e.g. Alvesson 1993; Deetz 1996; Townley 1993) in the area of knowledge-firms or in the construction of the subjectivity of knowledge-workers. In addition the literature on organizational learning has been identified as colluding with the 'ruling courts' which govern organizations (Coopey 1995) and to employ ideologically a discourse of democracy and liberation (Snell and Chak 1998). The exploitative ethos of many organizational learning discourses has been underlined by postmodern scholars (Boje 1994).

We summarize here a set of premises implicit in organizational learning theorization, which have been developed previously (Gherardi 1999) in order to highlight how they sustain a discourse which disciplines behaviour:

* *Organizational learning is always ameliorative and disinterested.* The alleged universality, neutrality and transparency of knowledge presume that humanity is its beneficiary, thereby neglecting power in the structuration of organizational knowledge. What is deemed worth learning has already been selected: only those in power learn the right things.
* *Organizational learning is intentional.* If learning resembles a process of appropriation and capitalization of something external, or of a known product, then the ways in which it is appropriated/produced can be specified and normatively sustained.

- *Organizational learning distorts.* Managerial requirements of work groups are that they 'learn' and transfer the knowledge thus acquired to organizational structures, and that it leads to an improvement in performance. The use of power in transferring knowledge is silenced. Organizational learning is conceived of as grounded on free transfer, on transparency, on voluntariness, and on the chain of authority, rather than in the murky depths of micro-conflictuality, micro-negotiation, and the systematic and more or less deliberate distortion/extortion of knowledge.
- *Organizational learning presumes change but not its understanding.* Learning proposes a change in the behaviour – actual or potential – of individuals or groups, or perhaps also a cognitive change. It does not necessarily require individuals to understand the logic that has led to a change (Child and Markoczy 1993). This amounts to saying that if some change is manifest, then a learning process has taken place, but also that change does not require any learning. The problem thus arises of how empirical evidence can be collected to demonstrate the relationship between change and learning.

The positive connotations associated with the word learning induce an *a priori* assumption of what needs to be empirically demonstrated. Learning, as the founding myth of the community of organizational learning scholars, obscures the myopia of learning from experience (Levinthal and March 1993) and silences the challenges to what counts as knowledge and how to sustain it that come from other communities.

Feminist claims to knowledge

It is impossible to use the word feminism in the singular, since there are many contemporary feminist positions. Our use of the singular here points to those post-structuralist feminist scholars working toward 'post-epistemological' conceptions of knowledge (Belenky *et al.* 1986; Barad 2003; Haraway 1991; Hawkesworth 1989). We outline in this chapter only the main claims to what counts as knowledge so as to highlight the set of theoretical assumptions that sustain our methodological framework for the workshop illustrated later:

- *Knowledge is engaged and self-critical participation in making the world in which we live.* Accounts of the world do not depend on a logic of discovery of inner laws, but on the subject's active construction and their power-based social relation in conversation with the world. Feminist studies are concerned with different ways in which knowers interact with the objects of knowledge, since knowing is embedded within specific ways of engaging the world, starting from the concrete particularity of bodies and social relations;
- *Knowledge is situated in historical practices.* Feminist studies take up a participatory stance toward knowing, reflecting, and learning. This is to say that feminist scholars conceive of 'knowing' as concretely situated in conversation among people, other organisms, machines and artefacts. That is, more interactional

than representational. They suggest that changes in knowledge are as much changes in practices as changes in beliefs and mental representations.

- *Knowledge is a multidimensional relationship between knowers and the known.* Knowing is neither external to knowers' thoughts, culture and interests, nor merely instrumental to representations. Feminist scholars construe knowledge as multidimensional relationships between knowers and knowns, rather than as a simple relation of representation and correspondence. Moreover such relationships are intertwined with complex relations among knowers as well as with the object of knowledge. This is an attempt to hold knowers accountable for what they do, and to make explicit to whom and to what they need to be accountable.

- *Knowledge is transformative and futural.* Feminists hope to have an impact on important aspects of the way the world is and to have an effect upon the culture of the practices they study in order to legitimate the changes they hope to effect. Therefore, they claim an alternative to the supposed neutrality and detachment of knowing, as portrayed in science, in favour of a reflective and self-critical participation in the production of knowledge.

One may reasonably object that we have overstated feminist claims to knowledge. Other traditions, as philosophy of science (Rouse 2002) or social studies of science and technology (Pickering 1992) emphasize that knowledge is situated within forms of life and is the outcome of interests, ideologies and the contingencies of social negotiations. However, our aim is not to deny a convergence with other positions in a critique of knowledge. It is to stress that feminism is a practice which aims to make knowledge more accountable, to contextualize questions of evidence and of what counts as evidence, and to show how evidential relations are produced in practice.

Fostering productive reflection on gendered leadership and its alternatives

Analysis of the organizational literature on leadership shows that it is constructed to maintain and reinforce hegemonic masculinity. Images of male sexual functions and of patriarchal paternalism are implicit in the way leaders' action is described. One observes a seductive game, modulated in the masculine, which seduces those who identify with the stereotypes of maleness and virility (Calás and Smircich 1991). Nevertheless, leadership in early organization studies has already been portrayed 'in a different voice' by Mary Parker Follet (1941). At the times of Taylor and the growing fortune of scientific management, she was writing of leadership in terms of participation, of power *with*, instead of power *over*, of the subject as a relational being. While scientific management became hegemonic, Parker Follet's contribution was marginalized and one of the reasons of its marginalization (Baritono 2001) was the 'different voice' heard through her message.

Leadership has long been a topic of central concern for organizational studies. However, attention has now shifted from the role and function of the leader to the practice of leadership, from a personalized and functionalist view to one that emphasizes the reflective and constructive dimension of leadership action and the process of the collective creation of meaning and consensus (Alvesson 1992). Among the emergent features of this new view of leadership there are some we believe to be of particular significance. The first is the growing awareness that leadership is not a personality trait or a natural gift or something that 'one does' by relating to others (Manz and Sims 1991). Thus, a prescriptive approach intended principally to identify categories and models (the charismatic leader, the participative leader, the transactional leader, and so on) was replaced by an experiential one in which the focus is on experiences of leadership, the relational dynamics involved in leadership, its motivational and emotional features, and especially its relationship with power.

The interweaving of leadership and power, and its gendered representation, has been emphasized by several authors (Kets de Vries 1993; Sievers 1996). It has been historically constructed as a male sub-text by producing images of leadership difficult to relate to femaleness (Alvesson and Billing 1997) or by describing styles and models of female leadership which stand as alternatives to traditional leadership (Hegelsen 1990; Loden 1985). Therefore our aim in designing an organizational intervention inspired by feminist claims to knowledge was to challenge the strong male ideology inscribed in mainstream literature.

A feminist critique leads to a redefinition of the concept of leadership and of training practices. Approaches more oriented to relationality, empowerment and reflexivity have appeared and courses and methods designed to re-elaborate personal and professional experience, create sense and consensus collectively, develop creativity and foster autonomy and self-awareness. The aim is no longer to teach efficacious leadership styles or models, nor to define skills to be developed; rather, it is to stimulate individual and collective reflection, for example, through the sharing of leadership stories recounted by workshop participants.

Recent years have seen the growth of a large body of literature on the use of *self case studies* and narratives in learning workshops (Griffith 1999). In these workshops, accounts of work experiences written by participants are discussed and analysed, and often rewritten. Alternatively, accounts are exchanged to foster 'dialogic conversation'. This can generate multiple points of view, stimulate analysis and deconstruct assumptions of canonical stories. It encourages the creation of alternative plots, thereby fostering a learning process that is at once dialogic, divergent, emergent and collaborative (Abma 2003).

We now describe a specific instance of a narrative workshop based on some of the assumptions just outlined. A large local authority organization in northern Italy asked us to design their in-house training for women managers to improve female leadership. Four cycles of the workshop were conducted; each attended by 12 women managers. Each workshop was divided into five daylong sessions designed around themes representing a core of leadership: rationality, control, decision-making, strategic thinking and their opposite. Each day was organized as follows:

- A short literary narrative for each theme was read to participants. This was intended to stimulate memory of similar experiences to prompt recall of situations connected with the day's topic.

- Following the narrative stimulus, each participant was invited to write a short story centred on the topic of the day relating to her professional experience.
- Narratives were exchanged and analysed in smaller groups. Following this they were discussed by the whole group in order to identify shared and divergent experiences in the organization, and underlying cultural models.

Cutting across the themes were a number of issues intrinsic to the topic of leadership. These included: leadership's relationship with power, recognition of its conflictual dimensions, the importance of learning to recognize and understand emotions connected with the exercise of authority in organizational contests and possibilities of individual or collective action for changing work situations.

The key component of the workshop was reflective learning, defined as 'a process which involves dialogue with others for improvement or transformation whilst recognizing the emotional, social and political context of the learner' (Brockbank *et al.* 2002: 75). Various writers have emphasized the need for reflective approaches to start from personal experience (Roberts 1981; Stanley and Wise 1983) and from self-awareness (Reinharz 1983; Held 1993) to question the traditional paradigms of 'objectivity' and 'detachment' that have supported the hegemony of maleness in the dominant models of knowing. Reflection and group analysis of situations in which the participants wielded authority in organizations furnish occasions for self-knowledge which involve not only the cognitive, cultural and affective dimensions of the individuals concerned but also the strategic and structural ones of the organization. The main assumption within productive reflection is that the group is a crucial learning resource because it enables different experiences to be shared and compared. And the means to foster reflective thought is indubitably narrative, owing to its ability to enhance retrospective glance and memory work.

An example of what is meant by retrospective thought and the methodology of memory work was provided on the first day of the workshop using the story of the stork told by Karen Blixen in *Out of Africa*. The story runs as follows. A man lived in a small house near a pond. One night he was woken up by a loud noise. He ran out of his house and in the darkness headed towards the pond, repeatedly tripping, falling and getting up again. Following the noise he found a leak in the pond wall, which he repaired and then went back to bed. When he looked out of the window the next morning, he saw that his footsteps had traced the outline of a stork on the ground. In this short story, the man looking out the window metaphorically represents 'retrospective glance'. His work of the night is finished, and it is only *a posteriori*, in the marks left on the ground, that he makes meaning of his movements, sees a pattern and shapes his experience. It is through recounting that the signs and traces of experience are pieced together and acquire complete meaning. The pattern of a life or an event emerges retrospectively when thought becomes reflective, when it turns onto itself to compose a narrative, to give shape to what was indistinct.

Besides the backward introspection that induces reflective thought to appropriate or re-appropriate personal history, of special importance in feminist methodology is 'memory work'. In the 1980s a group of German women published a collected volume which reconstructed, on the basis of individual experiences, the social processes that construct female sexuality (Haugh 1987). The methodology of memory work was then transferred to other contexts, for instance the socialization of women to academic work, or the therapeutic treatment of women victims of abuse. Put briefly, the expression 'memory work' refers to the process of recovering the historical-cultural self and gaining awareness of how it is interwoven with practical social relations. It looks at the self as a historical product, as an on-going trajectory, and as a cultural product (form of the discourse) and a social one (relational practice). It is based on the assumption that some change in the present can only be brought about if that past is subjected to 'dispassionate' and 'passionate' analysis.

Narrating is a way to re-appropriate experience, to 're-member' in the sense of reconstructing a 'dismembered' body (Brady 1990), and to gain new awareness. Narrating makes it possible to construct a memory and to retrieve something that would otherwise be lost. It is an opportunity for individuals to acquire collectively renewed projectuality and a more sophisticated ability to interpret and make sense of the events they encounter. In short, it is 'a practice of transformation, reflection, reconstruction, re-cognition and re-structuration of the self' (Gamelli 1995: 116).

The use of narrative methodology: an example

This section presents one aspect of our narrative workshop to illustrate the process leading to productive reflection. The subject (on the second day of the workshop) was the relationship between gender and leadership. The stimulus for reflection and narrative writing was a story entitled 'Fanta-Ghiro' taken from Italo Calvino's *Italian Folktales*, of which a summary follows.

A king had three daughters but no sons. The king was of a sickly disposition. One day a Turkish king declared war against his land, but the king was too ill to take command of his army. So his three daughters offered to take his place. The father at first refused, because commanding an army was not women's work. But then, given the seriousness of the situation, he agreed to send his eldest daughter, but on the condition that she dressed and behaved like a man. He warned her that if she started talking about women's things, his trusted squire would bring her straight home. The daughter left for the war, but during the sea voyage she saw a gaily-coloured fish and remarked that she wanted a ball gown in the same colours. So the squire took her straight back home. The same thing happened to the second daughter. During the voyage, when she saw the colourful sails of the fishing boats, she began talking about the fabrics she wanted to decorate her bedchamber. So the third daughter, Fanta-Ghiro, then set off to fight the war, even though she was still so small that her armour had to be padded before she could put it on. The sea voyage passed without incident, and the young princess went to parlay with the enemy king. The king was intrigued by the 'iron general' and set traps to see whether he was not really a woman. He took Fanta-Ghiro into the armoury and then into the garden, asking question to catch her out. Fanta-Ghiro passed all the tests until the king invited her to go for a swim. This forced her to find an immediate excuse to return home. But she left behind a letter explaining who she really was. The king, by now in love, followed Fanta-Ghiro and asked her to marry him. Peace was made, of course, and when Fanta-Ghiro's father died he left his kingdom to his son-in-law.

This story was particularly stimulating for the group, owing to various features that emerged from the written narratives and the plenary discussions. The first of these features concerned the symbolic order of gender apparent in the story, which the participants recognized as an organizational archetype (gender segregation) and a dilemma (whether to adopt male or female styles of behaviour) that all of them had encountered in their professional lives. Added to this was the fact that the plot of the story was substantially ambivalent. On the one hand, an unconventional figure of a woman was presented and valorized. On the other, the end of the story depicted a canonical scenario in which the conventional order was restored through matrimony and inheritance by the male offspring, thereby complying with one of the essential principles of narrative: the restoration of the violated order (Bruner 1990). The co-presence of these features elicited reactions ranging from admiration, through identification and frustration, to anger. It generated numerous stories that developed aspects and nuances of the relationship between gender and leadership as experienced by the women. Participants recounted experiences of discrimination, episodes of revenge and affirmation, introspective analyses of their relationships with leadership and power, and anecdotes about when they had to disguise themselves as men, or when they refused to do so.

The following is one of the stories produced:

That morning Allegra climbed the stairs to her office thinking that yet another of those days was about to begin. Tiredness due to work (positive) would be accompanied by the subtler, more insidious weariness (negative) that comes from fighting a losing battle.

Once again it was going to be the same old struggle, the one that since her promotion she had been fighting in a public organization still trapped in a formal, individualistic and – why not? – male mentality. Absorbed in her thoughts, Allegra turned the corner and ran into Dr Nero, her boss, who had always resented her promotion.

She tried to slip past him … too late! 'Allegra, good morning! I hope that today we can finally get that matter sorted out.'

'Right, that matter … for God's sake', thought Allegra.

The 'matter' concerned lessons on theory of organizations and old-style leadership that Nero based on his 20-year experience of leadership declined in the masculine.

As if leadership can be taught! And then, what leadership? As if there's a universal model of it!

'Remember that personnel management requires an iron fist!' Dr Nero's voice boomed in the background as Allegra remembered the altercation between them the previous day: 'You give too much importance to others, to personal aspects. You want to understand everything and everyone. Set value on differences! What rubbish. And then let me say, all that baloney that you think is so important: creating a climate, building a team. It's nothing but a waste of time, it's just women's stuff.'

The ringing of her mobile phone saved Allegra from her memories and from Dr Nero. She rushed into her office slamming the door behind her.

For a moment she teetered towards the idea that Dr Nero might be right, that there was no place for the emotions in work, no place for caring about others, for valuing differences. But then she shook her head, whispering 'But what sort of world would that be?' as she settled into her chair. 'No, I'm not the leader that Nero wants me to be, but what do I care? And then an iron fist would clash with my name!' she said to herself as she smiled and switched on her computer.

The story of Allegra is apparently an abstract and decontextualized story, for all its references to the narrator's personal and organizational experience. However, when set within the training context and shared with the group, it immediately assumed a situated character and an explicit organizational significance, eliciting shared reflection on individual experiences of leadership and on the leadership models of the organizations to which the participants belonged. The story discloses awareness that the female is constructed in the organization as the 'other' with respect to maleness still hegemonic in concrete and discursive practices. At the same time the story opened up a space for personal choice and for wondering about collective alternatives in thought and practice. The emphasis on the diversity of leadership styles between men and women, and the reference to valuing differences, prompted the group to reflect on an organizational culture doomed to double-bind situations in which women filling leadership roles are required to behave like men but without abandoning their femaleness.

Finally, the story highlighted that leadership is tied to a person's relationship with power, but being in a position of authority grants power to use it differently. But, how can this be done? The group elaborated a view of power as power *with others*, in a domain of relation, exchange, co-operation and responsibility where gender has citizenship. Not all women managers adopt a female style or all men a male one. The question of 'a gendered style' was criticized as a question badly framed, thus opening a space for reflecting on the partiality, openness and far-reaching possibilities for criticism and transformation of the dominant power relations.

To summarize, the following were the basic principles of the narrative workshop:

- A critical analysis of the historical context which produced a body of knowledge, i.e. leadership studies and within them a research of the voices and experiences that have been marginalized or excluded from the mainstream.
- Memory work as the practical engagement with personal and collective experiencing of leadership/followership.
- Writing of and listening to narratives of leadership themes grounded in the organizational culture.
- Opening of a discursive field for questioning the alternatives and confronting personal and collective choices.

The process of changing an organizational culture is neither easy nor fast, but in one session after the other we noted that participants were coming back to discussions they had had at their own workplace with their collaborators (mainly women). Small changes were introduced and attempts to find a practical application for the term 'participatory style' were supported by the awareness that within the managers an alternative model of leadership was looking for legitimation and had the support of the headquarters.

Unfortunately, we cannot say how great were the consequences of the lessons learned in the participants' work situations. Evaluation of the workshop through a questionnaire gave positive feedback, but this is not a good measure for estimating the changes introduced, rather it is a measure of participants' satisfaction. We are sure though that the workshop has had a strong impact in its symbolic value as a sign of the organizational commitment to gender citizenship.

How can our approach be applied in different contexts and what are the conditions in which such approach might be particularly appropriate? Based upon our experience in organizational development inspired by feminist reflective methodology it is the group of people which make the difference (their personal engagement in changing their workplace arrangements) together with the willingness of the organization to commit itself to the proposal of practical changes suggested by the group. In other words it is necessary for organizational culture to support a style of intervention that by its nature is critical of the status quo. Also, at the same time, it is necessary that when people are asked to engage themselves in a personal and organizational process of reflective learning, the psychological contract with the organization be in balance. Productive reflection cannot be another means for managerial exploitation.

Concluding remarks

The positive connotations of learning have legitimized it as the founding myth of a community of organizational scholars and have transformed it into a managerial technique for the control of workers and the reification of their expertise. Organizational learning, as a technique for extorting productive knowledge from those who create it, rests on several biases: the assumption that knowing is intentional, disinterested, always ameliorative and that learning presumes change. If 'reflective learning' is to avoid the fate of becoming another managerial technique, we have to learn the lesson and challenge what is the meaning of learning, knowing and reflecting.

Feminist reflective methodology argues for critical reflection on the politics of knowledge. Not only is feminism a concept, but it is a practice and as a practice it implies different ways of producing relevant knowledge and realizing ideas. Feminist claims to knowledge production can be summed up as: engaged and self-critical participation in the world we live in, knowing as transformative and futural, situated in the relationship among knowers and known. These principles can be put into practice and inform a methodology for enhancing workplace learning through critical reflection.

The outcome of feminist reflection in workplace learning is not a sudden revolutionary breakdown. It is a more modest and sound effort at making knowledge claims more accountable through a critical examination of how knowers are positioned in a network of human and non-human power arrangements and how the resulting 'author-ization' of knowledge constrains or enables people's lives.

Acknowledgements

We wish to thank all the participants to the workshop that gave us much insights and energy and our colleague Attila Bruni who worked with us in holding the workshop and commented on earlier versions of the paper.

References

Abma, T.A. (2003) 'Learning by telling: storytelling workshops as an organisational learning intervention', *Management Learning*, 34, 2: 221–40.

Alvesson, M. (1992) 'Leadership as social integrative action: a study of a computer consultancy company', *Organisation Studies*, 13, 2: 185–209.

Alvesson, M. (1993) *Cultural Perspectives on Organisations*, New York: Cambridge University Press.

Alvesson, M. and Billing, Y. (1997) *Understanding Gender and Organisations*, London: Sage.

Barad, K. (2003) 'Posthumanist performativity: toward an understanding of how matter comes to matter signs', *Journal of Women in Culture and Society*, 28, 3: 801–31.

Baritono, R. (2001) *La democrazia vissuta. Individualismo e pluralismo nel pensiero di Mary Parker Follett*, Torino: La Rosa.

Belenky, M., Clinchy, B. Goldberger, N. and Tarule, J. (1986) *Women's Ways of Knowing*, New York: Basic Books.

Blixen, K. (1937) *Den afrikanske Farm*, Copenhagen: Gyldendal (Engl. (1938) *Out of Africa*, London: Putnam).

Boje, D. (1994) 'Organisational storytelling: the struggles of premodern, modern and postmodern organisational learning discourses', *Management Learning* 25, 3: 433–61.

Brady, E.M. (1990) 'Redeemed from time: learning through autobiography', *Adult Education Quarterly*, 41, 1: 43–52.

Brockbank, A., McGill, I. and Beech, N. (2002) *Reflective Learning in Practice*, Aldershot: Gower.

Bruner, J.S. (1990) *Acts of meaning*, Cambridge: Harvard University Press.

Calás, M.B. and Smircich, L. (1991) 'Voicing seduction to silence leadership', *Organisation Studies*, 12, 24: 567–602.

Calvino, I. (ed.) (1956) *Fiabe italiane*, Torino: Einaudi (Engl. (1980) *Italian Folktales*, New York: Harcourt Brace Jovanovich).

Child, J. and Markoczy, L. (1993) 'Host-country managerial behaviour and learning in Chinese and Hungarian joint ventures', *Journal of Management Studies* 30, 4: 611–31.

Coopey, J. (1995) 'The learning organisation, power, politics and ideology', *Management Learning*, 26, 2: 193–213.

Deetz, S. (1996) 'Discursive formations, strategized subordination, and self-surveillance: an empirical case', in A. McKinlay and K. Starkey (eds) *Managing Foucault: A Reader*, London: Sage.

Gamelli, I. (1995) 'La conoscenza di sé e il pensiero introspettivo: la meditazione', in D. Demetrio (ed.) *Per una didattica dell'intelligenza. Il metodo autobiografico nello sviluppo cognitivo*, Milano: Franco Angeli, 113–23.

Gherardi, S. (1999) 'A symbolic approach to competence development', *Human Resource Development International: Enhancing Performance, Learning, and Integrity*, 2, 4: 313–34.

Gherardi, S. (2003) 'Feminist theory and organisational theory: a dialogue on new bases', in H. Knudsen and H. Tsoukas (eds) *The Oxford Handbook of Organisational Theory: Metatheoretical Perspectives*, New York: Oxford University Press.

Griffith, W. (1999) 'The reflecting team as an alternate case teaching model. A narrative, conversational approach', *Management Learning* 30, 3: 343–61.

Haraway, D. (1991) *Simians, Cyborgs, and Women: The Reinvention of Nature*, New York: Routledge.

Haugh, F. (ed.) (1987) *Female Sexualization: A Collective Work of Memory*, London: Verso.

Hawkesworth, M.E. (1989) 'Knowers, knowing, known: feminist theory and claims of truth', *Signs*, 14: 533–57.

Hegelsen, S. (1990) *The Female Advantage*, New York: Currency Doubleday.

Held, V. (1993) *Feminist Morality: Transforming Culture, Society and Politics*, Chicago: The University of Chicago Press.

Kets de Vries, M.F.R. (1993) *Leaders, Fools and Imposters*, San Francisco: Jossey-Bass.

Levinthal, D.A. and March, J.G. (1993) 'The myopia of learning', *Strategic Management Journal*, 14: 95–112.

Loden, M. (1985) *Feminine Leadership or How to Succeed in Business Without Being One of the Boys*, New York: Times Books.

Manz, C.C. and Sims, H.P. Jr. (1991) 'Super-leadership: beyond the myth of heroic leadership', *Organisational Dynamics*, 19: 18–35.

Parker Follett, M. (1941) 'Leader and expert', in H. Metcalf, and L.F. Urwick (eds) *Dynamic Administration: The collected Papers of Mary Parker Follett*, New York: Harper & Bros.

Pickering, A. (1992) *Science as Practice and Culture*, Chicago: University of Chicago Press.

Reinharz, S. (1983) 'Experiential analysis: a contribution to family research', in G. Bowles and R. Duelli Klein (eds) *Theories of Women's Studies*, London: Routledge and Kegan Paul.

Roberts, H. (ed.) (1981) *Doing Feminist Research*, London: Routledge and Kegan Paul.

Rouse, J. (2002) *How Scientific Practices Matter: Reclaiming Philosophical Naturalism*, Chicago: University of Chicago Press.

Sievers, B. (1996) 'Greek mythology as a means of organisational analysis. The battle at Larkfield', *Leadership and Organisational Development Journal*, 17, 6: 32–40.

Snell, R.S. and Chak, A.M.-K. (1998) 'The learning organisation: learning and empowerment for whom', *Management Learning*, 29, 3: 337–64.

Stanley, L. and Wise, S. (1983) 'Back into personal' or: our attempt to construct feminist research, in G. Bowles and R. Duelli Klein (eds) *Theories of Women's Studies*, London: Routledge and Kegan Paul.

Townley, B. (1993) 'Foucault, power/knowledge, and its relevance for human resource management', *Academy of Management Review*, 18, 3: 518–45.

16 Lessons and issues for practice and development

Peter Docherty, David Boud and Peter Cressey

Our point of departure with this volume is that reflection is an integral part of good work, a key to learning to improve production and to making life at work more satisfying. It is a necessary element in evaluation, sense-making, learning and decision-making processes in the workplace. Effective learning at the individual, group and organisational levels is achieved not through conventional programs but through acknowledging the learning potential of work and integrating learning activities in the workplace. An essential element in this learning is reflection in and on the work being carried out. This is what we term productive reflection. Productive reflection is a key to unlocking vital creative forces in employees (a new productive force) and at the same time a way of engaging workers in the creation of new identities, meanings and communities inside work (a new form of engagement), all of these are powerful intangible resources for the organisation. Productive reflection focuses the need to bring the thinking and active subject to the centre of work practices, to underline the importance of continuing learning and the necessity to prioritize personnel's quality of life issues if the organisation is to be sustainable in the long run. But, in order for reflection to achieve this position in working life today, it must be re-thought and re-contextualized so that it can fit more appropriately within group settings that have so far been insufficiently clearly named and acknowledged.

In this volume we have presented several of the key issues regarding the development of productive reflection in the workplace through a close examination of the ideas and concepts behind important perspectives on the issue, together with the analysis of specific contexts or cases in which special efforts have been made to create positive conditions for productive reflection. Given the complexity of the issues, the contributors are drawn from different professional backgrounds, educationalists, management scientists, psychologists, and sociologists. In this chapter we present our main lessons from our joint experiences under four heading: firstly, the nuancing of the concept of 'productive reflection', secondly the facilitation of productive reflection, thirdly, the tensions and balances involved in 'productive reflection' and fourthly, issues for further attention.

Nuancing the concept of 'productive reflection'

Our common point of departure was to address 'productive reflection' as collective reflection in the workplace. The distinctive interests and experience of individual contributors has helped to give a more detailed description of this concept. Earlier work has related reflection to professionals' thinking in action and development of skills and knowledge (Schön 1983), to experiential learning (Kolb 1984), and to adult and continuing education (Boud *et al.* 1985). The term 'collective' focuses the process of social interaction as distinct from aggregating individual cognitive processes. Thus Breidensjö and Huzzard, in adopting a union perspective in Chapter 12, conceptualize reflection as a means of 'contrasting and confronting experience with expectations through dialogue', where experience is experience of what employees have done in their work and how they have acted in a given context. This is part of an organizing process within a social collectivity or 'community of practice'. As such, it is part of a dynamic that has its own assumptions, institutionalizing tendencies and rules of belonging. Yet, these very same features of organizing that help enhance security and reduce uncertainty also have a constraining role. (We return to this in discussing tensions in section three of this chapter.)

On of the central points made throughout this volume is that 'making sense of one's work' is a critical issue for people in modern work organisations. This concerns finding meaning in one's work, a key factor for experiencing a sense of coherence, wellbeing and health at work (Antonovsky 1987). Elmholdt and Brinkmann point out in their discursive perspective on reflection in Chapter 14, that the modern humanistic discourse on reflection at work can merely be a camouflage for a dangerous form of control in which people are 'self-controlling' themselves in line with the old bureaucratic control models. They distinguish between two types of reflection: self-reflection directed inwards towards the self and separated from immediate action and reflection directed outwards at the ongoing situation in which somebody is acting. They give special weight to self-reflection as a potentially liberating mechanism for accomplishing the humanistic ideals of self-development and self-actualisation. It is also compatible with the current trend towards the conflation of humanistic and liberal motives found in the literature on learning organisations and lifelong learning, which may become a threatening demand on individuals for continuous learning.

An important temporal aspect addressed by Boud, and Elkjaer and Høyrup, is the separation of thought and action in reflection. Reflection is an assessment of how and why we have perceived, thought, felt and acted. Situations regarded as triggering reflection are states of perplexity, hesitation, doubt, ambiguity, equivocality or uncertainty. Other features of reflection processes that have been emphasized as important for its effectiveness are the productive use of differences and careful awareness of the elusiveness of reflection. The first point concerns the utilisation of the resources making up the collective that is reflecting. If possible the group should include all relevant stakeholders, competences and experience relevant to the issue under consideration and, in all events, the participants should be given the opportunity to make due contribution to the dialogue. Several authors pointed out that reflection is not to be treated as a formal learning intervention. While it can be structured, reflection can easily be eliminated by the rigid design of the context of reflection – thereby it is elusive. Its structuring must be done in ways sensitive to how people talk about learning at work and to the performance expectations of normal workflow. In addition to professional knowledge and experience, examples have been given regarding gender and national differences.

Nyhan argues in Chapter 11 that if reflection is to contribute to resolving the problem of meaning then it must include an ethical dimension. Genuine collaborative work requires the capacity for collective ethical reflection for everybody to find meaning and realize their goals. Ethics are essential if organisations are to achieve social and economic and personal excellence. Nyhan distinguishes here between 'external codes of practice' and 'community-of-practice'-based ethics. It is the latter that are essential – building ethical communities founded on internal convictions about the values of excellence and the practice of the virtues associated with these values. Ethical practices must be built from within organisations. Developing such a capacity for reflection is a holistic and prolonged 'living' of a practice. This capacity is acquired through sharing in and contributing to the excellence of the practice of one's community.

Reflection is relevant in most contexts. While earlier writers have focused on reflection in non-routine situations, Breidensjö and Huzzard suggest that reflection may well occur on routine actions on a regular basis and that 'reflection routines' might become an essential activity of a learning workplace union. Examples of non-routine actions were the radical changes presented in Chapters 7, 8 and 9. These were regarded by management as essential for the development, in some cases the survival, of the organisations concerned. Although learning should be an important component of or process parallel to such change processes, it is frequently very difficult to pay sufficient attention to the long-term concerns of learning when facing the short-term pressures of change. Thus, some of the examples given were 'curates' eggs' from the standpoint of reflection, i.e. the examples are good in parts. Other examples illustrated the development of relations, regarding participation in Chapter 5, communities of practice in Chapter 6 and dialogue in Chapters 8, 10 and 15.

What do the issues focused and the examples given tell us about conditions conducive to 'productive reflection' and their design? This question is addressed in the next section

Conditions facilitating, promoting and supporting productive reflection at work

In summing up his review of work on informal learning in Chapter 5, Ellström draws the conclusion that learning at work (like learning in formal educational settings) is a matter of design not evolution (Ellström 2001; Fenwick 2003; Shani and Docherty 2003). Design in this context means conscious, active decisions on measures to promote, facilitate and support reflection and learning. However, the issues of reflection and learning are often not formally allotted clear priority on the management agenda in many organisations and the prerequisites for these activities will in fact be steered by values, norms and practices that have simply evolved and are not given a thought. Stebbins *et al.* in Chapter 9 discuss the proactive measures for reflection and learning as learning mechanisms. These mechanisms may be cognitive, cultural, structural or procedural. Learning mechanisms are formalized strategies, policies, guidelines, management and reward systems, methods, tools and routines, allocations of resources and even the design of the physical facility and work spaces. Management's concern for the creation and maintenance of learning mechanisms in individual organizations may vary from total unawareness of their possible existence to ranking them a primary means of competition (De Geus 1992; Garvin 2000; Friedman *et al.* 2003; Shani and Docherty 2003). The contributors to this volume have addressed learning mechanisms in terms of culture, management systems, organisational structures, procedures and resources. The experiences reported are both positive and negative, i.e. have helped or hindered reflection.

Culture and reflection

Cultural or cognitive mechanisms provide or are the bearers of language, concepts, symbols, theories and values for thinking, reasoning and understanding learning issues. These mechanisms may be manifested in company value statements, strategy documents, management–union joint agreements, and the adoption of organizationally specific adaptations of management systems such as the balanced scorecard. The concepts, ideas and values incorporated in these mechanisms may originate from many sources: organisational, professional, national, or gender.

The two case studies presented in Chapters 7 and 9 clearly illustrate the impacts of the professional and organisational cultures. In PrimeOptics (Chapter 7) the organisation had a strong science/engineering culture that resulted in the project members giving low priority and little attention to human resource and work organization aspects of the organizational redesign. Their self-imposed timeframe for the project was cited as the reason for not evaluating current progress and alternative solutions, a feasible opportunity for reflection and learning. As a defence contractor the company had strong secrecy norms – information was only shared on a need-to-know basis. This norm clearly limited collective reflection and learning at work. In the second case, HPO, the health care provider (Chapter 9), top management felt it necessary to prioritize short-term goals of rapidly turning the business around and radically reducing costs. This entailed emphasizing the short-term at the expense of the long-term, static at the expense of dynamic efficiency and effectiveness. Thus learning and reflection were 'tailored' to that necessary to complete the project. Different learning mechanisms were designed to each stage of the project and were dismantled at on completion of the stage.

Nyhan's emphasis on ethics as a key value base in organisations has been cited earlier. Recent revelations of the absence of such a basic value foundation in parts of industry, commerce and the public sector have been a rude awakening for many people. The absence of 'community of practice'-based ethics has led politicians to strengthen code/rule-based ethics via new legislation, for example in the United States following the Enron and World Com cases.

Management systems and reflection

The cultural values and norms of an organisation are embedded in many of its practices. Key practices in management systems concern power, control, surveillance and leadership. In Chapter 6, Schenkel illustrated how the management system included formal routines for handling deviations/contingencies in production in a major construction project that determined the scope for collective reflection and learning available to different groups of engineers. Meeting quality and safety criteria set by external stakeholders meant most engineers abstaining from many learning opportunities through solving unexpected problems at work. The surveillance system was based on reinforcing dominant formal procedures at the expense of developing informal communities of practice in which reflection played a key role.

In Chapter 14, Elmholdt and Brinkmann raise the issue of self-surveillance or participatory surveillance, which in many situations is replacing management surveillance (Driver 2002). Growing complexity and the pressures of time cannot be handled adequately by communicating up and down the hierarchy. The devolution of authority to the shop floor in various forms of semiautonomous teams managed by objectives or targets, is becoming more common in Europe, even if it is still widespread in only a few countries (Benders *et al.* 1999). A current development in leading Swedish firms is the involvement of front-line personnel in development work. In the more advanced cases, the range of tasks handled by team members only stops short of marketing and legal matters (Shani and Docherty 2003). This includes emotional labour at work as the workers now shoulder responsibility for solving problems and reaching agreements with fellow team members, other teams along the line, suppliers and customers. These were all tasks previously conducted by supervisors or support departments prior to the teams. Thus new social as well as technical and administrative skills are required of the workers.

A key aspect of power in organizations is reflected in the relationship between management and personnel, i.e. participation practices. Cressey describes the development of employee participation in the post-war period in Chapter 5. The initial phase was characterized by the unions' focus on conditions of employment, especially security of employment and safety. This was basically achieved through representative bodies establishing rights through central negotiations and legislation. Participation took place at a distance from workplaces and the majority of union members. By the 1970s central representation was complemented by a trend of personnel representation in different problem-solving bodies within companies. Unions became more interested in conditions of work, such as work organization and competence development. Employers came to see the benefits of personnel participation. The latest developments, as noted above, have moved to direct participation, whereby many workers, in both industrial and service sectors, are both multi-skilled and shoulder broad responsibilities. In some countries and sectors this has meant the replacement of representative by direct participation, whereas in others the development of direct participation has been achieved in close co-operation with the unions to establish a dual solution of representative and direct participation. Breidensjö and Huzzard see a new potential role for the unions now as competent suppliers and guarantors of reflective practices at workplaces as an alternative to the doctrine of leanness. This may well engage underutilized capacities in the workforce, deploying them to add value.

The cases of PrimeOptics and HPO illustrate that participation is an issue that does not solely concern employees who will still have their jobs in the redesigned organization. The HPO case illustrated the need actively to plan for the future of those members of the organization whose employment will be terminated due to the changes in their organization. Many difficulties may be avoided by involving customers and other stakeholders. The PrimeOptics case illustrated the need for top management to be involved in the change process and not simply to be mailed a solution. In this case, the top manager missed opportunities for synergy and reflection at all management and employee levels. Thus the various taskforces had a restricted view of the internal environment and shifting priorities. Lack of dialogue up and down the hierarchy seriously limited productive reflection, learning and commitment to the strategic design. Management and the taskforce did not regard design work as iterative or that it should receive attention beyond the rather 'closed' taskforce membership.

In primarily addressing the shortcomings of male-dominated leadership in working life, Gherardi and Poggio point out that much of the current theorizing on organizational learning sustains a discourse that disciplines behaviour (Gherardi 1999). Departing from Mary Parker Follet's (1941) writing on leadership as exercising power *with*, instead of power *over*, co-workers, they focus on a view of leadership that emphasizes its reflective and constructive dimension in action and the process of collective creation of meaning and consensus.

They have used narrative-based intervention to fuel dialogue among women managers on themes representing the core of leadership, such as rationality and control, in order to challenge the strong male ideology inscribed in mainstream literature.

Structural mechanisms and reflection

Structural learning mechanisms may be organizational, technical or physical. The most common organizational forms are forums or arenas that provide legitimacy for reflection and the formal opportunity for a collective or group to meet and 'discuss things'. These may exist 'until further notice', such as work group meetings or continuous improvement group meetings, or be coupled to a specific assignment, such as a development project, a policy revision or a planning task. The formation of specific project groups may also be coupled to learning and collective reflection. Parallel learning structures are an organizational strategy for facilitating experiential learning for broad groups of personnel (see Chapter 9) (Bushe and Shani 1991).

Technical learning mechanisms are generally based on the use of information and communication technology. The Internet has given rise to virtual communities which are essential for many people in their daily work. Virtual networks are often more important to professionals than their social networks at their workplace – it is to them they turn with queries and problems (Teigland 2003). The Internet and organizational databases provide access to with full-text references, statistical data, links to important data sources, computer programmes for data analysis. These may be shared and worked on jointly by members of the collective.

The physical design of the workplace can be designed to support interaction between the members of an organization and collective reflection. Apart from formal meeting rooms there are the 'free areas' where coffee and meal breaks are held, places where one can sit informally, even with access to a whiteboard. Boud draws attention in Chapter 13 to where reflective dialogues occur in the work context, e.g. chatting in the car to and from work. (We get an association to Pettigrew's (1974) participant observation study of two departments competing to gain control of a firm's new computer centre. He participated in both groups' collective reflection/planning arenas: the football club changing room in the one case, and a local pub in the other).

The need for 'space for learning' was advanced by Nonaka and Konno (1998) based on a Japanese concept '*ba*' that is defined a context in which knowledge is shared, created, and utilized. Nonaka *et al.* (2001) maintain that *ba* does not necessarily mean a physical space. They suggest that it can be a physical space (e.g. an office space), a virtual space (e.g. a teleconference), a mental space (shared ideas) or any combination of these. A critical aspect of *ba* is space for interaction. As such *ba* is viewed as interaction between individuals, between individuals and the environment, and between individuals and information, but not necessarily the space itself. Fulop and Rifkin (1997: 46) have a similar concept of 'learning spaces' which occur 'when people in the organization communicate in certain reflective and "authentic" ways about information, experiences and feelings'. In their case learning spaces might conceivably involve joint reflection on decisions such as outsourcing, new technology and job redesign.

Procedural mechanisms and reflection

Procedural learning mechanisms concern the routines and methods that may be used to promote and support learning. As productive reflection concerns social interaction and communication, several of the contributions in the book concerned supporting dialogue in the collective. Bjerlöv and Docherty focused on the concepts of differentiation and decentration in conversations to promote the development of shared understanding in work group meetings. Stebbins *et al.* underlined the importance of a continual dialogue between project group members and the project stakeholders, be they senior management or customers who will use the interface being created by the project group in the form of a new product or a new service organization. The lack of dialogue up and down the hierarchy seriously limited productive reflection, learning and commitment to top management's strategic design. Not engaging management was just one example of the project group's avoidance of conflict, the discussion of differences, and the consideration of emotional and non-technical issues. These contributions emphasized the difficult, but often very necessary roles, to be played in these processes by in-house or external facilitators. The impact of facilitators on the dialogues and their outcomes naturally depend greatly on their roles, legitimacy, discretion and resources as well as professional competence and experience.

Two other contributions took examples, not of natural work groups, but of groups of managers and professionals in more formal educational settings in which the dialogues concerned their personal work life experiences. Berthoin Antal and Friedman address productive reflection in work contexts involving individuals from different national cultures involved in complex tasks. They underline that an interactive process of critical reflection lies at the core of 'intercultural competence'. It requires people to break out of their own cultural frameworks and expand the range of interpretations and behaviours they can call on. They coin the term 'negotiating reality' for the unique handling of each interaction and the solving of problems through observation, listening, experimentation, risk taking and active involvement with others. This does not, however, imply cultural neutrality, but ascribing equal importance and respect to all people (cf. Bjerlöv and Docherty).The goal of a 'negotiating reality' strategy is to maximize learning while not sacrificing long-term effectiveness. It is based on Argyris and Schön's (1974) model II values: valid information, free and informed choice, and internal commitment.

Gherardi and Poggio's approach to a gender perspective on 'productive reflection' is based on a critical stance to the mainstream work in organizational learning. They maintain that if 'reflective learning' is to avoid the fate of becoming another management technique then knowledge claims must be made more accountable through a critical examination of the position of 'knowers' in power arrangements and of how knowledge impacts on people's lives. They use a narrative intervention to create a dialogue to examine these issues. This entails a critical analysis of the historical context, analysis of personal and joint experiences and writing and listening to narratives on the theme in question, in this case leadership. Even here, they point out the important of the organizational culture to support this style of intervention that by its nature is critical to the status quo.

Resources and reflection

What use may be made of opportunities for productive reflection is naturally dependent on the resources available to the particular collective that is involved. We have already mentioned the issues of formal discretion, legitimacy and support, both moral support and support from facilitators and experts and formal organizational and physical arenas for discussion. An additional highly important resource is time. Reflective activities focusing on the content, processes and outcomes of actions need time – time to observe, to exchange ideas and experiences with others, and time to think – this time is not usually available in contexts of 'lean production' (Eraut 1995; Richtnér 2004).

However, the availability of time, though necessary, is not sufficient. An important factor is how time is used, more specifically, how its allotment to different tasks, such as production or reflection, is regarded by members of the organization. From this perspective, time is a product of prevailing beliefs and cultural practices (Antonocopoulou and Tsoukas 2002; Hassard 2002). Thus a change in the use of time may be seen as a result of collective learning, rather than a consequence of a management decision on the use of time. Fenwick (2003) concludes that an increased subjective awareness of the learning opportunities encountered at work and how these were handled, proved more important than the allocation of 'objective' learning time for the promotion of learning from everyday activity. Subjects seemed to 'learn how to learn' from their own practice and, thereby, also how to find time for this learning. Thus, again culture comes in. Learning and development issues must be clearly prioritized in the organization so that personnel have the knowledge, skills and commitment to identify and handle these issues as an integral part of ongoing activities.

Tensions and balances in productive reflection

What learning for whom?

Many authors on organizational learning define their own typology of learning. Pawlovsky (2001) lists 10 such typologies in his review of organizational learning in management science. There are strong similarities between the typologies, which basically rest on the assumption that there are differences between learning as a conditioned response and learning as a result of reflection, insight and maturation. Several of the contributions here make reference to different types of learning that are occurring in the workplace. In Chapter 4, Ellström presents a typology of 'adaptive' and 'developmental' learning which he relates to the interplay between levels of action and reflection. He emphasizes the need to attain a balance between adaptive and developmental learning, basically by countering the tendency to 'drive out developmental learning and reflective activities from organizations' official arena and into the "shadow system", or perhaps to outside the workplace'.

Similarly, Breidensjö and Huzzard in Chapter 12 use March's (1991) concepts 'explorative' and 'exploitive' learning when formulating their concerns regarding the potential (or real impact) of the 'lean production' model on learning in organizations. This model may well focus learning solely on exploitive learning to achieve cost reduction and customer value, to the exclusion of a broader explorative learning. Again a balance must be attained by ensuring the latter is on the agenda. As they indicate, unions can play an important role.

Many chapters, especially the critical and discourse-based contributions, focus on the ownership of workplace learning; who are its beneficiaries? The authors are concerned about the risks that learning in the workplace may well become a further tool in management's control of the workforce and that it will mainly lead to developments in employees' situations entailing greater work intensity and stress, more constraints and less coherence. The creation of a 'win-win' requires a keen and open appreciation of these risks and the involvement of personnel and their unions in policies and programmes for personnel development (Cressey *et al.* 1999).

Balancing ways of establishing 'productive reflection'

Learning contexts may be grouped on many dimensions. One of the most relevant and important in this context is the dimension of 'informality – formality'. Colley *et al.* (2003) provide a current and excellent review and analysis of research on formal and informal learning. Much of the research reviewed deals with individual learning, though the collective reflection in our focus is included in the continuous learning continuum of Stern and Sommerlad (1999). However, we feel that the locus of control in the creation and maintenance of propitious conditions for productive reflection are of key importance. We have already noted that Ellström's observation that learning at work is a matter of design and not evolution. Stebbins *et al.* have addressed this design approach in terms of the formation of 'learning mechanisms', which we have utilized in this chapter. However Boud has provided a clear warning of the dangers of an overutilization of the design approach: taken too far, this will create anxiety and stress that destroy the climate for reflection. Schenkel (Chapter 6), on the other hand has referred to the informal development of reflective practices in communities of practice. In would seem therefore necessary to attain a balance between the formal design of conditions for productive reflection and the provision of leeway for the development of informal practices. To use our interpretation of Amin and Cohendet's (2004) terms in this context, this would mean striking a balance between 'management by design' and 'management by communities'.

It is quite difficult to draw clear lines between the formal and the informal in facilitating reflection. There are three simple paradoxes in this context. Firstly, learning mechanisms may function best when they are not formally labelled as such, but rather as debriefing sessions, project follow-up and evaluation sessions, continuous improvement sessions, and weekly work group meetings. For many people, reflection and learning are inhibited as soon as the terms are mentioned. Secondly, many people have difficulty seeing themselves as being competent, and as being in need of learning, at the same time. A third paradox is that reflection needs to be legitimized as a part of work, while simultaneously being rejected if it is a formal expectation.

Issues for further attention

The topic of collective reflection and learning at the workplace in organizations has been gaining increasing attention in the past few years. While striving to put the issue of collective reflection more clearly on the agenda, this volume has not, for reasons of space, addressed all aspects. There is also considerable work still to be done on the issues we have taken up. Some of the issues are as follows.

How can space for reflection be created?

Important reflection takes place naturally at work, but also outside work. Reflection outside work, either because it is natural and the conditions and opportunities are favourable – in the car to work, at home, on the internet, in the pub, in the changing room or because there are no appropriate or adequate conditions at work. How can these be created and couple up and draw benefit from the 'outside' reflection networks? At work, there are the formal learning mechanisms, arenas, routines, methods and the informal communities. How are different kinds of learning, for different groups taking place on the different scenes? Another feature of learning is that it seems to occur at interfaces between people from different levels, professions, milieux, for example between experts (with theoretical knowledge) and practitioners (with tacit knowledge), or, between development and production staff. The study of different 'social learning interfaces' needs to be extended. Another term besides 'interfaces' is 'in between' spaces that are neither fully in work, nor out of work that seem to be fruitful arenas for productive reflection (Solomon *et al.* forthcoming). Indeed, we need new ways of theorizing spaces for reflection.

Whose concern is productive reflection?

We maintain it concerns the main stakeholders in working life, namely workers and their representatives, management and society. Society can legislate to create a favourable framework for the other stakeholders' actions. For example, work environment legislation in Sweden stipulates that the work shall support individuals' development to their full capability. This legislation is a key support for competence development in working life. Unions and management are now beginning to discuss 'security of employability' as an alternative to 'security of employment', employ-ability entailing a joint understanding and responsibility between workers and their employers to maintain their knowledge and skill levels so that they are attractive on the labour market and should be able find employment.

What is required of individuals to be able to take advantage of the learning opportunities offered by their workplace? Personal factors would include the individual's knowledge and understanding of the task at hand. Awareness of learn-ing opportunities and self-awareness of how one has dealt with such opportunities in the past, as well as a number of emotional and social factors. The former issue of emotions has not been specifically addressed here, and is a field which requires specific attention. The latter include motivation, self-efficacy, personal and occupational identities. Taken together these constitute important factors in what Ellström calls a 'learning readiness'. How is the emergence of productive reflection practices affected by professional, religious, national and gender values and attitudes? Learning readiness and, by extension, readiness for reflection is not a fixed attribute of individuals or environments, but needs to be continually constructed in the light of the various inclinations and desires of stakeholders.

How is productive reflection to be promoted, developed and maintained?

Important concepts here are leadership, management and culture. Leadership and management concern not least the value base and norms characterizing top management, especially regarding participation and partnership, and learning and development. Organizational culture and climate, strategy and policies will determine the framework for emerging routines and practices for collective reflection. Modern management systems attempt to take a more holistic approach to organizational performance than the more limited financial reports required by government legislation and sought by stockmarket analysts. These newer systems also address such 'intangibles' as an organization's learning, 'intellectual capital', flexibility and innovativeness. Such a category of systems are 'balanced score card systems'. In addition such systems are not utilized simply as control systems, but also as the basis for dialogue between different levels in the organization to create a common understanding and development of strategy (Olve *et al.* 2003).

The interplay between these variables in different contexts needs further study. Which resources are required? What is the relation between time, organizational slack, and the development of reflective practices? What are the relations between objective resources and attitudes towards the use of resources, for example time? Which types of learning mechanisms are most efficacious in different contexts? What roles should different facilitators and experts take in different contexts? As we have suggested earlier, care needs to be taken that in operationalizing the answers to these questions, the necessary co-construction of productive reflection by workers and management and the need for it to be responsive to local concerns is not compromised.

When is productive reflection relevant and what form does it take in different contexts?

Certain event-driven contexts, such as organizational redesign occasioned by crises, changes in ownership, technology or institutional frameworks present different prerequisites for reflection than those existing in stable conditions. Ironically, when major change is in progress pressures of time and the anxieties of senior management to implement immediate solutions can inhibit productive reflection at just the point when it is most needed and can potentially have the greatest impact.

The growing attention to learning in the academic world is well matched by its growth in the fields of industry and commerce, not least with the talk of the 'knowledge economy'. The need to handle growing complexity, turbulence and change and to accommodate the short term and the long term, mean that learning and reflection in the workplace are receiving increased priority. As with the development of work organizations towards multi-skilling and direct representation, this follows not primarily from changing values, but from the realization that this is the most feasible alternative. Considering learning, management must find ways to integrate learning in or at the workplace, because it is more relevant, effective and less costly. By exploring some of the issues in certain detail, we have obtain a more nuanced understanding of 'productive reflection', of some solutions and pitfalls, and have a better picture of the challenges facing decision makers at all levels in organizations. The challenges are many, but there are positive experiences and clear issues to address.

References

Amin, A. and Cohendet, P. (2004) *Architectures of Knowledge: Firms, Capabilities and Communities*, Oxford: Oxford University Press.

Antonocopoulou, E. and Tsoukas, H. (2002) 'Time and reflexivity in organization studies: an introduction', *Organisation Studies*, 23, 6: 857–62.

Antonovsky, A. (1987) *Unraveling the Mystery of Health: How People Manage Stress and Stay Well*, San Francisco, CA: Jossey-Bass.

Argyris, C. and Schön, D.A. (1974) *Theories in Practice: Increasing Professional Effectiveness*, San Francisco, CA: Jossey-Bass.

Benders, J., Huijgen, F., Pekruhl, U. and O'Kelly, K. (1999) *Useful but Unused. Group Work in Europe*, Dublin: European Foundation for Living and Working Conditions.

Boud, D., Keogh, R. and Walker, D. (eds) (1985) *Reflection: Turning Experience into Learning*, London: Kogan Page.

Bushe, G.R. and Shani, A.B. (Rami) (1991) *Parallel Learning Structures: Increasing Innovation in Bureaucracies*, Reading, MA: Addison Wesley.

Colley, H., Hodkinson, P. and Malcom, J. (2003) *Informality and Formality in Learning*, London: Learning and Skills Research Centre.

Cressey, P., Della Rossa, G., Docherty, P., Kelleher, M., Kuhn, M., Reimann, D. and Ullstad, C. (1999) *Partnership and Investment in Europe: The Role of the Social Dialogue in Human Resource Development*, Consolidated report, Brussels: EC Leonardo project EUR/96/2/1071/EA/III.2.a/FPC.

De Geus, A. (1992) *The Living Company*, Boston, MA: Harvard Business School Press.

Driver, M. (2002) 'The learning organisation: Foucauldian gloom or Utopian sunshine?', *Human Relations*, 55: 33–53.

Ellström, P.-E. (2001) 'Integrating learning and work: conceptual issues and critical conditions', *Human Resource Development Quarterly*, 12, 4: 421–35.

Eraut, M. (1995) 'Schön shock: a case for re-framing reflection in action?', *Teachers and Teaching*, 1, 1: 9–22.

Fenwick, T.J. (2003) 'Professional growth plans: possibilities and limitations of an organization-wide employee development strategy', *Human Resource Development Quarterly*, 14, 1: 59–77.

Friedman, V.J., Lipshitz, R. and Overmeer, W. (2003) 'Creating conditions for organizational learning', in M. Dierkes, A. Berthoin Antal, J. Child and I. Nonaka (eds) *Handbook of Organizational Learning and Knowledge*, Oxford: Oxford University Press, 757–74.

Fulop, L. and Rifkin, W.D. (1997) 'Representing fear in learning in organizations', *Management Learning*, 28, 1: 45–63.

Garvin, D.A. (2000) *Learning in Action*, Boston, MA: Harvard Business School Press.

Gherardi, S. (1999) 'A symbolic approach to competence development', *Human Resource Development International: Enhancing Performance, Learning, and Integrity*, 2, 4: 313–34.

Hassard, J. (2002) 'Organizational time: modern, symbolic and postmodern reflections', *Organization Studies*, 23, 6: 885–92.

Kolb, D.A. (1984) *Experiential Learning: Experience as a Source of Learning and Development*, Englewood Cliffs, NJ: Prentice-Hall.

March, J.G. (1991) 'Exploration and Exploitation in Organizational Learning', *Organizational Science*, 2, 1: 71–87.

Nonaka, I., Toyama, Y. and Byosière, P. (2001) 'A theory of organizational knowledge creation: understanding the dynamic process of creating knowledge', in M. Dierkes, A. Berthoin Antal, J. Child and I. Nonaka (eds) *Handbook of Organizational Learning and Knowledge*, Oxford: Oxford University Press, 491–517.

Nonaka, I. and Kunno, N. (1998) 'The Concept of "Ba": Building a Foundation for Knowledge Creation', *California Management Review*, 40, 3: 40–54.

Olve, N.-G., Petri, C.-J., Roy, J. and Roy, S. (2003) *Making Scorecards Actionable: Balancing Strategy and Control*, Chichester: Wiley.

Parker Follet, M. (1941) 'Leader and expert', in H. Metcalf and L.F. Urwick (eds) *Dynamic Administration: The Collected Papers of Mary Parker Follett*, New York: Harper & Bros.

Pawlovsky, P. (2001) 'The treatment of organizational learning in management science', in M. Dierkes, A. Berthoin Antal ,J. Child and I. Nonaka (eds) *Handbook of Organizational Learning and Knowledge*, Oxford: Oxford University Press, 61–88.

Pettigrew, A. (1974) *The Politics of Organisational Decision Making*, London: Tavistock Publications.

Richtnér, A. (2004) *Balancing Knowledge Creation: Organizational Slack and Knowledge Creation in Product Development*, Stockholm: Stockholm School of Economics.

Shani, A.B. (Rami) and Docherty, P. (2003) *Learning by Design: Building Sustainable Organizations*, Oxford: Blackwell Publishers.

Schön, D.A. (1983) *The Reflective Practitioner. How Professionals Think in Action*, New York: Basic Books.

Solomon, N., Boud, D. and Rooney, D. (forthcoming) 'The in-between: exposing everyday learning at work', *International Journal of Lifelong Education*.

Stern, D. and Sommerlad, E. (1999) *Workplace learning, culture and performance*, London: Institute for Personnel and Development.

Teigland, R. (2003) *Knowledge Networking: Structure and Performance in Networks of Practice*, Stockholm: Stockholm School of Economics.

Index

Keen, P.G.W. 107, 115, 119
Keep, E. 135, 143
Kelleher, M. 11, 14, 25, 56, 59, 64, 65,
133, 139, 144
Kennedy, J. 158, 169
Keogh, R. 33, 34, 37, 42, 44, 45, 52, 158,
166, 168, 194, 205
Kets de Vries, M.F.R. 185, 191
Kilmann, R.H. 82, 91
Klein, G.A. 51, 53
Kluckhohn, F.R. 126, 130
knowledge: economy 148, 204; society
172
Kochan, T.A. 106, 108, 119
Kohlberg, L. 140, 144
Kolb, D.A. 31, 159, 169, 194, 206
Kuhn, M. 56, 64
Kunda, G. 51, 52
Kvale, S. 172, 179, 180

Landau, D. 82, 91
Lash, S. 19, 25, 139, 143
Lave, J. 21, 25, 61, 62, 65, 70, 71, 72, 79,
134, 137, 140, 144, 149, 157, 162, 180
leadership, and power 185; women's
181–91, 198
Leadership, Organization and
Co-determination 60–1
lean production 58–9, 136, 146, 147, 151,
153, 155, 201
leanness, versus learning 147–8
learning, situated 61, 63
learning: assumptions 39; cycle 159;
danger of formalizing the informal
166; denial of 161, 162–3; despite
staff development 161–2;
developmental (creative) 44–5, 48–50;
developmental 201; discourse 177;
double-loop 12, 122, 172; everyday 29,
160; exploitative 201; from experience
158; from mistakes 37, 39; informal
43–51; journal 163, 164; mechanisms
107–9, 116; non-reflective 172, 173,
179; organization 12, 106, 133, 134,
135, 136, 146, 156, 173; organization
theory 14, 16; promoting at work 49–
51; resistance to 164; spaces 146, 153,
152–3, 199; subject in communities of
practice 179; turn 18, 19; Type 1 and
Type 2 69–70; *see also* organizational
learning
Levinthal, D.A. 183, 192
Lewin, K. 60, 65
life world 166, 167

Lilley, S. 13, 14, 16, 25
Liontios, M. 164, 169
Lipshitz, R. 129, 130, 196, 205
Loden, M. 185, 192
looping-effect 170, 176–7
Luckman, T. 72, 79

MacInnes, J. 63, 64
Macintosh, C. 30, 42
MacIntyre, A. 134, 138, 139, 143, 144
Mackenzie, K.D. 80, 92
Magnusson, Å. 118, 119
Malcolm, J. 165, 169
Malinen, A. 32, 34, 35, 42
Manz, C.C. 185, 192
March, J.G. 12, 25, 45, 50, 53, 94, 105,
151, 157, 183, 192
Markoczy, L. 182, 191
Marquardt, M. 173, 180
Marsick, V.J. 11, 25
Martin, J.S. 120, 130
Martin, M.W. 135, 139, 141, 143, 144
McGill I. 186, 191
McHugh, D. 13, 26, 147, 157
McKinlay, A. 175, 180
McKinley, W. 148, 157
McLain Smith, D. 44, 52, 122, 129
Meaning Work: Rethinking Ethics 139
memory work 186, 189
Mendus, S. 143, 144
Mezirow, J. 33, 35, 42, 44, 45, 48, 53
Mitroff, I.I. 82, 91
Mohrman, S.A. 90, 91
Moon, J. 31, 42, 158, 169
Moon, W. 109, 110, 119
Moran, R.T. 120, 130
Morris, F. 59, 65
Morris, M.W. 121, 130
Morris, T. 137, 144
Mueller, F. 58, 65
mutual engagement 71–2

Nadler, D.A. 83, 85, 91
narrative: approaches 71–2, 181–91, 198,
200; methodology, use of 187–9;
workshop 185–7
National Institute for Work Life 7
negotiating reality 120–2, 128–9
networks, social 72, 74–7
Nonaka, I. 14, 25, 167, 169, 199, 206
Nyhan, B. 11, 14, 25, 59, 65, 133, 139,
144

O'Kelley, K. 197, 205